Evening Standard

LONDON PUB GUIDE

1995

Evening Standard

LONDON PUB GUIDE

Angus McGill

Foreword by Willie Rushton

Cartoons by Frank Dickens

First published in Great Britain in 1994 by
PAVILION BOOKS LIMITED
26 Upper Ground, London SE1 9PD

Designed by Alyson Kyles

Additional reporting by Brian Angel, Nicholas Bond, Richard Bruton, Joan Cawston, Ben Colman, James Hughes-Onslow, Peter Morrison, Ann Morrow, Kenneth Hughes, Tom Pocock, Edward Sullivan, David Weston, Peter Williams.

Commissioning Editor for the Evening Standard: Joanne Bowlby

A CIP catalogue record for this book is available from the British Library.

ISBN 1 85793 3265

Printed and bound in Great Britain by
Butler & Tanner Ltd, Frome and London

2 4 6 8 10 9 7 5 3 1

Typeset in Palatino and Helvetica

This book may be ordered by post direct from the publisher. Please contact the Marketing Department. But try your bookshop first.

Maps designed by Footprints Design,
5 Dryden Street, London WC2E 9NB

Corporate editions and personal subscriptions of the Evening Standard London Pub Guide are available. Call us for details. Tel: 071-620 1666

CONTENTS

Foreword	6
Introduction	7
Maps	8
Reviews	14
Eros Awards	219
Pubs with Theatres	220
Gay Pubs	220
Pubs with Late-Night Opening	221
Pubs with No-smoking Areas	221
Riverside Pubs	222
Pubs with Car Parks	222
Pubs with Live Music	223
Pubs with Beer Gardens	224

FOREWORD

I HAVE BEEN SENIOR JUDGE of the Evening Standard Pub of the Year Contest for a quarter of a century now, man and woman. I know this because my son Toby was born in the middle of a particularly severe bout of judging, and I know he was born in 1969. I remember staggering home after a licensee in the Dover area had tried to bribe me with endless Drambuies. My wife, Dorgan, was lying on our four-poster. I lay down beside her, and passed out. She shook me awake, told me that the whole miraculous business was underway and asked me to ring St George's Hospital. I didn't think this was advisable, given that the Drambuies had unhinged my teeth and the Hospital might well think that I had gone into labour. As it turned out the gynaecologist was even more inebriated than I was. Suffice to say that that all happened a long time ago, and Toby is now older than I am, and St George's Hospital is now a luxury hotel.

Being a Senior Judge is an enormous privilege. It is a prestigious, if unpaid, position and indeed in the traditional Pecking Order of Things, for instance when the Management and Staff of the Evening Standard gather, as they do every All Fools's Day, to beat the bounds of Peter McKay and raise their eyebrows to the Lord, the Senior Judge parades in front of the Editor, but some distance, of course, behind the Proprietor with his long, felt wand. This is quite proper as I and my rich and varied collection of colleagues hover above the everyday hackery of Grub Street. After all, we make History, they simply record it.

'Rich and varied' my colleagues certainly have been. To pluck a few at random – Susan Hampshire, Stephanie Lawrence, Sheila Hancock, the lovely Nigella Lawson, the exotic Carol Thatcher, the fiery hooker and solicitor Brian Moore, Tim Rice, Kingsley Amis and his boy, Martin, Gavin Thing of That's Life – how the memories flood back. And ever at my shoulder, my faithful Watson, 'the one fixed point in a changing age', the one and only Angus McGill. Angus, it rhymes with 'mongoose', a journalist who has never blunted his nib probing for smut and muck in the danker reachers of our once-great City, who was never that interested in the dark side of anything as long as the light was on, the band was playing and it was someone else's round. Too good for the Nobel prize, too rare for a Pulitzer, Angus is what young journalists should aspire to, but, alas, they don't, they fall far short and become gossips or awful women columnists with hyphens and massive chips on their padded shoulders.

To have simply known and conversed with Angus McGill would seem enough excitement for one lifetime, to have done this in a multitude of public houses and over a good number of drinks is Paradise Enow. My word, we've been to some fine hostelries and indeed to some right sinks, but always in questing mode, and this essential book is the sum of our experience. Armed with this tome you need never draw another sober breath in a lousy pub or dull company.

Good health!

W. RUSHTON, CHIEF JUDGE

PS Haven't you got homes to go to?

INTRODUCTION

I HAVE TO SAY straight away that this is not a Good Pub Guide. Goodness, as Mae West would have said, has nothing to do with it. If I have done it right you will think some of the pubs in this book are just the sort of pub you like, others you would only enter with a gun to your head. That is because, well they are pubs. There are 300 of them in this guide and no one could possibly like them all.

There are pubs in London for just about every section of the adult community. Some are as hushed as gentlemen's clubs, others deafen you. Some don't let you in unless you are dressed entirely in leather. At least one still asks for a jacket and tie. The pierced and tattooed biker has his pub and the Westminster Cathedral chorister his.

Bearing this in mind I have tried not to say whether I like the pub in question or not though, reading the guide through, I find I have done so far too often. Take no notice. My role is to tell you about each pub and leave liking it or not to you. 'A sado-masochist stamp-collecting pub with William Morris wallpaper!' I hear you say. 'Smashing!' I haven't actually found this pub though I bet it's out there somewhere.

There are other pubs in here that are almost as specialized, some of them bizarre. You are not going to believe this but there are pubs in London that cater entirely for men and women who want a quiet drink. Some of these have got into this guide as well. As for the pubs I personally like, well there are quite a few of those in here. Twelve of them get Eros awards for no better reason than that I think they are terrific. The biker, the chorister and the sado-masochist stamp collector would each have chosen quite a different list and some of these will be in here too. There are, as I hope to show, some very interesting pubs in London.

ANGUS MCGILL

A
B
C
4
3
2
1
MARYLEBONE RD.
CRAWFORD ST.
PADDINGTON ST.
MARYLEBONE H. ST.
GLOUCESTER PLACE
BAKER STREET
GEORGE ST.
EDGWARE RD.
SEYMOUR ST.
WIGMORE STREET
OXFORD
Marble Arch
Bond Street
CUMBERLAND GATE
PARK LANE
UPPER BROOK ST.
BROOK
GROSVENOR SQUARE
UP. GROSVENOR
GROSVENOR ST.
NEW BOND ST.
STREET
CONDUIT ST.
CURZON ST.
PICCADILLY
ST. JAMES'S ST.
PALL
Hyde Park Corner
HYDE PARK CORNER
18
130
135
124
53
225
237
178
117
245
226
MAP 1

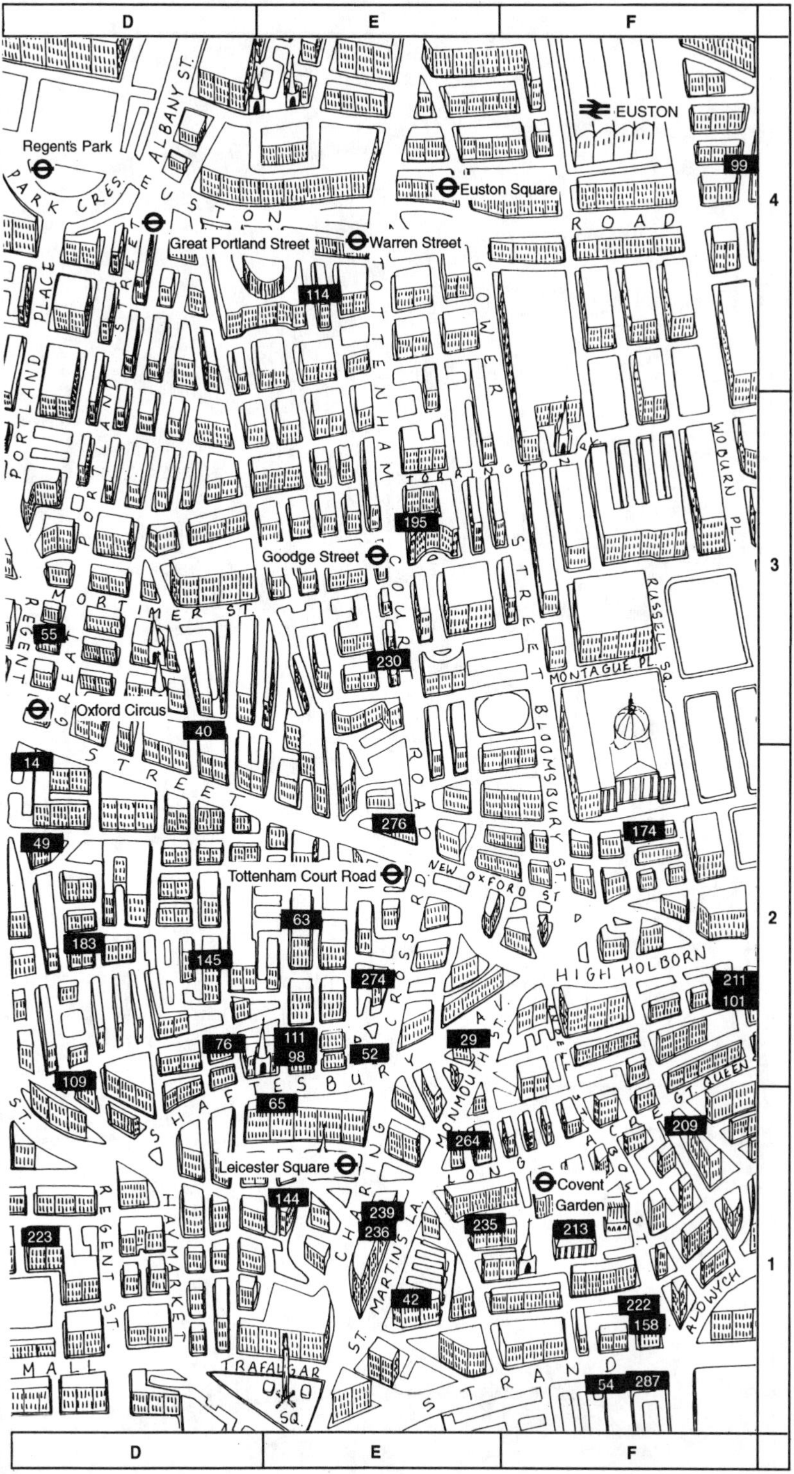
D
E
F
4
3
2
1
EUSTON
99
Regent's Park
PARK CRES.
ALBANY ST.
Euston Square
EUSTON ROAD
Great Portland Street
Warren Street
114
PORTLAND PLACE
GREAT PORTLAND STREET
TOTTENHAM COURT ROAD
GOWER STREET
TORRINGTON PL.
WOBURN PL.
195
Goodge Street
RUSSELL SQ.
MORTIMER ST.
REGENT ST.
55
230
MONTAGUE PL.
Oxford Circus
40
14
OXFORD STREET
BLOOMSBURY ST.
276
174
49
Tottenham Court Road
NEW OXFORD ST.
63
183
145
HIGH HOLBORN
274
CHARING CROSS RD
211
101
76
111
98
52
29
SHAFTESBURY AV.
MONMOUTH ST.
109
65
GT. QUEEN ST.
209
264
LONG ACRE
Leicester Square
Covent Garden
HAYMARKET
144
239
236
235
213
223
ST. MARTINS LA.
42
ALDWYCH
222
158
MALL
TRAFALGAR SQ.
STRAND
54
287

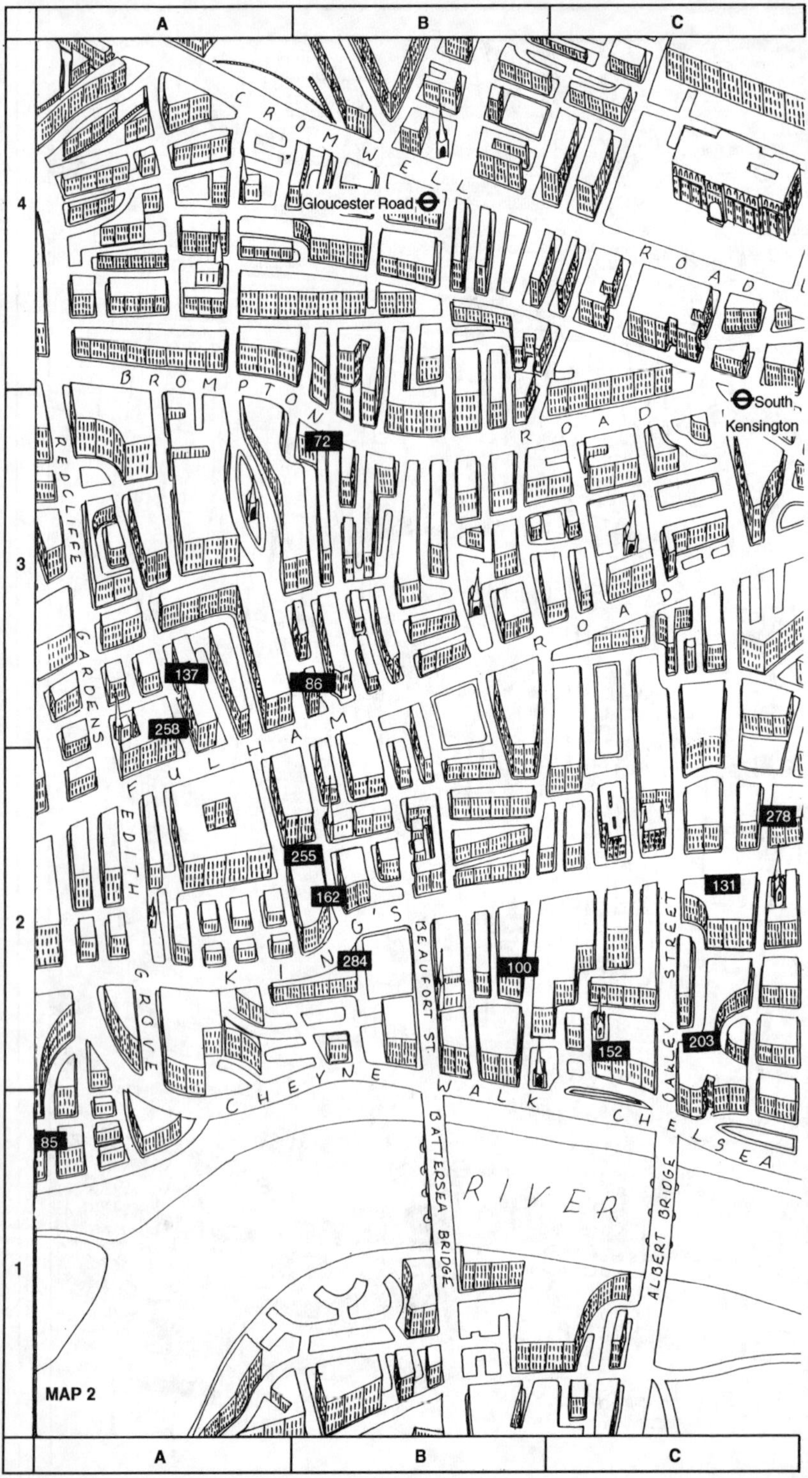
A
B
C
4
3
2
1
CROMWELL ROAD
Gloucester Road
BROMPTON ROAD
South Kensington
REDCLIFFE GARDENS
FULHAM ROAD
EDITH GROVE
KING'S ROAD
BEAUFORT ST.
OAKLEY STREET
CHEYNE WALK
CHELSEA
BATTERSEA BRIDGE
ALBERT BRIDGE
RIVER
72
137
86
258
255
162
284
100
152
203
131
278
85
MAP 2

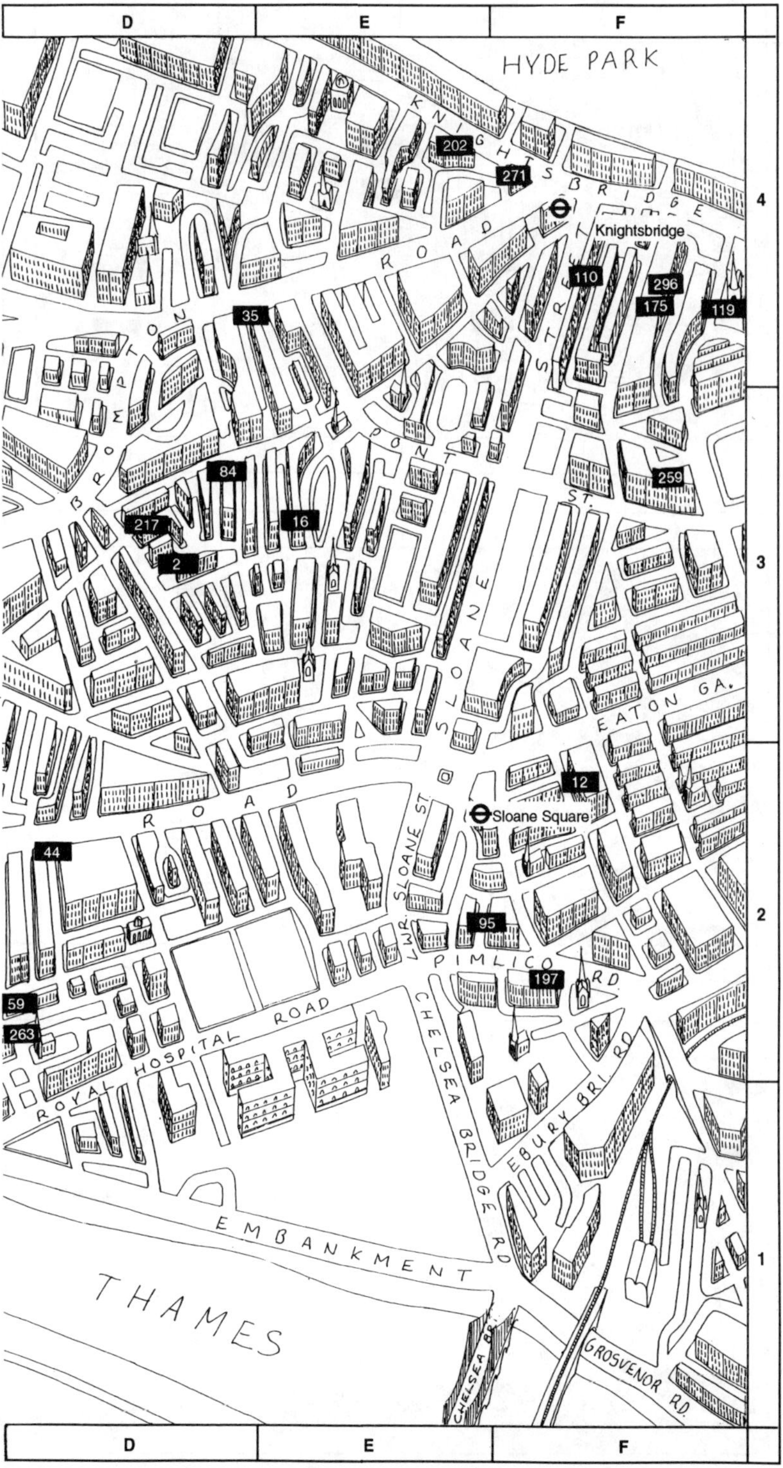
D
E
F
HYDE PARK
KNIGHTSBRIDGE
Knightsbridge
ROAD
BROMPTON
PONT ST.
SLOANE ST.
SLOANE SQ
EATON GA.
Sloane Square
LWR. SLOANE ST.
PIMLICO RD
ROYAL HOSPITAL ROAD
CHELSEA BRIDGE RD
EBURY BRI. RD
EMBANKMENT
THAMES
CHELSEA BR.
GROSVENOR RD.
202
271
110
296
175
119
35
84
217
16
2
259
12
44
95
197
59
263
4
3
2
1

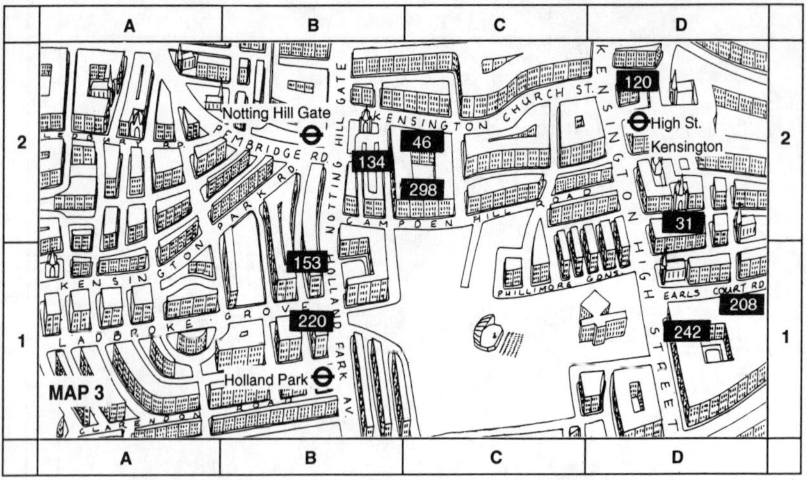
A
B
C
D
1
2
MAP 3
Notting Hill Gate
High St. Kensington
Holland Park
KENSINGTON CHURCH ST.
PEMBRIDGE RD.
NOTTING HILL GATE
CAMPDEN HILL ROAD
KENSINGTON PARK RD.
KENSINGTON
LADBROKE GROVE
HOLLAND PARK AV.
CLARENDON ROAD
PHILLIMORE GDNS.
EARLS COURT RD
KENSINGTON HIGH STREET
120
46
134
298
31
153
220
208
242

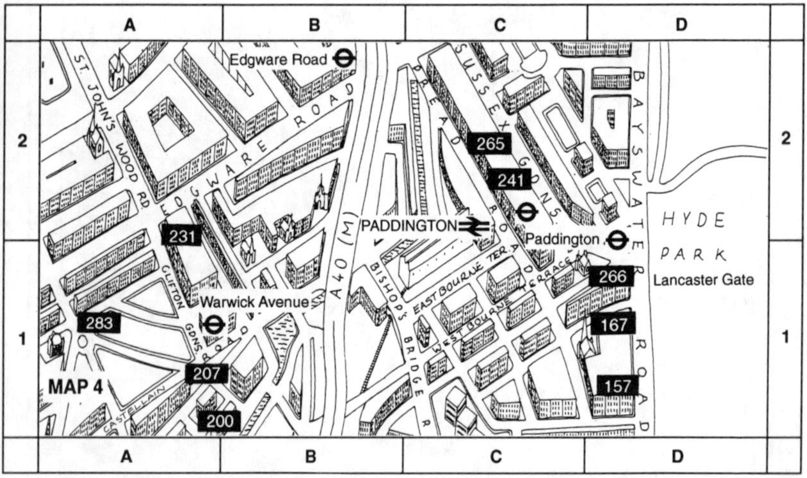
A
B
C
D
1
2
MAP 4
Edgware Road
PADDINGTON
Paddington
Lancaster Gate
Warwick Avenue
HYDE PARK
ST. JOHN'S WOOD RD
EDGWARE ROAD
PRAED
SUSSEX GDNS.
BAYSWATER ROAD
A40 (M)
BISHOPS BRIDGE R
EASTBOURNE TERA
WESTBOURNE TERRACE
CLIFTON GDNS.
CASTELLAIN ROAD
265
241
231
283
266
167
207
157
200

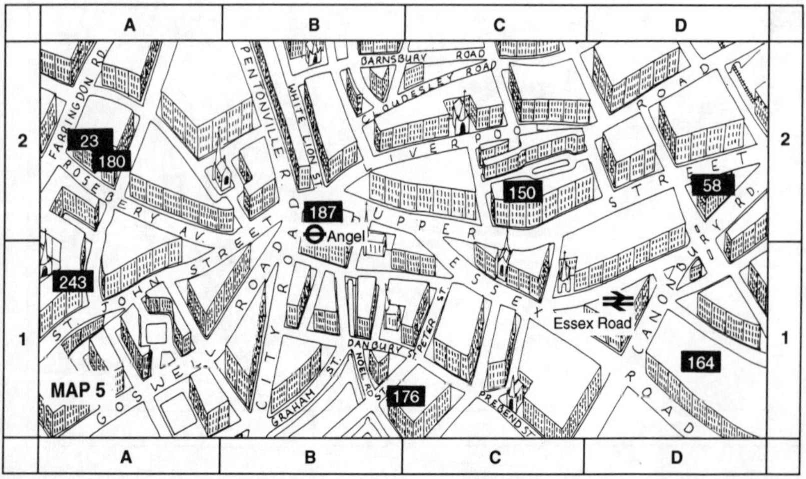
A
B
C
D
1
2
MAP 5
Angel
Essex Road
FARRINGDON RD
ROSEBERY AV.
PENTONVILLE R
WHITE LION S
BARNSBURY ROAD
CLOUDESLEY ROAD
LIVERPOOL ROAD
UPPER STREET
ESSEX ROAD
CANONBURY RD.
ST. JOHN STREET
GOSWELL ROAD
CITY ROAD
DANBURY ST.
GRAHAM ST.
NOEL RD.
ST. PETER ST.
PREBEND ST.
23
180
243
187
150
58
164
176

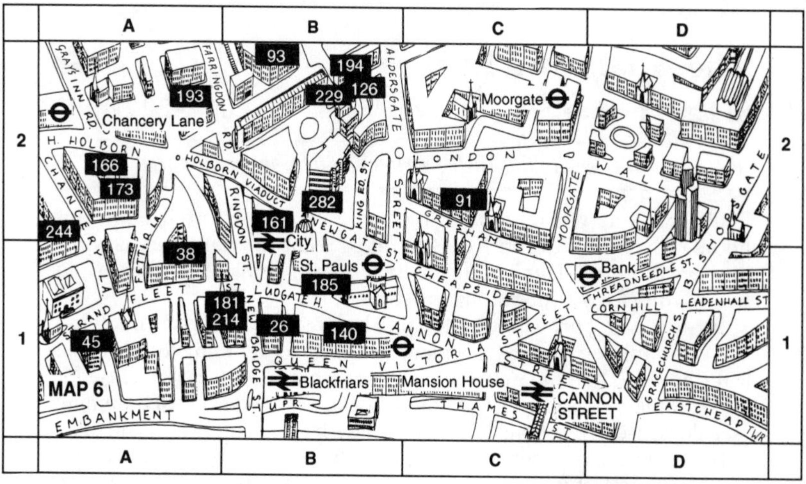

A
B
C
D
2
1
MAP 6
93
194
126
229
193
166
173
244
38
161
282
91
185
181
214
26
140
45
Chancery Lane
Moorgate
City
St. Pauls
Bank
Blackfriars
Mansion House
CANNON
STREET
GRAY'S INN RD.
FARRINGDON RD.
ALDERSGATE
H. HOLBORN
HOLBORN VIADUCT
CHANCERY LA
FETTER LA
RINGDON ST.
NEWGATE ST.
KING ED. ST.
LONDON WALL
GRESHAM ST.
MOORGATE
BISHOPSGATE
STRAND
FLEET ST.
LUDGATE H.
NEW BRIDGE ST.
CHEAPSIDE
THREADNEEDLE ST.
CORNHILL
LEADENHALL ST.
CANNON STREET
QUEEN VICTORIA STREET
UPR. THAMES ST.
GRACECHURCH S.
EASTCHEAP
TWR
EMBANKMENT

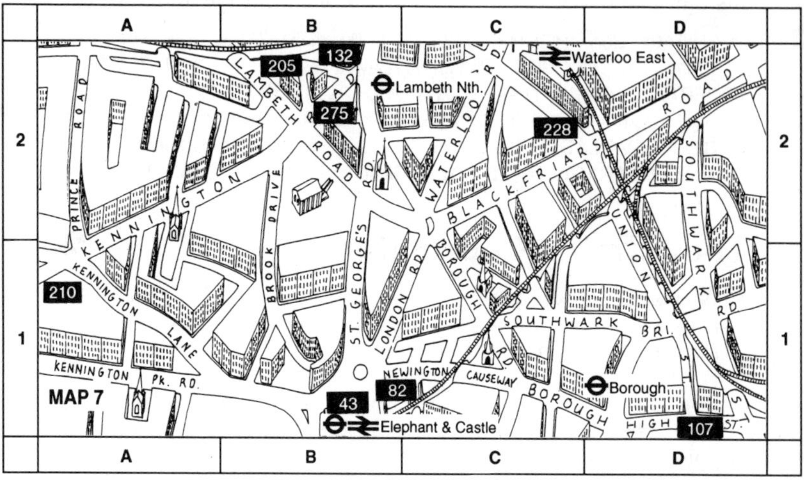

A
B
C
D
2
1
MAP 7
205
132
275
228
210
82
43
107
Lambeth Nth.
Waterloo East
Borough
Elephant & Castle
LAMBETH ROAD
PRINCE ROAD
KENNINGTON
KENNINGTON LANE
KENNINGTON Pk. RD.
BROOK DRIVE
ST. GEORGE'S RD.
LONDON RD.
WATERLOO RD.
BLACKFRIARS ROAD
BOROUGH RD.
SOUTHWARK BRI. RD
UNION ST.
SOUTHWARK ST.
NEWINGTON CAUSEWAY
BOROUGH HIGH ST.

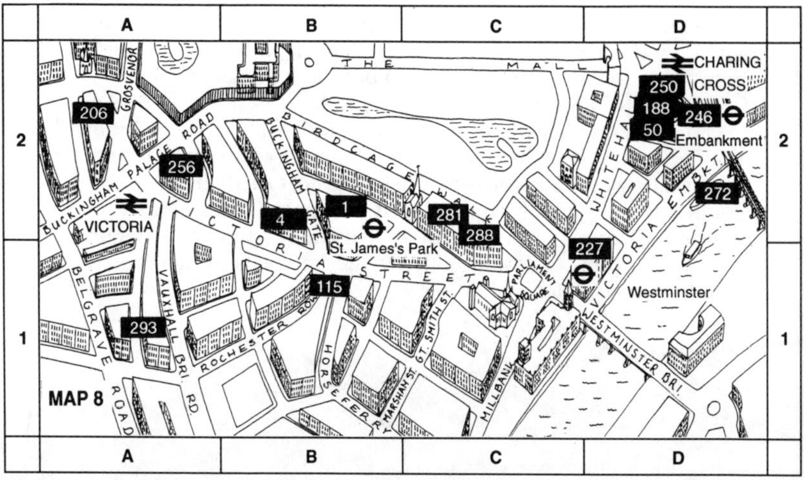

A
B
C
D
2
1
MAP 8
206
256
4
1
281
288
227
250
188
50
246
272
115
293
CHARING
CROSS
Embankment
VICTORIA
St. James's Park
Westminster
THE MALL
GROSVENOR
BUCKINGHAM PALACE ROAD
BUCKINGHAM GATE
BIRDCAGE WALK
VICTORIA STREET
WHITEHALL
VICTORIA EMBKT.
PARLIAMENT SQUARE
WESTMINSTER BRI.
BELGRAVE ROAD
VAUXHALL BRI. RD.
ROCHESTER ROW
HORSEFERRY
MARSHAM ST.
GT. SMITH ST.
MILLBANK

The Adam and Eve

1

81 Petty France, SW1 **071-222 4575**

'If you haven't been to this little pub lately it may surprise you'

Petty France is where you go to change your passport. This means hours of hard chairs and forms to fill so what we want here is some positive thinking. Think of the holiday ahead. Think of the Adam and Eve waiting for you just along the street.

If you haven't been to this little pub lately it may surprise you. It has had a complete personality change. It used to be a fair to middling lager house. Then the new owners, Scottish and Newcastle, closed it for six weeks, and when it reopened, hey presto it was one of their new real ale houses, bare boards, quick pies with flaky pastry lids and all.

It has eight cask beers on the hand pumps and these now account for 60 per cent of its turnover. There has been a marked turnover in customers too. New ones have been moving in, old ones moving on . . .

OPEN: Mon-Sun. **HOURS:** 11.00am-11.00pm (12.00-3.00pm and 7.00-10.30pm Sun). **CLOSED:** Christmas Day, Boxing Day. **CREDIT CARDS ACCEPTED:** Visa, Access. **BAR FOOD AVAILABLE:** 11.00am-10.00pm (12.00-2.00pm and 7.00-9.00pm Sun). Wheelchair access. Private room seats 15. **BEERS AVAILABLE:** Theakston, Courage Best, Courage Directors, Holsten, Carlsberg. **NEAREST TUBE STATION:** St James's Park. **MAP REF:** 8, B/2

The Admiral Codrington

2

17 Mossop Street, SW3 **071-581 0005**

'Perhaps the Cod's day will dawn again'

During the years of swinging London the Admiral Codrington swung. In the seventies and eighties successive waves of Sloanes and Yuppies made it their own. It was panelled and lit by gas AND it had a cocktail bar, a grill and carvery, a popular manager and a lovely garden. It was socially a smash.

Fashion comes and fashion goes. Perhaps the Cod's day will dawn again. Linda and Dean, new young managers, have been brought in from Essex to spark things up again but these things take time . 'The Cod is BACK,' says Dean. Well, that's good . . .

Did it always have this dark panelling and small, leaded windows? Yes, it did. And what has happened to the lovely garden? It is under a conservatory now and Mossop Street does not exactly help.

Could anyone possibly guess that it was once Green Lettuce Lane, wandering among market gardens? Nowadays almost the whole of one side is a John Lewis warehouse. In the days of its social success this didn't seem to matter.

OPEN: Mon-Sun. **HOURS:** 12.00-11.00pm (12.00-3.00pm and 7.00-10.30pm Sun). **CREDIT CARDS ACCEPTED:** Visa, Access, Mastercard, Eurocard, AmEx. **BAR AND RESTAURANT FOOD AVAILABLE:** 12.00-3.00pm and 6.00-8.00pm. Wheelchair access. Beer garden seats 32. **BEERS AVAILABLE:** Worthington Best, Charrington, Bass, London Pride, Carling Black Label, Tennent's Extra, Tennent's Pilsner, Grolsch, Fuller's, Mitchell. **NEAREST TUBE STATION:** South Kensington. **MAP REF:** 2, D/3

The Albany

3

Queen's Road, Thames Ditton **081-398 7031**

'My Thames Ditton correspondent thinks we should be told'

Is Thames Ditton London? No it is Surrey. My Thames Ditton correspondent however says that the view from the garden of this little pub on the river bank is so lovely, Hampton Court Palace in the near distance, the home park across the water, the jeunesse dorée sailing and rowing, punting and skiffing, that he thinks we should be told.

OPEN IN SUMMER: 11.00am-11.00pm (12.00-3.00pm and 7.00-10.30pm Sun). **OPEN IN WINTER:** 11.00am-3.00pm and 5.00-11.00pm (12.00-3.00pm and 7.00-10.30pm Sun). **CREDIT CARDS ACCEPTED:** All major cards except Diner's Club. **BAR FOOD AVAILABLE:** 12.00-2.30pm. **RESTAURANT FOOD AVAILABLE:** 12.00-2.30pm and 6.30-8.30pm (12.00-2.30pm and 7.00-8.30pm Sun; 12.00-2.30pm in Winter). No smoking area. Beer garden seats 150. **BEERS AVAILABLE:** Courage Best, Charrington, Flowers IPA, Carling Black Label, Tennent's Extra, Tennent's Pilsner. **NEAREST BR STATIONS:** Hampton Court, Thames Ditton.

The Albert

4

52 Victoria Street, SW1 **071-222 5577/7606**

'The very essence of middle-class respectability'

When it comes to Victorian values let me commend to you the Albert. It is the very model of a high-Victorian public house. No larking about here, sir, if you please.

The Albert started out in 1845 as the Bluecoat Boy, a modest sort of pub, but slummy, dissolute Victoria was in the grip of a major redevelopment – to whit the building of Victoria Street – and everyone was straightening their ties and adjusting their clothing. Was the Bluecoat Boy good enough for the grand new mansion flats? It seems not. The Artillery Brewery virtually rebuilt it and when it reopened in 1862 it was the Albert we see today, the very essence of middle-class respectability.

The Albert is a big successful pub. It needs a staff of 25 to keep running smoothly, more in the summer. There is quick food in the bar and a very English restaurant on the first floor, always white tablecloths, always roast beef. Tourists with much to see in the neighbourhood find there a welcome respite from sore feet and history.

This is New Scotland Yard's local and MPs use it a lot. With the Houses of Parliament just up the street they appreciate the division bell in the restaurant and, after a drink or two, they may well start to think that one day their picture may join the portraits of Prime Ministers, from the Marquis of Salisbury to John Major, lining the broad mahogany staircase. Mrs Thatcher unveiled her portrait herself.

The pub sign in Victoria Street shows the young Prince Consort in pensive mood, holding a rose. The route has been changed now but when the Queen met heads of state at Victoria Station she would often point it out to her guests as they bowled along Victoria Street in the state landau. Albert was her great-great-grandfather.

OPEN: Mon-Sun. **HOURS:** 11.00am-11.00pm (12.00-3.00pm and 7.00-10.30pm Sun). **CLOSED:** Christmas Day, Boxing Day. **CREDIT CARDS ACCEPTED:** All major cards. **RESTAURANT FOOD AVAILABLE:** 7.45-10.30am (Mon-Fri only) and 12.00-9.30pm. **SET PRICE LUNCH AND DINNER:** £13.95. Wheelchair access (but not lavatory). Private room seats 24. **BEERS AVAILABLE:** Ruddles, Webster's, John Smith's, Courage, Wadworth, Guinness, Holsten, Budweiser, Foster's, Miller. **NEAREST TUBE STATION:** St James's Park. **MAP REF:** 8, B/2

The Albion

5

2 Clissold Road, N16 — **071-241 0360**

'Goth Night Thursdays'

One time biker's pub, now a rocker and punk pub. The 73 bus to Stoke Newington still takes you right to the door.

The bar's the same, counter in the middle, disco floor to the right, pool tables to the left and the music never stops. Goth Night Thursdays, the eighties Fridays, blues and rock Saturdays, rave Sundays and Newcastle Brown every night of the week.

OPEN: Mon-Sun. **HOURS:** 11.00-12.00am Mon-Thur; 11.00-1.00am Fri-Sat; 12.00-3.00pm and 7.00pm-12.00am Sun. **CREDIT CARDS ACCEPTED:** None. Wheelchair access (disabled lavatory). Tables outside seat 25. **BEERS AVAILABLE:** Tetley, Pedigree, Webster's, Foster's, Castlemaine, Lowenbrau, Holsten, Carlsberg. **NEAREST TUBE STATION:** Angel.

The Albion

6

10 Thornhill Road, N1 — **071-607 7450**

'worth any number of detours'

Nice old Thornhill Road with its Georgian houses and little shops is a bit bothered by all the cars but then just about everyone in this agreeable bit of Islington has one if not two and they spend a lot of time squeezing past this graceful ivy-covered coaching inn which belongs to a quieter more rural time. People drinking at the oak tables in front of the pub whenever it's not actually raining take no notice.

If going to the Albion means a detour then make it, though of course if you do you will be increasing the traffic in Thornhill Road. It is an elegant prosperous pub with a roomy bar doing well with Ruddles County and Webster's Yorkshire Bitter and there is a restaurant area with an open fire in winter and smaller panelled rooms behind, one for non-smokers. Hearty home-cooked lunches and suppers emerge from a busy kitchen. Beware fattening old-fashioned puddings covered in custard.

The star turn at the Albion though is the beer garden at the back – big, quiet and extraordinarily pleasant in the summer with its trellis and roses and picnic tables. This really is worth any number of detours.

OPEN: Mon-Sun. **HOURS:** 11.00am-11.00pm (12.00-3.00pm and 7.00-10.30pm Sun). **CREDIT CARDS ACCEPTED:** All major cards. **BAR FOOD AVAILABLE:** 12.00-2.30pm and 7.00-9.30pm. No smoking area. Wheelchair access (disabled lavatory). Beer garden seats 180. **BEERS AVAILABLE:** Carlsberg, Holsten, Molsen, Becks, Budweiser, Theakston XB, Webster's, Foster's, Ruddles County. **NEAREST TUBE STATION:** Angel, Highbury and Islington.

The Alexandra

7

33 Wimbledon Hill Road, SW19 **081-947 7691**

'An institution in the busy centre of Wimbledon'

The Alex is one of Young's flagships, number one for liquor sales they say in ringing tones. My man in Wimbledon is not surprised. He writes: 'The Alex is an institution in Wimbledon, a busy town-centre pub, classically Victorian and over recent years thoroughly refurbished. The old public bar, for instance, is the Wine and Ale Bar now, all beams and brickwork and huge barrels to put plates and glasses on, an open log fire spit-roasting beef and turkey and a staircase leading to the new roof garden. There's a barbecue up there on sunny days.

'A no-smoking bar leads the Green Bar, now predominantly red actually, and go past the counter where pub meals are served and you are in the wine bar, Young's first, where you can eat and drink till 1am on Friday and Saturday nights.

'It is, as it always was, a place where people do business, do lunch, recover from shopping. The station is only a few minutes' walk away and some regularly break their journeys to the further-flung outposts of network SouthEast for a little something at the Alex. They can always catch the next train. Or the one after that . . .'

OPEN: Mon-Sun. **HOURS:** 11.00am-11.00pm (12.00-3.00pm and 7.00-10.30pm Sun). **CREDIT CARDS ACCEPTED:** All major cards. **BAR AND RESTAURANT FOOD AVAILABLE:** 12.00-3.00pm and 7.00-10.00pm. No smoking area. Wheelchair access (but not lavatory). Tables outside seat 85. **BEERS AVAILABLE:** Michelob, Rolling Rock, Castle Lager, Peroni, Tiger, Grolsch. **NEAREST TUBE STATION:** Wimbledon.

The Alma Tavern

8

499 Old York Road, SW18 **081-870 2537**

'Rugby nights are terrific occasions'

Every Victorian schoolboy knew what the Alma was. Alma, battle of; famous victory; Crimean War, 1854. The Alma Tavern was built in Old York Road twelve years later, a hotel at first but now a much-admired Victorian pub.

It stands directly opposite Wandsworth Town station and after victory or defeat at Twickers rugger buggers bound for Waterloo see the Alma's elegant Frenchified dome and pour off the train and straight into the bar. They tend to get home a little later than intended.

The Alma is a prosperous pub faced by shiny glazed tiles, bright green, and inside there are lovely painted mirrors, gold mosaic medallions, a classical plaster freize and a fine mahogany staircase leading out of the bar. They have all been scrupulously restored. In winter a fire blazes in the art deco fireplace and a handsome 1920s range heats the separate dining room. There are morning papers on the bar, a huge baker's dough table and a little French cash kiosk in the dining room. They cultivate Frenchness at the Alma, sell croques monsieur (£2.35), croques madame (£2.65) and cassoulet (£5.25) and a lot of wine. Indeed they have now taken to printing, 'hôtel de la gare' on the menus. 'Tongue in cheek,' says Charles Gotto, the licensee.

The Alma has become a big rugger pub and rugby nights are terrific occasions there. Doesn't the pub fear for the health of its painted mirrors? 'Why?' says rugger fan Gotto. 'They are as good as gold.'

OPEN: Mon-Sun. **HOURS:** 11.00am-11.00pm (12.00-3.00pm and 7.00-10.30pm Sun). **CREDIT CARDS ACCEPTED:** All major cards. **RESTAURANT FOOD AVAILABLE:** 12.00-3.00pm and 7.00-10.30pm. **SET PRICE LUNCH AND DINNER:** £9.95. Wheelchair access. Private room seats 70. **BEERS AVAILABLE:** Young's Special, Tennent's Extra, London Pride, Castlemaine, Oatmeal Stout, Beamish. **NEAREST BR STATION:** Wandsworth Town.

The Anchor

9

Bankside, SE1 **071-407 1577**

'Excuse me, is this the way to the stews?'

Things have certainly changed on Bankside. In Shakespeare's day it was brothels and slums and look at it now, a famous old inn, immaculate in every particular, five bars, a minstrels' gallery, a private 18th-century dining room, a new riverside terrace, a garden terrace, a barbecue and a most superior restaurant.

It was all warehouses and breweries on the river bank by the time the Anchor was built. The new tavern was small but respectable. Henry Thrale, the rich Southwark brewer, owned it and his friend Dr Johnson went there sometimes. He was a man who liked taverns. Oliver Goldsmith, it is said, went too and David Garrick and Edmund Burke.

I'm afraid the Anchor cannot always offer conversation on quite such a high level but it is a fine old pub, much bigger than it looks and full of interest. It takes its beer and its food seriously and the Thrale Bar and the Ale Bar seem hardly to have changed in 200 years. It is not a pub you can leave quietly. In the creaking Olympics the Anchor's floorboards would get the gold.

The restaurant is well known in its own right. Sam Wanamaker often ate there, bringing the likes of Mel Gibson and Michael Caine. He always had table 7, the one in the window. The big new riverside terrace with its serried ranks of picnic tables is a great asset too. As for the view of St Paul's . . .

OPEN: Mon-Sun. **HOURS:** 11.30am-11.00pm (12.00-3.00pm and 7.00-10.30pm Sun). **CLOSED:** Christmas Day, Boxing Day, New Year's Day. **CREDIT CARDS ACCEPTED:** All major cards. **BAR FOOD AVAILABLE:** 11.30am-3.00pm and 5.30-9.00pm. **RESTAURANT FOOD AVAILABLE:** 12.00-2.30pm and 6.00-9.30pm. **SET PRICE DINNER:** £14.95. Wheelchair access (but not lavatory). Beer garden seats 200. Private room seats 50. **BEERS AVAILABLE:** Anchor Bitter, John Smith's, Courage Directors, Courage Best, Adnams, Ruddles County, Kronenbourg, Foster's, Budweiser. **NEAREST TUBE STATION:** London Bridge.

The Angel

10

101 Bermondsey Wall East, SE16 **071-237 3608**

'The haunt of sailors, pirates, smugglers, press gangs, bawds'

There has been an inn here in Rotherhithe, built on piles at the water's edge, since the 17th century, perhaps much earlier, always in the thick of things, around it a warren of tenements, workshops, boatyards, and general riverside carrying-on. There were at least four little bars on the ground floor, the haunt of sailors, pirates, bawds, I suppose bawds, there were always bawds. Pepys knew it well, it appears in his diaries, and Judge Jefferies, they say, watched the hangings on Execution

Dock from the balcony. Sometimes he watched the hangings in one pub, sometimes in another but, disagreeable to the last, he appears to have chosen the Angel to haunt.

Well it has been rebuilt a few times in its day but it has done well to survive at all what with hard times and the Blitz and sundry disasters. In more recent years it was a busy and popular dockers' pub but they too have gone now and the Angel looks a bit lonely in its historic place on the river bank.

The new young landlady reports that old Bermondsey and Rotherhithe residents meet the new incomers in the bar and start to mingle and there's a serious restaurant upstairs with an ambitious menu, venerable and formally dressed waiters and a fine view of Tower Bridge. This attracts business lunchers from the City, not far off, and is open in the evening too.

Almost at the front door is an outcropping of ruin in the centre of a field and a notice telling us that this is the remains of Edward III's moated manor house. Edward III was A Good Thing, in Antonia Fraser's view. He had nothing at all to do with the Angel Tavern.

Bob Hoskins has. He was blown up inside it in the closing shots of *The Long Good Friday*.

OPEN: Mon-Sun. **HOURS:** 11.00am-3.00pm and 5.30-11.00pm (12.30-3.00pm and 7.00-10.30pm Sun). **CLOSED:** Christmas Day, Boxing Day. **CREDIT CARDS ACCEPTED:** All major cards. **BAR FOOD AVAILABLE:** 12.00-2.00pm. **RESTAURANT FOOD AVAILABLE:** 12.00-1.45pm and 7.00-9.45pm (7.00-9.45pm Sat; 12.00-1.45pm Sun). **SET PRICE DINNER:** £15.50. Tables outside seat 20. Private room seats 50. **BEERS AVAILABLE:** Courage Best Bitter, Courage Directors, Webster's, Foster's, Kronenbourg, Beamish, Guinness. **NEAREST TUBE STATION:** Rotherhithe.

The Anglesea Arms (11)

15 Selwood Terrace, SW7 — **071-373 7960**

'everything substantial, nothing too smart'

An owner who will have no modish changes made has been the best possible friend to this lovely pub. It is an early Victorian Free House, an integral part of a prosperous South Kensington terrace and you will find no jukeboxes, fruit machines or television sets in it. There is a large saloon bar and a smaller bar down some steps known as the cubby, very cosy with a fire in winter. Neither ever seem to change. Then there is a stretch of forecourt that some would say was the jewel in its crown. It is a hugely popular place to drink in the summer.

Summer or winter the Anglesea Arms is wonderfully reassuring with its armchairs and buttoned leather settles, its deeply polished woodwork, its pictures and shaded lights, everything substantial, nothing too smart. The hours are unchanged too, time called at 3pm so that the bar gets a clean and a rest in the afternoon.

The owner is Lady Joseph whose late husband, Sir Maxwell Joseph, was chairman of Great Metropolitan. His company owned a great many pubs but this was her own, her personal pub and so it remains.

Pat and Mary Timmons run it immaculately for her. Mary takes charge of the food and Pat the beer.

The Anglesea Arms was the *Evening Standard*'s Pub of the Year in 1988.

OPEN: Mon-Sun. **HOURS:** 11.00am-3.00pm and 5.00-11.00pm. **CLOSED:** Christmas Day and Boxing Day. **CREDIT CARDS ACCEPTED:** Visa, Access. **BAR FOOD AVAILABLE:** 11.00am-3.00pm. **SET PRICE LUNCH:** £4.95 (Sun only). Wheelchair access. Beer garden. **BEERS AVAILABLE:** Adnams, Harveys, Boddingtons, Brakspear, Dorset IPA, London Pride, Young's, Greene King, Abbot Ale, Grolsch, Red Stripe, Foster's, Guinness, Murphys. **NEAREST TUBE STATIONS:** South Kensington, Gloucester Road.

The Antelope

12

22 Eaton Terrace, SW1 — **071-730 7781**

'deeply traditional'

The residents of Eaton Terrace are twice blessed. They live in Eaton Terrace and they have the Antelope on their doorsteps. It is a charming old pub, gentlemanly and understated. It doesn't want to swank but there was an inn on the site for, oh, ages, and the present building goes back to at least 1780, which means that modern Belgravia grew up around it. When the houses arrived the Antelope obligingly provided two front doors, one for the grander household staff led by the butler, the other for Other Ranks. Once safely inside partitions kept them decently apart. There are still the same number of front doors. Fewer butlers though.

The Antelope is deeply traditional. One tradition is good plain cooking. Fanny Craddock said its little panelled restaurant recaptured the flavour of the old chop-house. That is still the aim.

Some things change. For many years customers stood outside on the pavement every summer, enjoying a drink in the sun. There were complaints and they have to stay inside now. Shame.

OPEN: Mon-Sun. **HOURS:** 11.00am-11.00pm (12.00-3.00pm and 7.00-10:30pm Sun). **CLOSED:** Bank Holidays. **CREDIT CARDS ACCEPTED:** All major cards. **BAR AND RESTAURANT FOOD AVAILABLE:** 12.00-3.00pm. Wheelchair access (but not lavatory). Private room seats 40. **BEERS AVAILABLE:** 6 types of Real Ale, Tetley, Nicholson's, Adnams, Castlemaine. **NEAREST TUBE STATION:** Sloane Square. **MAP REF:** 2, F/2

The Archery Tavern

13

4 Bathurst Street, W2 — **071-402 4916**

'Once in a while, an archer might come in'

The Archery Tavern is a pretty country pub tucked away behind Bayswater Road, the archer's pub, rooted in the great days. It was built in 1839 on Thomas Waring's archery range and he is the chap on the inn sign. He was famous in his day, a celeb.

Waring is still there but I'm sorry to say he is just about the only archer who is. It is not that there aren't any archers these days. There are archery clubs all round London, in fact the London Archers are just across the park. They shoot three or four times a week on a strip of land attached to Kensington Palace. But, well, let's face it, there are any number of much nearer pubs. The London Archers go to them.

So the Archery Tavern has to depend on drinkers with other interests and it has no problem there. People love it. It is so genuinely old-fashioned and it has such interesting beers. Badger. Tanglefoot. Blackadder. There's champagne at £2.95 a glass and oysters to go with it in season.

Still the Archery Tavern stays loyal to the idea of archery. It keeps its name, Thomas Waring goes on drawing his bow and there are pictures of old archery occasions all over the walls. And once in a while, an archer might come in.

OPEN: Mon-Sun. **HOURS:** 11.00am-11.00pm (12.00-3.00 and 7.00-10.30pm Sun). **CLOSED:** Christmas Day. **CREDIT CARDS ACCEPTED:** Access, Visa, AmEx, Diner's Club. **BAR FOOD AVAILABLE:** 11.00am-11.00pm. Wheelchair access. Tables outside seat 30. **BEERS AVAILABLE:** Vice Beer, Tanglefoot, Badger Best, Wadworth, Blackadder, Eagle, Hoffbrau lagers. **NEAREST TUBE STATION:** Lancaster Gate.

The Argyll Arms

14

18 Argyll Street, W1 **071-734 6117**

'"Look at ME" is what it's saying'

Round the corner from Oxford Circus, actually squashed up against the side of the Underground station, is this spectacular Victorian pub. It gets packed at lunchtime. It is busy in the afternoon. You can't move in the evening.

This Argyll is the business. First of all it looks so great from the front, all that decoration, all that show. 'Look at ME' is what it's saying so of course you go in and Victoria Regina you are in a glittering mirrored corridor with etched glass partitions opening on small numbered bars. Straight ahead is the big saloon bar, bags of space, bags of swank and behind that is the dining room. Every room is full of people talking.

The small bars at the front are lovely. They give you your own bit of counter and, more important, your own space. People liked that in 1868 and they like it now but all over London grand Victorian pubs like this one have had the partitions they were born with taken away.

They haven't done it at the Argyll so cheers for it and back to our tour. Up the massive mahogany staircase and you are in another big bar, Victorian pastiche up here, recently done but in the spirit of things and a fine view of the London Palladium just across the road. That is where the Duke of Argyll's London house stood, a great mansion, but it came down in the 1860s and with it the original Argyll Arms. This Argyll Arms went up in its place.

It has not changed much. Well, it is not so smokey, there's hidden air conditioning at work and the upstairs bar is different, also the loos. They recently spent £50,000 on them. Gentlemen using the gents now find themselves facing framed pages of the *Financial Times*, thus enabling them, as Kipling advised, to fill each unforgiving minute with sixty seconds worth of distance run.

You might suppose a pub so near Oxford Circus to be on the front line, particularly on Saturday nights, but there is very little trouble. Mike Tayara, the landlord, has a dress code. He asks for 'an acceptable standard of dress' and puts the general absence of aggro on Saturday nights down to this. Others put it down to the large man on the door.

OPEN: Mon-Sat. **HOURS:** 11.00am-11.00pm. **CREDIT CARDS ACCEPTED:** All major cards. **BAR FOOD AVAILABLE:** 11.30am-7.30pm. No smoking area. Wheelchair access (but not lavatory). Private room seats 60. **BEERS AVAILABLE:** Tetley, Nicholson's Best, Wadworth 6X, Pedigree, Greene King IPA, Wells Bombadier Best, Everards Tiger Best. **NEAREST TUBE STATION:** Oxford Circus. **MAP REF:** 1, D/2

The Audley 15

41 Mount Street, W1 **071 499 1843**

'Built in a style that, in the opinion of the Duke, any gentleman's gentleman might enter'

Pubs do not come grander than the Audley. The address says it all: Mount Street, the heart of Mayfair, Berkeley Square at one end, Park Lane at the other. Even Lady Bracknell might have approved of that.

We have the first Duke of Westminster to thank for it. In the early 1880s he was having Mount Street rebuilt and his architects included drawings for a large glitzy public house. He sent them right back, giving them clearly to understand that a gin palace was not what he had in mind. So the Audley was built in a style that, in the opinion of the Duke, would not offend any gentleman's gentleman – neo-French Renaissance, red brick and pink terracotta like the rest of the street. It is, indeed, very imposing and when the British Tourist Board wanted a pub for its London brochure this was the one it chose.

Like all pubs of its generation the Audley mirrored the class divisions of the world outside. It was cut up into a parish of separate bars, each with its own social nuances. Mahogany and etched glass partitions hid each group of customers from the others, while narrow hinged screens hid customers from staff.

The screens and partitions have long gone, of course, and we can see, as the first customers could not, all of the superb plaster ceiling and the whole of the bar itself. The original chandeliers have survived, so have the clocks, so has its general air of being rather a cut above which, indeed, while in the Audley, we all are.

It is the perfect pub to take overseas visitors. It appears on the schedules of all up-market tours and sometimes in the summer it fills up with lively and appreciative American ladies. At other times Japanese, French or German groups take over. The panelled dining room upstairs is a great attraction for them all. You eat formally and substantially here in the well-known English manner, several courses, Stilton, port. The roast beef always goes well, as does the distinctly superior fish with chips.

OPEN: Mon-Sun. **HOURS:** 11.00am-11.00pm (12.00-3.00pm and 7.00-10.30pm Sun). **CLOSED:** Boxing Day. **CREDIT CARDS ACCEPTED:** All major cards. **BAR FOOD AVAILABLE:** 11.00am-9.30pm. **RESTAURANT FOOD AVAILABLE:** 12.00-3.00pm (Sun-Fri) and 5.30-9.30pm (Mon-Sat). **SET PRICE LUNCH AND DINNER:** £15. Wheelchair access. Tables outside seat 30. Private room seats 40. **BEERS AVAILABLE:** Courage, John Smith's, Holsten, Kronenbourg, Miller, Budweiser. **NEAREST TUBE STATIONS:** Green Park, Marble Arch.

The Australian

16

29 Milner Street, SW3 **071-589 3114**

'A golden age'

Brief cricketing interlude . . .

In 1878 Australia, on its second tour, played two matches on the smart new cricket pitch on Prince's Green, now occupied by Lennox Gardens. The first was against the Gentlemen of England. All three Grace Brothers turned out for the Gentlemen who won by an innings and one run. The Australians then played the Players of England. The match was unfinished.

It was a golden age. Dr Grace was in his prime, everyone was playing for the fun of it, England nearly always won and Australian cricketers far from home found a refreshment stop much to their liking in the wide, leafy street that led directly to the cricket ground.

The pub they adopted later renamed itself the Australian and successive licensees have filled the place with cricketing memorabilia. There are early banana-shaped cricket bats, antique cricket balls, a replica of the urn in which the ashes are kept, cigarette cards, an ancient box of Blakey's Cricket Spikes, a terrific carved figure of Don Bradman. Photographs of great cricketers are everywhere.

It is a fine looking pub built with the rest of Milner Street in the 1850s, a three-storey building covered in Virginia creeper with well-used tables on the pavement. It was given an expensive refurbishment early this year and is now a lot less Spartan than in days of old.

It is a serious beer pub with five regular ales but Pimms is a popular local drink and they get through a lot of champagne. Cricket remains an abiding interest, the staff wears the pub's own Australian t-shirts which are for sale and the food is substantial and very English. Double fried egg, gammon, pineapple and chips does well at the Australian.

OPEN: Mon-Sun. **HOURS:** 11.00am-11.00pm (12.30-3.00pm and 7.00-10.30pm Sun). **CREDIT CARDS ACCEPTED:** All major cards except AmEx. **BAR FOOD AVAILABLE:** 12.00-2.30pm (12.00-3.00pm Sat; not Sun). Wheelchair access (but not lavatory). Tables outside seat 25. **BEERS AVAILABLE:** Tetley, Nicholson's, Wadworth, Brakspear, Adnams, Lowenbrau, Carlsberg, Castlemaine. **NEAREST TUBE STATIONS:** Knightsbridge, Sloane Square. **MAP REF:** 2, E/3

The Backpacker

126 York Way, N1 **17**

'A phenomenal number of tinnies'

In the past few years this small pub in the grotty bit behind King's Cross station was first a local called the City of York, then a gay pub called Traffic. .

It is now the Backpacker, a pub famed among young Oz and Kiwi world travellers. They pack in and demolish a phenomenal number of tinnies. Lager is king but there's a big run on green stuff, a Backpacker concotion of celebrated potency. At weekends there's a late licence and a prime time charge to get in. It is not for contemplatives. Fortissimo is one word that comes to mind. Legless is another.

On Sunday afternons the action switches to a remarkable annexe, a large warehouse nearby known as the Church because it only opens on Sundays. Tickets and coupons for lager at the door, entry is Ozzies and Kiwis first, Poms last but once inside everyone equally whoops it up from 12 till 3 when even in this neck of King's Cross Sunday afternoon starts to wind down.

OPEN: Sometimes, probably Thurs-Sat; Sun pm at the Church (follow the crowd). **HOURS:** Flexible. **BEERS AVAILABLE:** Australian canned lager. **NEAREST TUBE STATIONS:** King's Cross, Kentish Town.

The Barley Mow **18**

8 Dorset Street, W1 **071-935 7318**

'The most popular bit of the pub'

The Barley Mow must sometimes miss the old days, lowing herds winding slowly o'er the lea and so on. It still looks every inch the farmers' pub it used to be.

It is full of reminders of days gone by. Brass price lists are still countersunk in the bar counter, so worn you can hardly read them which is as well as the prices are 100 years out of date and there is still an old brass tap behind the bar labelled Old Tom. It was for gin. You brought your own jug and they filled it up.

The Barley Mow's strong card then was English country ales and it still is. It gives you a choice of seven nowadays. The main relics of the past, though, are the three pine kiosks occupying the whole of the left-hand side of the bar. Each has its own bit of counter, a pair of facing benches, a table between and a door with a lock. They are pawnbroker booths. The idea was you slunk in with the family silver, locked the door and did a deal. Pawnbrokers stopped coming years ago but the booths were left and now they are the most popular bit of the pub. People lucky enough to find a free one tend to stay there the rest of the evening.

In late 1967 the Beatles opened their new Apple boutique round the corner in Baker Street and they sometimes popped in to the Barley Mow. Well, you can see it was the sort of pub they would like, plain, old-fashioned, unflash and, with teeny boppers out there in force, I bet the privacy of those nice old booths went down well.

OPEN: Mon-Sat. **HOURS:** 11.00am-11.00pm. **CREDIT CARDS ACCEPTED:** None. **BAR FOOD AVAILABLE:** 12.00-3.30pm. Wheelchair access. **BEERS AVAILABLE:** Becks, Labatts, Miller Lite, Sol, Carlsberg, Lowenbrau, Castlemaine. **NEAREST TUBE STATION:** Baker Street. **MAP REF:** 1, B/4

The Barley Mow

19

Narrow Street, E14 **071-265 8931**

'A dramatic turn of events for any building'

In the days when canals served most of the country the lock at the entrance to the Limehouse Basin was the way in from the Thames to the whole system. The basin had ten acres of water, four acres of quays and wharfs and the river lock, and the dockmaster controlled it all from the big customs house on the river bank.

The Limehouse Basin is a marina now with spankling new waterside houses, 50 berths for canal boats, 50 for seagoing yachts and

high hopes. As for the dockmaster and the customs house, both have new names and new roles. The dockmaster has become the harbourmaster, with new offices in the dock. The customs house has become the Barley Mow. This is a dramatic turn of events for any building, particularly one with such an official, not to say bossy past. It has to be said, though, that the customs house makes a surprisingly good pub. It is a listed building – 'red brick, domestic, early 18th-century style with rusticated stucco quoins' is how the list describes it – so when Taylor Walker took it over in the late 1980s it couldn't be altered too much. Still, it provides an extra-large bar, a spacious restaurant, a big function room upstairs and a huge riverside terrace, and there was a historic name waiting for it – the Barley Mow, after Taylor Walker's famous old brewery the Barley Mow. This was in Limehouse too. The dockmaster used to fly a blue flag if the dock was open, a red flag if it wasn't. His flagpole is still there, flagless at the moment but jaunty and optimistic as flagpoles are. And the views of the river, of course, are beyond price.

OPEN: Mon-Sun. **HOURS:** 11.00am-11.00pm (12.00-3.00pm and 7.00-10.30pm Sun). **CREDIT CARDS ACCEPTED:** All major cards. **BAR FOOD AVAILABLE:** 12.00-2.30pm and 6.30-9.00pm. No smoking area. Wheelchair access (disabled lavatory). Tables outside seat 100. Private room seats 40. **BEERS AVAILABLE:** Tetley, Burtons, Carlsberg, Castlemaine, Budweiser, Labatts. **NEAREST DOCKLANDS STATION:** Limehouse.

The Beaufoy Arms

20

18 Lavender Hill, SW11 **071-228 9246**

'Every night is reggae night'

The leading reggae pub. The sound is up to blast off. SPEAK UP!

An on-the-spot dancer writes: 'Big central bar has mixed crowd sitting and mingling. No room to move but who needs it? Dancing on the spot is the normal way to appreciate sounds from the wheels of steel. There's no live music here. Strictly for reggae lovers only with elements of dancehall, ragga and the safe side of jungle.

'Every night is reggae night but David Rodigan of Kiss FM DJs on Thursdays so walls bulge and punters spill out onto the pavement. Friday nights have Daddy Ernie of Choice FM and other well-known reggae DJs. Saturday is revival night with reggae from the 60s, 70s and 80s. This is Bob Marley time.

'There are exotic dancers during the day hence the large mirror at waist height on the platform.'

OPEN: Mon-Sun. **HOURS:** 11.00-12.00am (12.00-3.00pm and 7.00-10.30pm Sun). **CREDIT CARDS ACCEPTED:** None. **BAR FOOD AVAILABLE:** 11.00-12.00am (12.00-3.00pm and 7.00-10.30pm Sun). **AVERAGE COST:** £3. Wheelchair access. **BEERS AVAILABLE:** Tetley, Burton's, Carlsberg, Castlemaine, Budweiser. **NEAREST BR STATION:** Clapham Junction.

The Beehive

21

407-409 Brixton Road, SW9 **071-738 3643**

'The Beehive even switches off the sound in its games machines'

Until recently the Beehive was a shoe shop. Everyone tells the bar staff it used to be a shoeshop. The bar staff is surprised such a popular shoeshop closed down.

Did the shoeshop have music? Many shops have music in Brixton. Most pubs in Brixton have music non-stop but there is no music in the Beehive. The Beehive is a J D Wetherspoon pub and following its rules to the letter, even switches off the sound in its games machines.

It claims to be the most popular pub in Brixton.

OPEN: Mon-Sun. **HOURS:** 11.00am-11.00pm (12.00-3.00pm and 7.00-10.30pm Sun). **CREDIT CARDS ACCEPTED:** Visa, Delta, Switch. **BAR FOOD AVAILABLE:** 11.00am-11.00pm (12.00-3.00pm and 7.00-10.30pm Sun). **SET PRICE LUNCH AND DINNER:** £3.95. No smoking area. Wheelchair access. **BEERS AVAILABLE:** Theakston Best, Theakston XB, Courage Directors, Younger Scotch Bitter, Wadworth 6X, Becks, Foster's, McEwans. **NEAREST TUBE STATION:** Brixton.

The Bell and Crown

22

72 Strand on the Green, W4 **081-994 4164**

'The whole pub seems to turn towards the river when the sun shines'

Strand on the Green wanders for half a mile along the river bank at Chiswick with beech trees and weeping willows and lovely 18th-century houses. As if this wasn't enough it has three of London's most attractive pubs.

If you walk along this riverside path starting at Kew Bridge you come to the Bell and Crown first, then the City Barge, then the Bull's Head. Meanwhile you will have passed houses in which John Zoffany chose to live and later Hugh Cudlip, Nancy Mitford, Margaret Kennedy, Goronwy Rees and Dylan Thomas. Most of them will have known at least one of these pubs. Dylan Thomas, of course, will have known them all.

The Bell and Crown is marginally the biggest, a well-appointed, comfortable old pub with an air of no expense spared. The polished central counter serves a number of separate drinking areas and a big conservatory. This seems a bit cut off in winter but the whole pub seems to turn towards the river when the sun shines. The conservatory now becomes part of the outdoors with a terrace beneath it under a red and white striped awning and beneath that a patio by the towpath filled with picnic tables under umbrellas. If you can't get a seat in any of these places you can sit on the river wall. People do in great numbers.

At midnight, the pub safely put to bed, the manager and his wife are often out on the towpath. They are not only walking their great dane. They are keeping an eye open for the Bell and Crown's absconding glasses, missed on the staff's earlier glass-hunting sorties.

OPEN: Mon-Sun. **HOURS:** 11.00am-11.00pm (12.00-3.00pm and 7.00-10.30pm Sun). **CREDIT CARDS ACCEPTED:** None. **RESTAURANT FOOD AVAILABLE:** 11.00am-3.30pm and 6.00-10.00pm (12.00-3.00pm and 7.00-10.30pm Sun). **SET PRICE LUNCH:** £3.80. **SET PRICE DINNER:** £5.95. No smoking area. Wheelchair access (but not lavatory). Beer garden seats 30. Private room seats 40. **BEERS AVAILABLE:** London Pride, ESB, Chiswick Special, Hock, Mr Harry. **NEAREST BR STATION:** Kew Bridge.

The Betsey Trotwood

23

56 Farringdon Road, EC1 **071-253 4285**

'Not the waiter . . . the Circle Line'

The Betsey Trotwood is the home from home for journos from the *Guardian* and now from the *Observer* whose offices are just over the road. In the bar to greet them are several life-sized cardboard cut-outs of characters from *David Copperfield*, including young David, Uriah Heep and great-aunt Betsey herself. The pub has a beer exclusively its own called Guardian bitter. A secret brew says the young landlord.

There's a restaurant upstairs and a wine bar downstairs, Todd's, open at lunchtime only. You may notice a distant rumble. That's not the waiter, it's the Circle Line.

OPEN: Mon-Sun. **HOURS:** 11.30am-11.00pm (12.00-3.00pm and 7.00-10.30pm Sun). **CLOSED:** Christmas Day. **CREDIT CARDS ACCEPTED:** None. **RESTAURANT FOOD AVAILABLE:** 12.00-3.30pm. Wheelchair access (but not lavatory). Tables outside seat 20. Private room seats 45. **BEERS AVAILABLE:** Spitfire, Bishops Finger, Master Brew, Guardian, Hurlimanns, Steinbock. **NEAREST TUBE STATION:** Farringdon. **MAP REF:** 5, A/2

The Blackbird

24

209 Earls Court Road, SW5 **071-835 1855**

'No blackbird pies I notice'

If any customers of the Earls Court Road branch of Barclays Bank have been on a particularly long holiday they will get a surprise when they pop into their bank. It is a pub now.

Fuller Smith and Turner, the Chiswick brewer, is doing this to banks. It has launched a series of pubs it calls Ale and Pie houses and has found redundant banks ideal for its purpose. The first one was a National Westminster bank in Fulham Road, now the Stargazey. The Blackbird is its second. Others, apparently, are on their way.

To look at it you would never guess that the Blackbird had ever been anything but a pub. The builders knew all right, they had a terrible job converting it. The walls were feet thick and reinforced.

Down the stairs and their troubles redoubled. It took one man eight days to cut a reasonable opening between two vaults to make a decent-sized beer cellar. The kitchens are down here too and the manager's office. This is the old bank safe. There isn't a window but he keeps the big steel door propped permanently open.

Upstairs in the banking hall, I beg your pardon, the saloon bar the original pillars are in place and the mahogany panelling but the rest is a 1990s version of the 1890s, the golden age, say the designers of pub interiors.

That is just the building. Some would say that what it sells is the important thing, the Fullers beer and the new pie and ale pies. The best seller pie-wise is the steak and ale pie though the chicken and bacon pie is close behind. There are no blackbird pies I notice.

OPEN: Mon-Sun. **HOURS:** 11.00am-11.00pm (12.00-3.00pm and 7.00-10.30pm Sun). **CREDIT CARDS ACCEPTED:** All major cards. **BAR FOOD AVAILABLE:** 12.00-9.00pm. No smoking area. Wheelchair access (but not lavatory). **BEERS AVAILABLE:** ESB, London Pride, Chiswick Bitter, Hock, Summer Ale, Mr Harry. **NEAREST TUBE STATION:** Earls Court.

The Black Cap 25

171 Camden High Street, NW1 **071-485 1742**

'The London Palladium of late night drag'

Every day of the week, sometimes twice on Sundays, stars of the gay pub circuit will be performing somewhere. It might Lee Paris or H I H Regina Fong, Ceri Dupree, Sassy Stryker or Titti la Camp. Sometimes you might get two for the price of one as with the Trollettes, sometimes three as in the Twisted Sisters of Variety, Sandra, Lucia and Millie Turner.

Elaborately wigged, extravagantly gowned, tottering on the highest heels, such starry ladies are in great demand. Some sing, belting out standards like Ethel Merman but louder. Some mime to Shirley Bassey or k d lang but the top stars are the stand-up comics, formidable dames not to be crossed.

They have strong personalities and a large following. Wherever they play, the White Swan in Commercial Road, the Two Brewers in Clapham High Street, the Royal Oak in Hammersmith, the Salmon and Compasses in Islington, the Gloucester in Greenwich, the Father Redap in Camberwell Green, the Royal Vauxhall Tavern in Kennington Lane, they get a hero's welcome.

The Black Cap in Camden Town is the London Palladium of late night drag. Years ago the ground floor of this Victorian pub had a public and a saloon bar on its ground floor, snugs and taprooms too I shouldn't wonder. Now it has one long cabaret bar that opens at 9pm and closes at 2am–3am on Fridays and Saturdays. You pay to get in except on Sundays. It is dimly lit and crowded, with a bar counter running most of its length, stopping to make room for a wider open space and a stage at the far end. The audience – mostly gay men, some gay women – pack the space in front of the stage as midnight approaches.

Upstairs is Shufflewicks Bar, a pleasant bar with unpublike hours – 1pm to 2am Monday to Saturday, noon to 3pm and 7pm to midnight on Sundays. It is named after Mrs Shufflewick, aka Rex Jameson, one of the great drag artists who often appeared downstairs. His LP *A Drop of the Hard Stuff* was recorded live at the Black Cap. He died at 58 in 1983.

There is no one today to touch him.

OPEN: Mon-Sun. **HOURS:** 1.00pm-2.00am Mon-Thur; 1.00pm-3.00am Fri-Sat; 12.00-3.00pm and 7.00pm-12.00am Sun. **CREDIT CARDS ACCEPTED:** None. **BAR FOOD AVAILABLE:** All hours. Wheelchair access. **BEERS AVAILABLE:** Worthington, Grolsch, Tennent's Extra, Tennent's Pilsner, Carling Black Label. **NEAREST TUBE STATION:** Camden Town.

The Blackfriar

26

174 Queen Victoria Street, EC4 **071-236 5650**

'A wonderful gallery of bronze monks'

People seeing the Blackfriar for the first time tend to go quiet and feel the walls. It is a remarkable pub,an outstanding example of art-nouveau and funny with it.

The Blackfriar is a wedge-shaped building opposite Blackfriars station, built on the site of the old Dominican monastery you hear about. The building, put up in 1875, attracted little attention until the architect H Fuller Clarke and the sculptor Henry Poole were called in in the early 1900s. They absolutely transformed it.

Clarke used sumptuous marbles to brilliant effect outside and in and Poole produced a wonderful gallery of bronze monks. That must be the Abbot with hands folded over his tummy, beaming down over the front door. Inside jolly monks have the time of their lives in panels set into the multicoloured marble walls, drinking, singing, fishing, sleeping it off. Theirs, clearly, are the mock-serious wise saws: 'Wisdom is Rare', 'Industry is All'.

It is a leisurely pub with comfortable hours – 11.30am to 11pm, bar snacks lunchtime only. Office workers pop in for a drink on their way home so it has a busy time early in the evening and on warm evenings a happy crowd in business suits gathers on the pavement outside. It doesn't open at all at weekends. As the monks say, industry is all.

OPEN: Mon-Fri. **HOURS:** 11.30am-11.00pm (11.30am-10.00pm Mon-Tue). **CLOSED:** Bank holidays. **CREDIT CARDS ACCEPTED:** Visa, Access. **BAR FOOD AVAILABLE:** 12.00-2.30pm. Wheelchair access (but not lavatory). **BEERS AVAILABLE:** Tetley, Becks, Nicholson's, Adnams, Wadworth, Lowenbrau, Castlemaine, Carlsberg, Guinness, Lebatts, Molsen. **NEAREST TUBE STATION:** Blackfriars. **MAP REF:** 6, B/1

The Black Lion

27

2 South Black Lion Lane, W6 **081-748 7056**

'One of them minds about the ghost'

Walk along the river from Hammersmith Bridge, first the Lower Mall and then the Upper, and you pass five very different and very interesting pubs. This is the fifth you come to.

The Black Lion appears in A P Herbert's *The Water Gypsies* lightly disguised as the Black Swan and is, like the others, old. Like the others it has lovely views of the river and provides a pleasant place to eat and drink outside. In the Black Lion's case it is a garden shaded by a massive chestnut tree even older, they say, than the pub.

The Black Lion, though, has two attractions not offered by the other four. The first is its skittle alley. There are very few left now and the Black Lion's younger customers seem much taken with it.

The other is a more specialized attraction. I must report with some bewilderment that ancient rumours of a ghost at the Black Lion are stoutly defended by the current down-to-earth and largely Australian staff. They all say they have heard the ghost clumping round on the top floor. The manager says he actually saw it once. None of them minds about the ghost, differing in this regard from Mr Francis Smith, an excise officer, who set out from the Black Lion to investigate the ghost in 1804. He laid in wait for it, his fusee primed and loaded, and at midnight the phantom appeared. Mr Smith shot it. Beneath the apparition's shroud was found the dead body of Mr Thomas Milward, a bricklayer. The hauntings ceased.

The less sensational haunting of the top floor of the Black Lion, however, seems to continue and there is good news for the ghost. None of the current staff has a fusee.

OPEN: Mon-Sun. **HOURS:** 11.00am-11.00pm (12.00-3.00pm and 7.00-10.30pm Sun). **CLOSED:** Christmas Day, Boxing Day. **CREDIT CARDS ACCEPTED:** Visa, Mastercard. **BAR FOOD AVAILABLE:** 12.00-2.30pm and 6.00-10.00pm. Wheelchair access (but not lavatory). Beer garden seats 100. Private room seats 44. **BEERS AVAILABLE:** Theakston, Courage Best, Foster's, Kronenbourg, Holsten Export, Guinness. **NEAREST TUBE STATIONS:** Ravenscourt Park, Stamford Brook.

The Blind Beggar

28

337 Whitechapel Road, E1 **071-247 6195**

'A scene that has passed into legend'

On 8 March 1966 George Cornell of the Richardson gang was drinking in the Blind Beggar in Whitechapel Road when Ronald Kray walked into the bar and shot him dead.

It is a scene that has passed into legend: the crowded bar, the Walker Brothers hit on the jukebox, the shots in the air from Kray's minder, customers diving for the floor, the two gangsters facing each other for a long moment. 'Well, look who's here,' Cornell said, whereupon Kray raised his Mauser 9mm and shot him through the forehead.

The Blind Beggar already had a place in the history of the East End. In 1865 the young evangelist William Booth spoke at an open-air meeting on the pavement outside. This was the genesis of the Salvation Army.

Alas it is the other event that holds centre stage. The Blind Beggar has been refurbished time and again. A big conservatory has been added and a beer garden tacked on at the side and people drinking in the comfortable modern bar with its button-backed sofas and red-shaded wall lights talk of other things.

All the same, almost thirty years later, the Blind Beggar is still the pub where Ronnie Kray, hearing that George Cornell had called him a fat poof, sought him out and shot him down.

OPEN: Mon-Sun. **HOURS:** 11.00am-11.00pm (12.00-3.00pm and 7.00-10.30pm Sun). **CLOSED:** Christmas Day, Boxing Day. **CREDIT CARDS ACCEPTED:** None. **BAR FOOD AVAILABLE:** 11.30am-2.30pm Mon-Fri; 6.00-9.00pm Sat; 12.00-2.30pm and 6.00-9.00pm Sun. Wheelchair access. Tables outside seat 100. **BEERS AVAILABLE:** Ruddells County, Ruddells Best, Webster's Yorkshire Bitter, Courage Best, Budweiser, Foster's, Holsten, Carlsberg. **NEAREST TUBE STATION:** Whitechapel.

The Bloomsbury Tavern

29

236 Shaftesbury Avenue, WC2 **071-836 5065**

'Slip out in the interval for a quick half'

This small Victorian pub in Shaftesbury Avenue has just celebrated its 100th birthday. It is in the same block as the Shaftesbury Theatre, so it is handy for pre-theatregoers. Members of the orchestra often slip out in the interval for a quick half.

The panelled bar has wooden partitions which give a bit of privacy if this is what you want, in which case you will like the quiet piped music. There is a small room upstairs j-u-s-t big enough for the pool table.

OPEN: Mon-Sun. **HOURS:** 11.00am-11.00pm (12.00-3.00pm and 7.00-10.00pm Sun). **CREDIT CARDS ACCEPTED:** All major cards except Diner's Club. **BAR FOOD AVAILABLE:** 12.00am-7.00pm (12.00-3.00pm Sun). Wheelchair access (but not lavatory). Tables outside seat 14. Private room seats 20. **BEERS AVAILABLE:** Nicholson's, Bass, Brakspear, Tetley, Tennent's Extra, Carlsberg, Castlemaine, Guiness. **NEAREST TUBE STATIONS:** Leicester Square, Tottenham Court Road. **MAP REF:** 1, E/2

The Blue Anchor

30

13 Lower Mall, W6 **081-748 5774**

'Someone seems to have left their oars behind'

The Blue Anchor is the first of the pubs on Hammersmith's riverside, a handsome old place at least 300 years old. There have, of course, been changes along the way, not least to its name. It started out as the Blew Anchor and Washhouses but as time passed it gave up washing and its spelling improved. The Victorians installed a host of partitions, our generation took them down and so it goes. The old panelling survives though as does the beautiful pewter bar counter.

The Blue Anchor is popular with the rowing club next door and goes in for old rowing photographs. Someone seems to have left their oars behind. There is a rather sombre collection of World War One artefacts, helmets, gasmasks and so on, and banknotes of many lands are pasted up over the bar counter.

This is a busy pub in the summer. Its customers fill the picnic tables lining the river wall and there are cool marble topped tables for them inside. The Georgian bow window has a view of the bridge, the river and the riverside path which used to be much enjoyed by Gustav Holst who taught at the St Paul's Girls School in Hammersmith for thirty-five years. They say he was inspired to write his *Hammersmith Prelude* and *Scherzo for Military Band* sitting at this window.

OPEN: Mon-Sun. **HOURS:** 11.30am-11.00pm (12.00-3.00pm and 7.00-10.30pm Sun). **CREDIT CARDS ACCEPTED:** None. **BAR FOOD AVAILABLE:** 12.00-2.30pm and 6.00-9.00pm. **SET PRICE LUNCH:** £4.25. **SET PRICE DINNER:** £4.50. Wheelchair access (but not lavatory). Tables outside seat 60. Private room seats 38. **BEERS AVAILABLE:** Wadworth, Sol, Molson Dry, Newcastle Brown Ale, Kronenbourg, Brody, Budweiser, Victor Bitter, Diamond White, Holsten Pils, Carlsberg Special Brew, Foster's. **NEAREST TUBE:** Hammersmith Broadway.

The Britannia

31

1 Allen Street, W8 **071-937 1864**

'A series of facelifts'

The Britannia, like Allen Street where you will find it, has steadily improved its lot. The Britannia Brewery was once the main thing there with brewers' drays clattering over the cobbles and everything smelling of hops and just next to it was a little working pub where the men could sample the ale. They called it the Britannia Brewery Tap.

There is still a Britannia Tap in Warwick Road, the smallest pub in London until they made it bigger. The one in Allen Street became more grandly The Britannia and as the street went upmarket it did too. It more than doubled its size and got a series of facelifts, a smart new frontage, window boxes, shutters. The little back room became a big open lounge and a conservatory was built over the old stableyard. There are rings for horses still in the wall and you can see where the forge was.

It is a popular pub. The long-time landlord John Eaglestone collects toby jugs which stand ear to ear on a shelf behind the bar. Isn't that Mae West in the middle?.

OPEN: Mon-Sun. **HOURS:** 11.00am-11.00pm (12.00-3.00pm and 7.00-10.30pm Sun). **CREDIT CARDS ACCEPTED:** None. **BAR FOOD AVAILABLE:** 12.00-3.00pm and 6.00-9.30pm (except Sun). **SET PRICE LUNCH AND DINNER:** £3.50. No smoking area (12.00-3.00pm only). Wheelchair access (but not lavatory). Private room seats 60. **BEERS AVAILABLE:** Young's Bitter, Young's Special, Winter Warmer, London Lager, Premium Lager, Oatmeal Stout, Guinness. **NEAREST TUBE STATION:** High Street Kensington.

MAP REF: 3, D/2

The Bull

32

13 North Hill, N6 **081-340 4412**

'Bang goes the afternoon again'

There is not a moment's doubt about the name of this pub. A very large painting of a very large bull is attached to the wall over the front door. Those who, approaching the door, think that this is a pub called the Cow were not paying attention in biology.

A notice on the front wall tells us that the Bull at Highgate was established on this site 400 years ago and that it used to be called Bellamy's Inn. This name lacked visual possibilities. Then as now North Hill was rather steep at this point and people toiling up the hill were most grateful to find a handsome coaching inn half way up. Bang went the afternoon. Even now when you drive up the hill there is strong temptation to turn into the car park. Bang goes the afternoon again.

Hogarth apparently lodged here. So did Millais, Cruickshank, Morland and Landseer. The present landlord and his Polish wife Ewa, pronounced Ever, have two small children and a pub to run. They don't take lodgers.

In Hogarth's day the Bull had a lot of small bars. Now it has just one big one with lots of pictures of bulls. It also has a spacious terrace with benches and a shady garden, nice in summer when there are barbecues nightly and Punch and Judy shows for the kids.

Families, says landlord Dennis Hutt, very much a family man, are always welcome at the Bull.

OPEN: Mon-Sun. **HOURS:** 12.00-11.00pm (12.00-3.00pm and 7.00-10.30pm Sun). **CREDIT CARDS ACCEPTED:** None. **BAR FOOD AVAILABLE:** 12.00-9.30pm. **SET PRICE SUNDAY LUNCH:** £3.35. Tables outside seat 110. **BEERS AVAILABLE:** Burton Ale, Tetley, Adnams, Carlsberg, Castlemaine, Lowenbrau. **NEAREST TUBE STATION:** Highgate.

The Bull and Gate

33

386 Kentish Town Road, NW5 **071-485 5358**

'Musos are to music what foodies are to food'

A lovely ornate exterior hides two bars. One is a normal pub bar, the other is for musos. Musos are to music what foodies are to food. They take their chances at the Bull and Gate.

A muso writes: 'The Bull and Gate specializes in breaking new bands with at least three playing every night of the week in a music room beyond the little bar. The music room is without chairs, tables and bar counter, a comfort-free zone that often empties between and during acts. Consequently bands can find themselves playing to two mates and a dog.

'Nirvana, Carter and Suede all played here in their early days and a hot new act still draws an excited crowd. Pick your night.'

OPEN: Mon-Sun. **HOURS:** 11.00am-11.00pm (12.00-3.00pm and 7.00-10.30pm Sun). **CREDIT CARDS ACCEPTED:** None. **BAR FOOD AVAILABLE:** 12.00-3.00pm. Tables outside seat 25. Private room seats 150. **BEERS AVAILABLE:** Flowers IPA, Beamish, Toby, Budweiser, Becks, Caffreys, Tennent's Extra, Foster's, Carling Black Label, Newcastle Brown Ale, Rolling Rock. **NEAREST BR STATION:** Kentish Town.

The Bull's Head

34

Strand on the Green, W6 **081-994 1204**

'You don't take the Thames for granted'

The Bull's Head admires but does not altogether trust the river that runs beneath its windows at Strand on the Green. Every month it washes over the towpath. Four or five times a year it covers the benches against the pub walls. It has not got into the pub itself since New Year's Eve 1977 when it swamped the saloon bar and the experts say that this won't happen again. Still, you don't take the Thames for granted.

High tide, low tide, this is a lovely site for a pub. District Line trains rattle across the railway bridge almost overhead but it is surprising how quickly you get used to that and the swans on the foreshore take no notice, nor does the heron on the post in the river, the cormorants on Oliver Island nor, indeed, the customers of the Bull's Head.

It has been there for almost 400 years now and has been expanding lately. It took over two of the pretty cottages on its right for the staff and the one on its left for extra room but from the outside you could never tell. There's an old plan of the interior dated 1803 on the wall and the pub seems much the same.

There is meant to be a secret tunnel to Oliver's Island which is said to have saved Cromwell's bacon during the Civil War. There is some sort of ruin behind the trees but no one lives on the little island now.

Roger and Trish Smart who run the pub for Scottish and Newcastle have spent twenty years by the river. They ran the Ship at

Mortlake before coming here and the early morning rowers, the passing pleasure boats, the waterbirds and a flood every now and then has become part of their lives. It is the really high tides they like best. The river looks wonderful then, they say, and they have the flood boards ready.

OPEN: Mon-Sun. **HOURS:** 11.00am-11.00pm (12.00-3.00pm and 7.00-10.30pm Sun). **CLOSED:** Christmas Day. **CREDIT CARDS ACCEPTED:** All major cards except AmEx. **BAR FOOD AVAILABLE:** 12.00-10.00pm. Wheelchair access. Tables outside seat 30. **BEERS AVAILABLE:** Waddington, Wadworth, Theakston, Courage Directors, Courage Best, Holsten, Budweiser, Foster's, Carlsberg. **NEAREST BR STATION:** Kew Bridge.

The Bunch of Grapes

35

207 Brompton Road, SW3 **071-589 4944**

'Year after year it stays a very classy pub'

The Bunch of Grapes has always been a very classy pub. It is a protected building of course and looks it, granite piers, painted stucco Corinthian columns, a cast-iron balcony and what about the spectacular painted mirrors, the etched glass and the splendid mahogany set-piece in the bar, a hand-carved vine with the ripest grapes? There used to be two of these. The other is now in a pub in Galway or so they say. They don't say what it is doing there.

In its high Victorian days the Bunch of Grapes had six bars with a separate entrance to each. It still has four bars and three entrances and has kept a lot of the old partitions and a set of snob screens in good working order. It does well with food, stalwartly English with a roast every day and there is a firmly worded notice on one of the doors: 'The management regrets that people in dirty clothing will not be served.' The management rightly feels that people will want to look their best in the Bunch of Grapes.

OPEN: Mon-Sun. **HOURS:** 11.00am-11.00pm (12.00-3.00pm and 7.00-10.30pm). **CLOSED:** Christmas Day, Boxing Day. **CREDIT CARDS ACCEPTED:** Visa, Access, Mastercard. **BAR FOOD AVAILABLE:** 11.00am-8.00pm. Wheelchair access. **BEERS AVAILABLE:** John Smith's, Courage Best, Courage Directors, Budweiser, Holsten, Foster's, Carlsberg, Guinness. **NEAREST TUBE STATIONS:** Knightsbridge, South Kensington. **MAP REF:** 2, D/4

The Camden Head

36

Camden Walk, N1 **071-359 0851**

'Glittering and glowing with lovely engraved glass'

The dealers of Camden Passage, one of London's nicest antique markets, have a great prize in the Camden Head.

If an antique has to be 100 years old, well, the Camden Head is nearly there. It was built in 1899 with Queen Victoria nearing the end of her long reign and it is a beautiful public house, perfectly proportioned, richly appointed, glittering and glowing with lovely engraved glass and brilliant-cut mirrors.

It stands, a choice example of the high-Victorian golden age of pub design with exuberant hanging baskets and its terrace spread before it, at a commanding point in the market and if whatever you search for still eludes you, there at the critical moment is the Camden Head.

You can choose between a red plush banquette and one of the stools around the imposing island bar counter, or, on fine days, return with your glass to the terrace. It may be quite a while before you feel inclined to return to the fray.

OPEN: Mon-Sun. **HOURS:** 11.00am-11.00pm (12.00-3.00pm and 7.00-10.30pm Sun). **CLOSED:** Christmas Day. **CREDIT CARDS ACCEPTED:** None. **BAR FOOD AVAILABLE:** 11.00am-3.00pm. Wheelchair access (but not lavatory). Beer garden seats 50. Private room seats 45. **BEERS AVAILABLE:** Theakston Best, Younger IPA, Becks, Guinness. **NEAREST TUBE STATION:** Angel.

The Captain Kidd

37

108 Wapping High Street, E1 **071-480 5759**

'A fine addition to tourist London'

Captain Kidd is a large and exuberant theme pub built on a magnificent site on the river at Wapping just four years ago. The theme is, of course, Captain Kidd, the 17th-century privateer, and his story is told on the walls of the bar in words, pictures and enlarged photostats of original documents. Here is his letter to the Lords of the Admiralty from Newgate Jail pleading for his two black children, here his death warrant...

He was cruelly and, many now think, unjustly done to death on nearby execution dock hard by the Town of Ramsgate. The Town of Ramsgate, small and introvert, is the genuine article. This is an exuberant modern pastiche and it is proving a great success.

A seemingly ancient archway takes you down a cobbled path to a big, cheerful ground-floor bar with a flagstone floor and genuinely brand-new 17th-century features. Above it is another bar largely devoted to bar snacks and with a slightly separate area where children can have soft drinks. On the floor above there is a serious restaurant with an ambitious menu and a serviceable wine list. Each floor has fine river views though the big river terrace at the side has the best, with Canary Wharf mistily downstream.

There was an old warehouse here before but Captain Kidd seems to have been here for ever, massive timbers supporting the ancient structure, open-tread wooden stairs leading uncreaking from floor to floor, all bleached and split, you might suppose, by centuries of spray and sun. You would suppose wrong.

Captain Kidd is what you might call ship-shape and Sam Smith fashion and it is a fine addition to tourist London. It is sure to give the genuinely old pubs of Wapping a run for their money.

OPEN: Mon-Sun. **HOURS:** 11.00am-11.00pm (12.00-3.00pm and 7.00-10.30pm Sun). **CLOSED:** Christmas Day. **CREDIT CARDS ACCEPTED:** All major cards except Diner's Club. **BAR FOOD AVAILABLE:** 12.00-3.00pm and 6.00-9.00pm (12.00-3.00pm and 7.00-9.00pm Sun). **RESTAURANT FOOD AVAILABLE:** 12.00-2.30pm and 6.30-10.30pm (12.00-2.30pm and 7.00-10.30pm Sun). **SET PRICE LUNCH:** £10.95 (Sun). Wheelchair access (disabled lavatory). Beer garden seats 200. Private room seats 60. **BEERS AVAILABLE:** Samuel Smith variants including Old Brewery, Museum Ale, Ayingerbrau. **NEAREST TUBE STATION:** Wapping.

The Cartoonist

38

76 Shoe Lane, EC4 **071-353 2828**

'Robert Maxwell filled the pub with his elephantine bonhomie'

Members of the Cartoonist Club of Great Britain come to this bright modern pub for get-togethers and original cartoons cover the walls of the two bars and the staircase.

Enoch Powell, Margaret Thatcher, Tony Benn, Ken Livingstone, Jeffrey Archer, Ken Dodd, Frank Bruno and Terry Waite (twice, once before, once after) have all been here to receive the Cartoonist Club's annual award. Robert Maxwell filled the pub with his elephantine bonhomie and shook it with the noise of his helicopter.

OPEN: Mon-Fri. **HOURS:** 11.00am-11.00pm. **CLOSED:** Bank holidays. **CREDIT CARDS ACCEPTED:** All major cards. **BAR FOOD AVAILABLE:** 12.00-3.00pm. Wheelchair access. Tables outside seat 100. Private room seats 40. **BEERS AVAILABLE:** Courage Best, Courage Director's, John Smith's, Holsten, Foster's, Carlsberg, Hoffmeister, Guinness, Budweiser, Molsen, Becks, Grolsch, Newcastle Brown Ale. **NEAREST TUBE STATIONS:** Chancery Lane, Blackfriars.

MAP REF: 6, A/1

The Cat and Canary

39

1-24 Fisherman's Walk,
Canary Wharf, E14 **071-512 9187**

'You are not obliged to say grace'

For those who have chosen or been forced to work in or around Canary Wharf here is a refuge. For another see Henry Addington. The Dockland Light Railway takes you to both. You get off at the Wharf, go down the escalator and through the North Colonnade door and there it is, a dark pubby pub that has clearly been there for ever. In fact it sprang into being in June 1992. Most of the woodwork is pretty old, as it happens. It came from redundant Victorian churches and includes some impressive pews and a telephone kiosk that used to be a pulpit.

Despite the ecclesiastic background you are not obliged to say grace before imbibing the excellent beer (including mild) and wines (including French and Australian) but if you are in a confessional mood there is a cosy corner known as the cuddy or a room adjoining it that always seems to bear the notice 'Private Function'. This is said to be reserved for the exchange of rumours by *Daily Telegraph* personnel. The manager, Paul Sykes, is out of sight most of the time. He is the chef and a good one too but his wife Jennie is a welcoming presence in front of house.

While waiting to play bar billiards, darts or shove ha'penny customers can stroll round admiring the pictures including Holbein's *The Ambassadors*, the one with a skull viewed as through a distorting mirror. This is a disturbing image perhaps for more dedicated drinkers.

OPEN: Mon-Sun. **HOURS:** 11.00am-9.00pm Mon-Wed; 11.00am-10.00pm Thur-Fri; 12.00-3.00pm Sat-Sun. **CREDIT CARDS ACCEPTED:** Visa, Access. **BAR FOOD AVAILABLE:** 12.00-3.00pm. No smoking area. Wheelchair access (disabled lavatory). Patio seats 60. Private room seats 25. **BEERS AVAILABLE:** Fuller's, London Pride, ESB, Chiswick Bitter, Hock, Summer Ale, Mr Harry. **NEAREST DOCKLANDS STATION:** Canary Wharf.

The Champion

40

13 Wells Street, W1 — **071-323 1228**

'The main thing is the quite remarkable new windows'

The good news from what New Yorkers would call the garment district is that the Champion is a champion Victorian pub again. Partitions once more shelter the tables round the walls, snob screens have returned if only as a decoration and 18-gallon barrels are back on their perch of honour high above the bar counter.

The main thing, though, is the quite remarkable new windows. When Samuel Smith bought the Champion in the 1980s they commissioned a series of big stained-glass windows from Anne Sotheran of York. They are now splendidly in situ, filling two whole walls. Each celebrates a different champion, Fred Archer, Bob Fitzsimmons, Young Tom Morris, Captain Webb, W G Grace, and they fill the bar with an extraordinary light.

OPEN: Mon-Sun. **HOURS:** 11.00am-11.00pm (7.00-10.30pm Sun). **CLOSED:** Christmas Day, Boxing Day. **CREDIT CARDS ACCEPTED:** None. **BAR FOOD AVAILABLE:** 12.00-3.00pm and 5.30-9.00pm. Wheelchair access. **BEERS AVAILABLE:** Samuel Smith Old Brewery Bitter, Museum Ale, Ayingerbrau Pils, Prinz. **NEAREST TUBE STATIONS:** Tottenham Court Road, Oxford Circus.

MAP REF: 1, D/3

The Champion

41

1 Bayswater Road, W2 — **071-229 5056**

'Uncamp uncomplicated gay local'

This long-established uncamp uncomplicated gay local in Notting Hill Gate has quietly got on with its life on this busy main road for years, hardly attracting a second glance.

OPEN: Mon-Sun. **HOURS:** 12.00-11.00pm (12.00-3.00pm and 7.00-10.30pm Sun). **CLOSED:** Christmas Day, Good Friday. **CREDIT CARDS ACCEPTED:** None. Wheelchair access. Tables outside seat 15. **BEERS AVAILABLE:** Worthington Best, Carling Black Label, Tennent's Extra, Tennent's Pilsner, Guinness. **NEAREST TUBE STATION:** Notting Hill Gate.

The Chandos

42

29 St Martin's Lane, WC2 **071-836 1401**

'If you are merely passing, wave to the burly cooper working on the ledge'

Samuel Smith, the Yorkshire brewers, were taking no chances on unknown, untried Southern builders when they bought this busy London pub ten years ago. There was a lot to be done so they brought men up from Yorkshire to do it.

People hardly recognized the old Chandos when it reopened. The building seemed to have been totally refaced. It had a gleaming black and gold fascia and immaculate new stucco and it was quite different inside – new fittings, new panelling, new just about everything. Victorian mahogany drinking booths, handmade by the joiners from Tadcaster, lined the walls of the big downstairs bar. Pairs of button-back leather sofas faced each other across coffee tables in the grandly named Opera Room upstairs. The Yorkshiremen, well pleased, went home again.

The Opera Room has a long day. It has its own staircase to the street, opens for breakfast at 9am and subsequently offers coffee, lunch, tea and supper. The downstairs bar opens at 11am. Both stay open until 11pm with bar food always on the go.

It is a useful, well turned out pub in a great position. We all find ourselves at the corner of St Martins Lane and William IV Street sometime and if you go in look at the framed photographs in the bar. That is head joiner Bob Simpson and those are the Yorkshire craftsmen who came to London in 1984 and did the hard graft.

OPEN: Mon-Sun. **HOURS:** 9.00am-11.00pm (12.00-10.30pm Sun). **CLOSED:** Christmas Day, New Year's Day. **CREDIT CARDS ACCEPTED:** Visa, Access. **BAR FOOD AVAILABLE:** 9.30-10.30am, 11.00am-2.45pm, 5.30-9.30pm. Wheelchair access (but not lavatory). **BEERS AVAILABLE:** Samuel Smith Old Brown Bitter, Museum Ale, Cider Reserve, Extra Strong Beer, Dark Mild Beer, Ayingerbrau Prinz, Pils. **NEAREST TUBE STATION:** Charing Cross.

MAP REF: 1, E/1

The Charlie Chaplin

43

26 New Kent Road, SE1 **071-703 6117**

'A workaday local'

This is a newish pub, a workaday local tucked between the Elephant and Castle's film centre and its vast pink shopping centre. There is a large cut-out of Charlie on its front. He lived round here.

OPEN: Mon-Sun. **HOURS:** 11.00am-11.00pm (12.00-3.00pm and 7.00-10.30pm Sun). **CLOSED:** Christmas Day. **CREDIT CARDS ACCEPTED:** None. **BAR FOOD AVAILABLE:** 11.00am-2.00pm (Mon-Fri only). Wheelchair access. Beer garden seats 24. Private room seats 200. **BEERS AVAILABLE:** Ruddells, Foster's, Carlsberg, Becks, Holsten, Guinness. **NEAREST TUBE STATION:** Elephant and Castle.

MAP REF: 7, B/1

Chelsea Potter

44

119 King's Road, SW3 **071-352 9479**

'A seat in the stalls'

Since the dawn of time the Chelsea Potter has occupied a prime corner of King's Road, its two window walls providing a seat in the stalls on the sometimes exotic passing scene.

In 1994 it got a massive renovation. The inside was gutted, skips brimmed over, pub designers, pub fitters, pub decorators came and went. It is much smarter now.

OPEN: Mon-Sun. **HOURS:** 11.00am-11.00pm (12.00-3.00pm and 7.30-10.30pm Sun). **CLOSED:** Christmas Day, Boxing Day. **CREDIT CARDS ACCEPTED:** Visa, Diner's Club, Mastercard. **BAR FOOD AVAILABLE:** 12.00-5.00pm (12.00-2.30pm Sun). Wheelchair access. Tables outside seat 30. **BEERS AVAILABLE:** Sol, Molsen Dry, Budweiser, Becks, Special Brew, Holsten Pils, Carlsberg, Kronenbourg. **NEAREST TUBE STATION:** Sloane Square.

MAP REF: 2, D/2

The Cheshire Cheese

45

5 Little Essex Street, WC2 **071-836 2347**

'If there is a list of haunted inns it will be there'

This is not to be confused, as they say, with Ye Olde Cheshire Cheese though it often is. American visitors sometimes photograph it inside and out before discovering that there is a rather better known Cheshire Cheese ten minutes' walk away.

This, though, is quite an old pub too and well known in some quarters. If there is a list of haunted inns it will be there. Its ghost pushes the fruit machine around at night and managers, alone in the pub at weekends, sometimes hear the dumb waiter inexplicably on its way up.

The pub closes at weekends but during the week the saloon bar stays open all day. It has Sky TV Sport. The dive bar's customers are noticeably younger. This is where the music is.

OPEN: Mon-Fri. **HOURS:** 11.30am-11.00pm. **CLOSED:** Bank holidays. **CREDIT CARDS ACCEPTED:** Visa, Mastercard, Diner's Club, Switch. **BAR FOOD AVAILABLE:** 11.30am-11.00pm. **RESTAURANT FOOD AVAILABLE:** 12.00-2.30pm. Wheelchair access. Private room seats 30. **BEERS AVAILABLE:** Courage Best, Courage Directors, Theakston, Foster's, Kronenbourg, Holsten, Beamish, Budweiser. **NEAREST TUBE STATIONS:** Temple, Charing Cross.

MAP REF: 6, A/1

The Churchill Arms

46

119 Kensington Church Street, W8 **071-727 4242**

'Irish landlord, Thai chef and himself at his most cherubic'

Winston would have liked this pub, very English and distinctly eccentric as it is with its Irish landlord, Thai chef and himself at his most cherubic, beaming down from the pub sign on all who pass that way.

It was called the Marlborough once but there have been some changes made, particularly since Gerry O'Brien took over 10 years ago. He replaced the backyard and garage with a conservatory that has 70 people eating in it most lunchtimes and his various collections cover the walls and ceilings. There are umpteen pictures of Winston, Winston mugs and statuettes and the conservatory has his collection of mounted butterflies, 1600 of them from all over the world.

In the summer live butterflies, bought as chrysalises from the butterfly house at Syon Park, hatch out and flit among the luxuriant greenery, settling hither and yon. The windows are open and eventually they take their chances in Kensington Church Street.

In the bar you can't see the ceiling for baskets, hat boxes, jugs, steins, lanterns and the like and marching above your head is a double row of chamber pots. In this jokey pub which has a wall covered in prime ministers this is labelled the Chamber Lane.

But what has brought particular renown to the Churchill Arms is its Thai food. The kitchen has a staff of eight, all Thais and they have undoubtedly helped to transform its fortunes. It has been Fuller's top profit maker three years running.

OPEN: Mon-Sun. **HOURS:** 11.00am-11.00pm (12.00-3.00pm and 7.00-10.30pm Sun). **CREDIT CARDS ACCEPTED:** All major cards, except AmEx. **RESTAURANT FOOD AVAILABLE:** 12.00-2.30pm and 6.00-9.30pm. Wheelchair access (but not lavatory). **BEERS AVAILABLE:** Chiswick, ESB, London Pride, Carlsberg, Heineken, Grolsch, Castlemaine. **NEAREST TUBE STATION:** Notting Hill Gate. **MAP REF:** 3, C/2

The Cittie of Yorke

47

22 High Holborn, WC1 **071-242 7670**

'The great hall of a medieval manor'

When the Yorkshire Brewers Samuel Smith made their first sally into London in 1979 they bought Hennekey's, well known, long established, much respected. They thus acquired six fine London pubs. This one sold only wine for more than 100 years. It was surely the greatest prize.

It was the original Hennekey's and it was famous. It had evolved from an ancient inn built in 1430 and largely rebuilt every 200 years or so. It emerged in its present form in the 1890s, and such a form . . .

There is no pub in London quite like this one. The main bar resembles the great hall of a medieval manor rising to a soaring trussed roof and high Gothic windows. Along one wall is the bar, shorter than it used to be but still one of the longest in Britain. Above it huge iron-hooped wine butts sit on a stout timber gallery supported by fluted iron pillars. Each butt once held 1000 gallons of wine. They were in active use right up to the outbreak of the last war when they were carefully drained. A well-placed bomb might have carried off the customers in a tidal wave of amontillado.

Small cubicles line the facing wall, a table and four chairs in each. They were originally kept for lawyers and their clients but they now have to take their chances like everyone else. The cubicles are very popular, as is the massive stove on cold days. It was made in 1815 and still works perfectly. Each of its three sides has an open grate and there is no sign of a chimney. That is under the floorboards.

Samuel Smith's made some alterations. They made a second, smaller bar at the Holborn end and a long cellar bar downstairs and, of course, they gave it a quaint new name. Well, there was a pub called the Cittie of Yorke in these parts in times gone by. Furthermore, olde Sam Smith does come from Yorke or not far offe. He brews good beer at Tadcaster and this and only this is now sold at all his London pubs. There were 27 of these at last count. As for the Cittie of Yorke, it is clearly in good heart. It remains a spectacular pub.

OPEN: Mon-Sat. **HOURS:** 11.30am-11.00pm (11.30am-3.00pm and 5.30-11.00pm Sat). **CLOSED:** Bank holidays. **CREDIT CARDS ACCEPTED:** Access, Visa, Mastercard, AmEx. **BAR FOOD AVAILABLE:** 12.00-2.30pm and 5.30-10.00pm. Wheelchair access. Private room seats 300. **BEERS AVAILABLE:** Old Brewery Bitter, Museum Ale. **NEAREST TUBE STATION:** Holborn.

The City Barge

48

27 Strand on the Green, W4 **081-994 2148**

'Someone, incredibly, pinched Queen Elizabeth I's Charter'

I don't suppose the City Barge was a prime target during the war. Presumably the landmine that got it was meant for the railway bridge. It missed though and knocked down most of this nice old riverside pub instead. The authorities debated. Perhaps they should take the rest down too but the City Barge just carried on trading so that was all right. An elderly regular remembers the time well. He arrived at the pub for a drink and found it hadn't got a roof and the rubble was up to here. He got his drink as usual.

Someone, incredibly, pinched Queen Elizabeth I's Charter which had been on the wall and hasn't been seen since but the ancient fireplace with its grate raised to stop floods putting the fire out survived, so did the bar counter, so did the parliamentary clock made without glass to save tax.

So the City Barge was patched up and after the war it was rebuilt. on the original 1484 foundations. The pub was the Navigator's Arms in those days and Richard III was in the winter of his discontent. It is slightly bigger now. You go down a few steps to the old bar which is much as it was before the bombing, small, homely, old-fashioned. The new bar is up a few steps, larger with a long counter and drinking booths. They have live music up here every weekend.

Like the Bull's Head, its near neighbour, the City Barge has Oliver Cromwell stories. It has Beatles stories too. A sequence of *Help!* was filmed here and John, Paul, George and Ringo had a few days filming by the river. The bit where Ringo falls into the cellar was shot in the studio. The City Barge doesn't have a cellar. The river keeps trying to get in so the beer is safer higher up.

OPEN: Mon-Sun. **HOURS:** 11.30am-11.00pm (12.00-3.00pm and 7.00-10.30pm Sun). **CREDIT CARDS ACCEPTED:** Visa, Access, Mastercard. **BAR FOOD AVAILABLE:** 12.00-2.30pm Mon-Sun; 5.00-9.00pm Mon-Sat. Wheelchair access (but not lavatory). Tables outside seat 33. **BEERS AVAILABLE:** John Smith's, Wadworth 6X, Theakston Best, Old Peculier, Courage Directors, Courage Best, Holsten, Miller, Tennent's Pilsner, Foster's, Heineken Export, Guinness, Beamish. **NEAREST TUBE STATION:** Gunnersbury.

The Clachan

49

34 Kingly Street, W1 **071-734 2659**

'The old Scots word for meeting place, and Scots do on occasions meet there'

Kingly Street must always have been a pain for Liberty's, nipping in as it does and cutting the great department store in two. The three-storey bridge that crosses Kingly Street is just Liberty's trying to get from one bit of the store to the other.

Go under the bridge and on the left is a small but perfectly formed public house, rather romantic, faintly Scottish, a turret on the corner adding a green copper dome to the skyline. This, until quite recently, was the Bricklayers and Liberty's owned it.

What, though, was Liberty's to do with it? It did not want a pub. It did want more space for warehousing. Perhaps . . . But no. The Bricklayers was a protected building as Liberty's itself is. A pub it had to stay. So in 1983 Nicholson's bought it, smartened it up, and changed its name. It is now the Clachan, the old Scots word for meeting place and, Scots do on occasions meet there. There is a large air conditioned bar, at least six real ales on tap and a good-sized clachan.

The haggis is piped in on Burn's Night and there are pictures of bearded Highland worthies but apart from this Nicholson's has resisted smothering the Clachan in tartan.

OPEN: Mon-Sat. **HOURS:** 11.00am-11.00pm. **CLOSED:** Christmas Day. **CREDIT CARDS ACCEPTED:** Visa, AmEx. **BAR FOOD AVAILABLE:** 11.00am-8.30pm. **SET PRICE LUNCH:** £5.65. Wheelchair access (but not lavatory). Private room seats 35. **BEERS AVAILABLE:** Tetley, Nicholson's, Greene King, Marston's Pedigree, Adnams, Wadworth, Bass, Becks, Castlemaine, Carlsberg, Guinness. **NEAREST TUBE STATION:** Oxford Circus. **MAP REF:** 1, D/2

The Clarence

50

53 Whitehall, SW1 **071-930 4808**

'You won't get malmsey at the Clarence. It is a real ale house'

Ancient overhead timbers from a Thames pier, wonderful cellars under Whitehall, leaded windows throwing delicate patterns on the pale wooden floor, this is a most romantic old pub.

It has tremendous appeal for tourists. It used to provide a jester for them every summer but this seemed a bit over the top and anyway he retired. They are pleased to find the settles and benches still there and the panelled restaurant upstairs with its view of Big Ben and come the evening the gas lights are lit and the lanterns outside come into their own and the place looks, if anything, even better.

Inigo Jones's famous banqueting hall is just two blocks away. It was from one of its windows that Charles I stepped onto the scaffold to face the executioner. Every year Roundheads and Cavaliers mark the anniversary of this grisly event with a toast in the Clarence.

I suppose the Clarence who gave his name to the Clarence was William IV, the sailor king. He was Duke of Clarence at the time. But this was the king who gargled two gallons of water every morning. Is he a suitable role model? Richard III's brother, poor perjured Clarence, won't do either, drowning, as he did, in a butt of malmsey.

You won't get malmsey at the Clarence. It is a real ale house – seven real ales on the handpumps, two more to follow. A butt of Brakspear's old ale, now . . .

OPEN: Mon-Sun. **HOURS:** 11.00am-11.00pm (12.00-3.00pm and 7.00-10.30pm Sun). **CREDIT CARDS ACCEPTED:** All major cards. **RESTAURANT FOOD AVAILABLE:** 11.00am-9.00pm. Wheelchair access (not lavatory). Beer garden seats 24. Private room seats 25. **BEERS AVAILABLE:** Wadworth, Brakspear, Theakston, Abbot Ale, Courage Directors, Courage Best, Ruddells County, John Smith's, Foster's, Holsten. **NEAREST TUBE STATIONS:** Charing Cross, Embankment. **MAP REF: 8, D/2**

Clutterbuck's Ale House

51

329 Edgware Road, W2 **071-723 3899**

'Used, it is said, by Dick Turpin on his way to York'

Clutterbuck's (Est 1721) it says boldly on the brand-new facias. But isn't this a new chain of real ale houses (Est 1992)? Ah yes, Taylor Walker would say, but there was a Thomas Clutterbuck and it was his brewery that was est 1721. So that has cleared that up.

There are six Clutterbuck's to date – Romford, Camden Town, Tottenham, Wanstead, Whitechapel and this one in Edgware Road. They were all ordinary working pubs that had passed their sell-by date and they have all been much improved. They provide wholesome old-time surroundings and plain old-fashioned pub food. There is no music, no tv, no gaming machines. There isn't even darts.

This one was the Wheatsheaf, a reasonable local in its day, used, it is said, by Dick Turpin on his way to York, but latterly in the grip of terminal seediness. So it got a new look, a new role and a new name. It seems to have got older rather than younger, emerging as an agreeable old-fashioned ale house with no fewer than eight real ales at the bar led by Clutterbuck bitter at £1.10 a pint.

The one thing they kept from the old Wheatsheaf days was the ceramic relief of Ceres, the Corn Goddess, on the wall. She had a daughter by Jupiter. [No gossip please. Ed.]

OPEN: Mon-Sun. **HOURS:** 11.00am-11.00pm (12.00-3.00pm and 7.00-10.30pm Sun). **CLOSED:** Christmas Day. **CREDIT CARDS ACCEPTED:** None. **BAR FOOD AVAILABLE:** 12.00-6.30pm. Wheelchair access. **BEERS AVAILABLE:** Clutterbuck's Bitter, Tetley, Adnams, Marsden Pedigree, Lowenbrau, Carlsberg, Castlemaine, Guinness. **NEAREST TUBE STATION:** Edgware Road.

The Coach and Horses 52

29 Greek Street, W1 **071-437 5920**

'"YOU'RE BANNED!"'

The Coach and Horses, now one of Soho's most celebrated pubs, stands opposite Kettners on the corner of Romilly Street and Greek Street and with its Victorian pillars looks sober enough. Inside, though, its red plastic stool covers, black Formica table tops and Basic Food Hygiene Certificate announce that this is a pub for serious drinkers. It owes its new-found fame to the painter Francis Bacon, to the cartoonist Michael Heath, to the staff of *Private Eye* but mostly to Jeffrey Bernard, serious drinker *in excelsis*. Bernard, of course, was the central character in *Jeffrey Bernard is Unwell* and wherever it is performed there is the Coach and Horses on the stage, Bernard himself locked in and its irascible proprietor Norman Balon a powerful off-stage presence.

For many years *Private Eye* had its offices opposite the pub and it became a haunt of Richard Ingrams, Peter Cook, William Rushton, Michael Heath – and Jeffrey Bernard. *Private Eye* still has its fortnightly lunches in an upstairs room although lunches in the pub itself have been stopped. The Heath cartoons on the wall all feature life in the Coach and Horses. Most show a little man, in one case from the Inland Revenue, peering round the door and saying 'Jeff bin in?' The other recurring figure is Norman Balon booming at regulars, some of them prostrate and used as footrests. 'Don't you have no homes to go to?' he'll be shouting or 'YOU'RE BANNED!' He claims to be London's rudest landlord and no one disputes it.

Balon is sometimes taken for Walter Matthau. This annoys him, as do most things, a discovery soon made by playgoers arriving at the pub in search of Jeffrey Bernard.

'Sorry I was rude last night but I was sober,' says one of Heath's Coach and Horses characters.

'Let me through, I'm an alcoholic,' says another, fighting his way to the bar.

OPEN: Mon-Sun. **HOURS:** 11.00am-11.00pm (12.00-3.00pm and 7.00-10.30pm Sun). **CREDIT CARDS ACCEPTED:** None. Wheelchair access (but not lavatory). **BEERS AVAILABLE:** Burton Ale, Tetley, Dorchester Bitter, Castlemaine, Lowenbrau, Carlsberg, Guinness. **NEAREST TUBE STATION:** Piccadilly Circus. **MAP REF:** 1, E/2

The Coach and Horses

53

5 Bruton Street, W1 **071-629 4123**

'Much smaller than you think'

Observe the jolly Christmas card exterior of this Mayfair pub, black-and-white Tudor, diamond-paned heraldic windows, cascades of ivy from ancient first-floor window boxes, what marvellous nick it seems to be in for a building of its age.

Ah well yes. It is said to be have been built in 1741 but in fact it was knocked about so badly in the war that it is mostly new really and much smaller than you might think from the outside. It has a single, narrow bar on the ground floor, cosy but often crowded, and a rather more roomy dining room upstairs where traditional pub lunches and suppers are served.

They do quite well with weddings. If you want to be married from the Coach and Horses you hire the whole pub.

OPEN: Mon-Sat. **HOURS:** 11.00am-11.00pm (11.00am-6.00pm Sat). **CLOSED:** Bank holidays. **CREDIT CARDS ACCEPTED:** Visa, Access. **BAR FOOD AVAILABLE:** 11.00am-2.30pm and 6.00-8.00pm. Private room seats 36. **BEERS AVAILABLE:** Theakston, Flowers IPA, McEwan Export, Becks, Harp. **NEAREST TUBE STATIONS:** Bond Street, Green Park. **MAP REF:** 1, C/2

The Coal Hole

54

91 Strand, WC1 **071-836 7503**

'The coalheavers moved on'

In the distant days of the Coal Hole's notoriety it was a coalheavers' hang-out in old converted cellars off the Strand. The coalheavers drank and carried on, word got round and others started going. Actors and the like . . .

Edmund Kean, the great tragedian of the day, liked a bit of low life and loved the Coal Hole. He started the Wolf Club there, a club dedicated to carrying on. Byron came once but didn't like it. Then there was a craze for mock trials there, described as 'clever but disgusting Judge and Jury Entertainment'. They might do well now.

The coalheavers moved on to the Ship and Shovel and the Coal Hole moved further along the Strand to proper premises in the Savoy buildings and that is where it is today. The old Coal Hole makes the present Coal Hole seem very respectable which, though I would not want to hurt its feelings, I believe it is.

The main bar on the Strand is high and handsome with large windows, hanging banners and marble reliefs of frisking maidens – Muses perhaps, or seasons. A recent refurbishment made a pleasant little gallery out of what was the manager's office.

The cellar bar has been much smartened up lately. It has its own entrance on the Strand and its own lively following. It is an interesting bar, wandering off downhill a bit, and at its far reaches is a locked gate beyond which some steps lead down to a little windowless snug.

This, they will tell you, is the coal hole. It certainly could be a coal hole. People drink in it sometimes. It is not for claustrophobics.

OPEN: Mon-Sat. **HOURS:** 11.00am-11.00pm. **CLOSED:** Bank holidays. **CREDIT CARDS ACCEPTED:** Visa, Access, AmEx. **BAR FOOD AVAILABLE:** 11.30am-2.30pm. **SET PRICE LUNCH:** £5. Wheelchair access (but not lavatory). Tables outside seat 12. **BEERS AVAILABLE:** Tetley, Brakspear, Bass, Wadworth, Nicholson's, Castlemaine, Lowenbrau, Carlsberg, Oranjeboom. **NEAREST TUBE STATIONS:** Covent Garden, Charing Cross.

MAP REF: 1, F/1

The Cock Tavern

55

27 Great Portland Street, W1 **071-631 5002**

'The lanterns were the thing'

All self-respecting Victorian and Edwardian pubs had lanterns over the door and as time passed they got bigger and bigger, symbols of status, conspicuous consumption and virility.

When the Cock Tavern opened in 1904 it had not one lantern but four, all of them immense. It also had a turret, a terracotta frieze and bearded heads of bacchants, not to mention five bars, each with a separate entrance to the street, but the lanterns were the thing. No one could miss the message. There was nothing henpecked about the Cock Tavern.

And yet somewhere along the line these huge lanterns went missing. Whatever happened to them? Surely they weren't nicked. I mean, four gargantuan lanterns, someone would have noticed. Anyway, they certainly weren't there when Samuel Smith bought the pub in the eighties and once you saw the old photographs the Cock Tavern just didn't look right without them.

The new owners saw what they must do. They put back partitions in the bar, resurfaced the frontage in polished granite, got new bacchants carved and, most essentially, had replicas of the lanterns made.

They are back up now, all four of them. They are huge. The Cock Tavern, not a modest pub, thinks they are the biggest lanterns in London.

OPEN: Mon-Sun. **HOURS:** 11.30am-11.00pm (12.00-3.00pm and 7.00-10.30pm Sun). **CLOSED:** Christmas Day. **CREDIT CARDS ACCEPTED:** AmEx. **RESTAURANT FOOD AVAILABLE:** 12.00-2.30pm. Wheelchair access (but not lavatory). Tables outside seat 36. Private room seats 100. **BEERS AVAILABLE:** Old Brewery Bitter, Museum Ale, Ayingerbrau. **NEAREST TUBE STATION:** Oxford Circus. **MAP REF:** 1, D/3

The Cocoanut

56

16 Mill Street,
Kingston

081-546 3978

'There aren't many cocoanuts left with this spelling'

The Cocoanut, as the landlord will tell you, is the only pub with this name in the country and there aren't many cocoanuts left with this spelling either. This, though, is how you spelled coconuts in the days when they were unshipped at Kingston in large numbers for the local coconut matting factory. The management put up a beer shed for its workers who called it the Cocoanut. Welcome to the pub...

The current building was begun just before the war. Then Hitler intervened with a novel planning objection and all work stopped until that little matter was settled. Eventually, the war over, the builders returned and a brand new Cocoanut opened on Coronation Day. Hilary and Tensing were so pleased they climbed Everest.

The Cocoanut, then, is a fairly recent addition to a noticeably bosky scene but it nestles so comfortably among pretty cottages that you hardly notice that it is so much younger than they are.

There is a homely public bar with pool, darts, crib, dominoes and even shove-ha'penny, a comfortable lounge bar and a pretty paved garden at the back with a pergola and a barbecue.

Benji, a large golden retriever with a taste for crisps, is in charge.

OPEN: Mon-Sun. **HOURS:** 11.00am-3.00pm and 5.30-11.00pm Mon-Fri; 11.00am-11.00pm Sat; 12.00-3.00pm and 7.00-10.30pm Sun. **CREDIT CARDS ACCEPTED:** None. **BAR FOOD AVAILABLE:** 12.00-2.00pm. **AVERAGE COST:** £5. **SET PRICE LUNCH:** £3.40. Wheelchair access. Beer garden seats 30. Car park. **BEERS AVAILABLE:** Hock, Chiswick Bitter, London Pride, Mr Harry, ESB. **NEAREST BR STATION:** Kingston.

The Coleherne

57

261 Old Brompton Road, SW1

'Full biker gear'

This is the most famous gay pub in the world and one subject to affectionate community jokes among gay men. The butt of the joke is the guy in full biker gear who rides a push bike; the lean leather-clad thug who is really the bank manager.

The Coleherne is a dark, cavernous, rather gloomy Victorian pub in Earls Court. The atmosphere is macho and slightly menacing with little of the gaiety of the usual gay pub. The leather boys gather on one side of the big U-shaped bar. They have their own entrance and loo. A large picture of Hells Angels glowers down. Less flamboyant customers line the baron the other side.

Serial killer Colin Ireland, now serving life, met his victims here. During his trial there were said to be more reporters in the Coleherne than regular customers.

In the Coleherne you either stand or lean. There are bare wooden floors and next to no furniture. In the far room is a large wooden cube which, when pulled forward, makes an apron stage for the strippers on Thursday nights.

The noise level is moderate, all things considered. There is no conversation at all among the leather boys. They hold pints and stare straight ahead. Things get jollier as the main body of the pub fills up and the music gets louder.

To the disappointment of tourists and reporters there is no how's your father.

OPEN: Mon-Sun. **HOURS:** 11.00am-11.00pm (12.00-3.00pm and 7.00-10.30pm Sun). **CREDIT CARDS ACCEPTED:** None. **BEERS AVAILABLE:** Worthington Best, Toby, Tennent's Extra, Tennent's Pilsner, Carling Black Label. **NEAREST TUBE STATION:** Earls Court.

Compton Arms

58

4 Compton Avenue, N1 **071-359 2645**

'Under a friendly sycamore tree . . .'

A quiet little pink-washed country pub hidden away off Canonbury Square. There's a small cosy low-ceilinged bar where local artists show their work and benches round cask tables under a friendly sycamore tree at the back. Crib and dominoes but not a jukebox or gaming machine in sight . . .

OPEN: Mon-Sun. **HOURS:** 11.00am-11.00pm (12.00-3.00 and 7.00-10.30pm Sun). **CREDIT CARDS ACCEPTED:** Access, AmEx, Eurocard. **BAR FOOD AVAILABLE:** 11.00am-10.00pm. Wheelchair access (but not lavatory). Beer garden seats 20. **BEERS AVAILABLE:** Molsen, Stella, Miller, Greene King, Flowers IPA, Abbot Ale, Rayment's, Harp, Kronenbourg, Guinness. **NEAREST TUBE STATION:** Highbury and Islington. **MAP REF:** 5, D/2

The Coopers' Arms

59

87 Flood Street, SW3 **071-376 3120**

'Denis must have looked in sometimes, surely'

Good mannered, good natured, we have here a thoroughly well-bred pub with staff and customers in complete accord. Parents may raise an eyebrow to find Justin or Julian serving behind the bar but it is usually an enjoyable interlude, to be dined out on later. For the moment the City can wait.

A massive buffalo head, a gift from a customer, presides over the bar, a baker's dough table occupies an extravagant amount of floor space, a splendid LMS long-case clock looks as though it was made for the end wall and two massive air filters on the ceiling keep the air clear and smokers and non-smokers in harmony. The brasserie style food is a major attraction. Upstairs is a useful room for special occasions, graced by a magnificent 17-foot table (originally a draughtsman's table from a Jarrow shipyard).

Lady Thatcher used to live in Flood Street. This then was her local. No one recalls seeing her in the Coopers' Arms but Denis must have looked in sometimes, surely.

OPEN: Mon-Sun. **HOURS:** 11.00am-11.00pm (12.00-3.00pm and 7.00-10.30pm Sun). **CLOSED:** Christmas Day and Boxing Day. **CREDIT CARDS ACCEPTED:** All major cards, except Diner's Club. **BAR FOOD AVAILABLE:** 12.00-3.00pm (Mon-Sun) and 6.00-9.00pm (Mon-Fri only). Wheelchair access. Private room seats 30. **BEERS AVAILABLE:** Young's, Castlemaine, Tennent's Extra, Holsten, Lowenbrau, Becks, Labatts, Rolling Rock, Steinlager, Stella Artois, Red Stripe. **NEAREST TUBE STATION:** Sloane Square.

MAP REF: 2, D/2

Crocker's Folly

60

24 Aberdeen Place, NW8 **071-286 6608**

'You would have to have a heart of stone not to feel for Mr Crocker'

At the height of the Victorian railway boom someone gave Mr Frank Crocker a hot tip. Marylebone Station was going to be built in Maida Vale.

Such information could make a man of energy and foresight rich and Mr Crocker was such a man. He worked out where the station would go and built an hotel right opposite. He opened it with the highest hopes in 1892 and waited for the Great Central Railway to arrive. Well, of course, we know that Marylebone Station was built in Marylebone but the news came as a terrible shock to poor Mr Crocker. A railway hotel without a railway station was at a peculiar disadvantage. Mr Crocker, despairing, jumped from one of the many upstairs windows.

The Crown Hotel – the name he gave it – faced difficult times but you should see it today. New owners, Regent Inns, spent £250,000 on it a couple of years ago and gave it a new name. It is called Crocker's Folly now and it is looking marvellous.

Mr Crocker was not one for penny pinching. His hotel looks splendid from the outside but inside it is magnificent. Marble columns, marble-lined walls, a sumptuous marble counter in the amazing saloon bar, massive baronial fireplaces, rich coffered ceilings, carved mahogany fittings everywhere . . .

There was originally a billiard room with two full-size tables. This is now a carvery with the biggest of the fireplaces and a bust of the Emperor Caracalla.

The public bar is almost as impressive as the saloon bar. It has bar billiards, games machines and an only slightly less imposing ceiling, also the original clock. Here and in the saloon bar there are always nine cask ales on the handpumps. The cellars are as roomy as everywhere else.

You would have to have a heart of stone not to feel for Mr Crocker.

To have built such a building and to have met with such a disappointment . . . His ambition was the death of him but he left London one of its most impressive public houses.

OPEN: Mon-Sun. **HOURS:** 11.00am-11.00pm (12.00-3.00pm and 7.00-10.30pm Sun). **CREDIT CARDS ACCEPTED:** All major cards. **BAR FOOD AVAILABLE:** 12.00-3.00pm. **RESTAURANT FOOD AVAILABLE:** 12.00-3.00pm and 6.00-10.00pm. **SET PRICE LUNCH:** £4.95. **SET PRICE DINNER:** £5.95. Wheelchair access (disabled lavatory). Tables outside seat 12. Private room seats 20. **BEERS AVAILABLE:** Crocker's, Adnams, Brakspear, Theakston, Bass, Wadworth 6X, Abbot Ale, John Smith's, Courage Best, Courage Directors, Foster's, Tennent's Pilsner, Tennent Extra, Kronenbourg, Holsten, Grolsch, Guinness. **NEAREST TUBE STATIONS:** Edgware Road, Warwick Avenue.

The Crooked Billet

61

14 Crooked Billet, SW19 **081-946 4942**

'The heart of Cromwell's Half-Acre'

The Crooked Billet is in the tiny hamlet of that name hard by Wimbledon Common and it has been in and out of local records for nearly 500 years. It first appears in 1509: a brewery and inn. Then we hear of Walter Cromwell, the father of Henry VIII's Lord High Chamberlain, retiring to the inn in 1513 and dying there. His bit of land gets called Cromwell's Half-Acre. A few years pass and the old inn is being rebuilt a little way off. Then it is rebuilt again. The builders seem hardly to have been out of the place.

The latest lot emerged only on Good Friday 1994, having given the old pub a thorough going-over. Breath was held while the oldest regular, a customer for more than 60 years, inspected his new local. The best he'd seen it, he said. Sighs of relief all round.

The newly refurbished pub is so tactfully done that you can't tell ancient from modern. In fact, the only original fittings that survive are the settles in what is now the no smoking area. In the restaurant at the back the menu takes in four continents, ranging from dim sum to fajitas, and there is a list of some 21 Old and New World wines and champagnes served by the glass or the bottle. What would old Walter Cromwell have made of that?

There is some outside seating to the rear and side of the pub but in fine weather most people will do what they have done for centuries. They will sit on the green opposite the Crooked Billet at the heart of Cromwell's Half-Acre.

OPEN: Mon-Sun. **HOURS:** 11.00am-3.00pm and 5.30-11.00pm (11.00am-11.00pm Sat; 12.00-3.00pm and 7.00-10.30pm Sun). **CREDIT CARDS ACCEPTED:** Visa, Access, AmEx. **RESTAURANT FOOD AVAILABLE:** 12.00-2.30pm and 7.00-10.00pm (12.00-2.30pm and 7.00-9.30pm Sun). No smoking area. Wheelchair access (but not lavatory). Tables outside seat 20. **BEERS AVAILABLE:** Rolling Rock, Labatts, Stella Artois, Red Stripe. **NEAREST TUBE STATION:** Wimbledon.

The Crown and Shuttle

62

Shoreditch High Street, E1 **n/a**

'... exotically round the pool table'

Respectable East End local with a popular regular feature. At lunchtime and in the early evening exotic dancers dance exotically round the pool table, taking off all their clothes except their shoes. City workers in suits watch without comment or expression and applaud politely as the dance concludes. Pool players then resume their interrupted game.

OPEN: Mon-Sun. **HOURS:** 11.00am-11.00pm (12.00-3.00pm and 7.00-10.30pm Sun). **CREDIT CARDS ACCEPTED:** None. **BEERS AVAILABLE:** Webster's, Courage Best, Holsten, Budweiser, Becks, Carlsberg, Newcastle Brown Ale. **NEAREST TUBE STATION:** Liverpool Street.

The Crown and Two Chairmen

63

31 Dean Street W1 **071-437 8192**

'Queen Anne seems to have been uncommonly stately. The chairmen would have need a drink'

This is the story. Queen Anne was having her portrait painted. The painter was James Thornhill and he had a studio opposite this pub. She arrived for the sittings in a sedan chair. The chairmen would put her down in Dean Street and while she tripped into the studio they would stagger into the pub.

The Queen Anne portrait in the House of Commons is by Thornhill. Perhaps that was the one. She seems to have been uncommonly stately. The chairmen would have needed a drink. Anyway the picturesque name brings in the passing trade and the pub flourishes.

OPEN: Mon-Sun. **HOURS:** 11.00am-11.00pm (12.00-3.00pm and 7.00-10.30pm Sun). **CLOSED:** Christmas Day, Boxing Day. **CREDIT CARDS ACCEPTED:** AmEx, Visa, Mastercard. **BAR FOOD AVAILABLE:** 12.00-3.00pm. Wheelchair access. Tables outside seat 12. Private room seats 30. **BEERS AVAILABLE:** Tetley, Wadworth, Brakspear, London Pride, Castlemaine, Carlsberg, Lowenbrau. **NEAREST TUBE STATION:** Piccadilly Circus.

MAP REF: 1, E/3

The Cutty Sark Tavern

64

Ballast Quay, SE10 **081-858 3146**

'People sometimes travel miles to be here'

Walk far enough along the river bank at Greenwich and you will come across a charming quay, a row of picturesque old houses, an ancient cherry tree and the Cutty Sark Tavern.

If it's fine people will be sitting on the river wall having a drink. If not they will be in the bar with its old beams and comfortable wooden furniture or in the old panelled room upstairs having red mullet perhaps or grilled sardines for lunch.

People sometimes travel miles to be here. The Cutty Sark has a sort of fan club and you can see why. It is a true period piece, a small riverside tavern that has hardly changed over the years.

It was the Union Tavern when it was built in 1804 and for most of its life it was a small working man's pub used mainly by seafarers and riverboat men. Nowadays it belongs to an entrepreneur called Sydney Haines and is a protected building – protected by him and by having a Grade II listing. 'I have resisted all advice to alter it,' he says.

Changing the name in 1954 to welcome the last of the great tea clippers to her new home in Greenwich was his idea but such other changes as there have been have been forced upon him. There was the matter of the loos, for instance. His customers did as their fathers and grandfathers had done, went into the yard and gazed up at the stars. The local council insisted on a more up to date procedure and he reluctantly put up a lavatory block in the 1960s.

Haines has other interests, a wine bar in Blackfriars, another tavern in Dorking, a vineyard in France. But his grown-up children still live on the quay and the Cutty Sark is the apple of his eye.

OPEN: Mon-Sun. **HOURS:** 11.00am-11.00pm (12.00-3.00pm and 7.00-10.30pm Sun). **CREDIT CARDS ACCEPTED:** All major cards except Diner's Club and AmEx. **BAR FOOD AVAILABLE:** 12.00-2.30pm Mon-Sun; 6.00-9.30pm Tue-Fri. Wheelchair access. Beer garden seats 60. **BEERS AVAILABLE:** Charrington, Bass, Worthington, Flowers IPA, Tennent's Extra. **NEAREST BR STATION:** Maze Hill.

De Hems

65

11 Macclesfield Street, W1 **071-437 2494**

'"Orangeboom Gezondheid"'

De Hems claims to be London's only Dutch pub. Does anyone doubt it? It looks Dutch. See its gable. It behaves Dutch. Proost. It's Dutch all right.

The De Hems used to be called the Macclesfield – you find it in Macclesfield Street on the very edge of Chinatown. A few more yards down the street and it could have been London's only Chinese pub but a Dutch sailor called de Hems took it over in the 1920s so it's Dutch plates, Dutch photographs, Dutch old masters. 'Oranjeboom Gezondheid' declares the mirror behind the bar counter, a friendly greeting apparently.

It is a very friendly pub, this one. The noise level rises as the evening goes on and the evening goes on until midnight, courtesy of a music license. The ceiling is a subtle shade of nicotine though the ceiling fans do their best and in the summer the doors fold right back, opening the whole bar to the air and other delights of Macclesfield Street.

They call the upstairs bar 't Oude Trefpunt', the old meeting place, and on the first Thursday of every month many Dutchies living in

London meet there for Nederlandse Avond, a Dutch evening, and the De Hems is known for its comedy club nights on Wednesdays.

You see people tucking into delicious-looking Dutch food. Bitterballen, deep-fried savoury balls served with mustard, six for £1.95; loempia, pancake rolls; groteborrelhap, a platter of chicken wings, crispy vegetables, bitterballen and loempia, £9.95. They put mayonnaise on their chips at De Hems. You can't get more Dutch than that.

Orangjeboom means orange tree, the symbol of the Orangjeboom Brewery in Rotterdam, and there's a huge Orangjeboom pump on the bar pouring out prime Dutch ale at £2.20 a pint.

There's a good demand for Dutch bottled beers too, not to mention draught Oranjeboom Geneva gin, but you don't have to drink any of these. De Hems has English beers too and English food if that is what you want in London's only Dutch pub.

OPEN: Mon-Sun. **HOURS:** 11.00-12.00am (12.00-3.00pm and 7.00-10.30pm Sun). **CLOSED:** Christmas Day and Boxing Day. **CREDIT CARDS ACCEPTED:** All major cards. **BAR FOOD AVAILABLE:** 12.00pm-12.00am. Wheelchair access (but not lavatory). Tables outside seat 16. Private room seats 120. **BEERS AVAILABLE:** Oranjeboom, Chimay, Amstel, Wittraff, Mort Suibte, La Trappe, Budweiser, Sol. **NEAREST TUBE STATIONS:** Piccadilly Circus, Leicester Square. **MAP REF:** 1, E/1

The Devereux

66

20 Devereux Court, WC2 **071-583 4562**

'Upstairs there are four rooms to let, bed and breakfast. This is unusual in a London pub'

Devereux Court is a quiet courtyard between the Strand and the Middle Temple. Here, in this elegant public house, lawyers gather, others too. There's a very nice restaurant, a pleasant bar, a room with books and comfortable chairs.

The pub was built in 1844, a good year for building things. It is very nice looking. It is caramel and white at the moment and suits it. Upstairs there are four rooms to let, bed and breakfast. This is unusual in a London pub. A single room with breakfast costs £40 a night, reasonable considering.

The little mews got its name from Robert Devereux, the Earl of Essex who owned the land around here. That is his bust high on the frontage. He was played by Errol Flynn in the movie. Bette Davis, as Queen Elizabeth, gave him a tremendous slap across the face, not faking it at all. It brought tears to poor Errol's eyes.

OPEN: Mon-Fri. **HOURS:** 11.00am-9.30pm Mon-Wed; 11.00am-11.00pm Thur-Fri. **CLOSED:** All bank holidays. **CREDIT CARDS ACCEPTED:** All major cards. **BAR AND RESTAURANT FOOD AVAILABLE:** 12.00-2.30pm. Wheelchair access (but not lavatory). Private room seats 100. **BEERS AVAILABLE:** Theakston XB, Theakston Best, Courage Best, Courage Directors, Wadworth 6X, Foster's, Kronenbourg, Holsten, Guinness, Beamish. **NEAREST TUBE STATION:** Temple.

The Dickens Inn

67

St Katharine's Way, E1 **071-488 1226**

'Trundled, creaking and groaning, to its new home'

Dickens loved pubs and wrote about them like no one else. Here, though, is a pub he had nothing to do with, knew nothing about. It is called the Dickens Inn.

It is cashing in on his name I suppose but I wish he could have watched as this massive old wood-framed warehouse was lifted onto wheels and then trundled, creaking and groaning, to its new home by Tower Bridge. Think what he could have made of that.

The old warehouse now stands brimming with life on a superb site in St Katharine's Dock, a huge inn, three-storeys high, each storey with a deep balcony the whole length of the building, each balcony crowded with people. It is a wonderful – well – Dickensian sight.

St Katharine's Dock with its marina crowded with yachts and dinghies is an outstandingly attractive part of London and the Dickens Inn, there for almost twenty-five years now, has been such a hit that they made it a third bigger eight years ago though you would never know just by looking. It now has five separate bars and restaurants, a staff of 55 and this year it won a major battle to let its customers drink outside. You would hardly believe it but there are people who go to great lengths to stop London drinking in the open air. Here is a rare victory for the good guys so a hat or two in the air please for two terraces full of tables, the tables full of people whenever the sun shines.

The Dickens Inn has changed hands once or twice in its short life. Charles Forte has it now and it is a place to see. The ground floor is a vast bar, dark, low ceilinged, the windows filled with the waving masts of the marina. There's a bustling snack bar on the ground floor too. You take your tray and find yourself a table inside or out. Upstairs and a pizzeria occupies the whole floor with tables all along the balcony. Up another floor and it's a grill and fish restaurant, the tables crisply tableclothed and again a long balcony full of people eating.

Cask ales and lager compete in the bar, the views are of boats and water, cobblestones and an apple tree pergola. It is an outstanding addition to the general jollity.

OPEN: Mon-Sun. **HOURS:** 11.00am-11.00pm (12.00-3.00pm and 7.00-10.30pm Sun). **CREDIT CARDS ACCEPTED:** All major cards. **BAR FOOD AVAILABLE:** 11.30am-5.00pm (11.30am-8.30pm Sat; 12.00-3.00pm Sun). **RESTAURANT FOOD AVAILABLE:** 12.00-3.00pm and 6.30-10.30pm. Wheelchair access. Beer garden seats 100. Private room seats 110. **BEERS AVAILABLE:** Courage Best, Courage Directors, Adnams, Wadworth, Carlsberg, Foster's, Kronenbourg, Budweiser. **NEAREST TUBE STATION:** Tower Hill.

Dirty Dick's

68

202 Bishopsgate, EC2 **071-283 5888**

'Goodbye dirty days'

Dirty Dick's is one of London's top tourist pubs. It is full of character and has an interesting story to tell but I'm sorry to say that nowadays tourists are often disappointed. It is not nearly dirty enough for them. It is, in fact, not dirty at all. It used to be but these are the hygienic nineties. The original Dirty Dick's would have been in deep trouble. As for Dirty Nat . . .

Dirty Nathaniel Bentley, an 18th-century dirty person, had a hardware shop in Leadenhall Street. The story goes that his bride-to-be died on their wedding day. Rather put out, he locked the room in which the wedding breakfast was set, swore it would never be reopened and thereafter neither changed his clothes nor washed. 'If you wash today,' he would say reasonably, 'you just have to wash again tomorrow.'

He became quite a celebrity. People flocked to his shop which daily grew more spectacularly dirty and when his landlord eventually got him out the owner of Ye Olde Port Wine House in Bishopsgate bought the entire contents, rotting wedding breakfast, dead cats and all and displayed them in his cellar. Ye Olde Port Wine House became Dirty Dick's.

Poor dirty Nat died broke five years later but Dirty Dick's prospered and when it was rebuilt in 1870 all the grisly artefacts were stored and then carefully put back. There they stayed until just ten years ago and a ghastly sight the old bar was with two mummified dead cats and other frightful things hanging from the black rafters. Customers would sometimes ask if the long-dead cats were real. A wire behind the bar would be pulled and a cat would twitch . . .

Finches owned the old pub for years and eventually decided that the time had come for a clean-up. Out went poor Nathaniel's vile household goods and a cleaner was taken on. Goodbye dirty days.

Young's has Dirty Dick's now and it remains a very successful pub. The main bar with its wooden floor, old beams and copper counter is crowded and notably cheerful, you have to book for the restaurant these days and the candle-lit cellar bar seems roomier and some may think a great deal more congenial than it did.

There's a photograph of it as it was. You will recognize the beams, the settles and the old wooden benches. If you miss the dead cats look in the glass case at the bottom of the staircase.

OPEN: Sun-Fri. **HOURS:** 11.00am-11.00pm (12.00-3.00pm Sun). **CLOSED:** Bank holidays. **CREDIT CARDS ACCEPTED:** All major cards. **BAR FOOD AVAILABLE:** 11.00am-3.00pm. **RESTAURANT FOOD AVAILABLE:** 11.30am-3.00pm. Wheelchair access. Private room seats 30. **BEERS AVAILABLE:** Young's Bitter, Young's Special, London Lager, Castlemaine, Tetley, Beamish, Red Stripe. **NEAREST TUBE STATION:** Liverpool Street.

The Dog and Fox

69

24 High Street, SW19 **081-946 6565**

'You can be too big, that seems clear'

The Victorians were used to these things but even they must have been impressed by the Dog and Fox. Such a display of turrets, decorated gables and pillared porticoes and its size! It occupies an enormous site, dominating its bit of Wimbledon Village.

Young's, whose pub it is, points out, that the bar isn't all that big considering. It is just that it is backed up by what seems an acre or two of terrace between pub and High Street, a Chinese restaurant and a ballroom, not used for balls much these days but essential for conferences, weddings and the like.

It comes as a shock to hear that it used to be even bigger, that it once had eight public rooms, two butteries, two barns, a stable and several hundred acres of land. You can be too big, that seems clear, and Young's must be relieved that with good Queen Victoria safely on the throne it was rebuilt in its present modest proportions and set back a bit so that the High Street could be widened. It wasn't exactly pokey even then. It still included gardens, a bowling green and a paddock, now all absorbed into Wimbledon Village, a lovely place on its hill top.

As for the bar, it would be considered a good size in a pub of more usual dimensions and it has just been totally refurbished in the modern Victorian style that Young's and its customers like so much.

OPEN: Mon-Sun. **HOURS:** 11.00am-11.00pm (12.00-3.00pm and 7.00-10.30pm Sun). **CREDIT CARDS ACCEPTED:** All major cards. **BAR FOOD AVAILABLE:** 12.00-3.00pm and 6.00-9.00pm. Wheelchair access. Beer garden seats 70. Private room seats 160. **BEERS AVAILABLE:** All Young's bitters; Tennent's, Red Stripe, Premium, London Lager, Castlemaine. **NEAREST TUBE STATION:** Wimbledon.

Doggetts Coat and Badge 70

1 Blackfriars Bridge, SE1 **071-633 9057**

'As in life the higher you go the better the view'

A modern pub on the river hard by Blackfriars Bridge, custom-built for Allied Lyons in 1976.

A wine bar on the ground floor spills out onto the Embankment in the summer with picnic tables and a river-boat view of the bridge. The main bar is on the floor above, there's a restaurant on the floor above that and a conference centre, board room and terrace at the top. There is a lift. Not many pubs have lifts. As in life the higher you go the better the view.

The name refers to Doggett's Coat and Badge Race, rowed every July between London Bridge and Chelsea by six young watermen. This has been going on since 1715 which makes it the oldest single sculls race in the world. There were only four competitors this year. Young watermen on the Thames grow fewer.

OPEN: Mon-Fri. **HOURS:** 11.00am-11.00pm. **CLOSED:** Bank holidays. **CREDIT CARDS ACCEPTED:** All major cards. **BAR FOOD AVAILABLE:** 11.00am-3.00pm. **RESTAURANT FOOD AVAILABLE:** 12.00-3.00pm. No smoking area. Wheelchair access (but not lavatory). Beer garden seats 100. Private room seats 30. **BEERS AVAILABLE:** Tetley, Nicholson's, Adnams, Wadworth 6X, Carlsberg, Castlemaine, Tuborg, Guinness. **NEAREST TUBE STATIONS:** Blackfriars, Waterloo.

The Dove Inn 71

19 Upper Mall, W6 **081-748 5405**

'I bet they all loved it, these famous faces'

A roll call of just some of the people who have visited the Dove hangs over the fireplace in the bar. It is a remarkable list, a who's who of the theatre and cinema, life and letters and I bet they loved it, these famous faces. This is, after all, the Pigeons of *The Water Gypsies*, the perfect riverside pub.

It has always attracted artists and writers. William Morris lived next door, James Thomson, in an on-rush of patriotism, wrote 'Rule Britannia' upstairs, Ernest Hemingway drank here and so did Graham Greene. This, then, is the calibre of person you must expect to find as you step inside from the narrow alleyway but first look in the the room immediately on your right. If you can squeeze in you will be in what the *Guinness Book of Records* says is the smallest bar in the UK, 4ft 2in by

7ft 10in, big enough for four medium-sized drinkers, two of them sitting on stools at the bar. The four medium-sized drinkers are there most of the time.

You will have to back out again into the dark, low-ceilinged, oak-beamed saloon bar, all black panelling, cushioned wall settles and copper-topped tables and you may well decide to stay right there, particularly in winter when the fire is on.

Up those steps though are rooms serving food and rooms for eating in and past them is the Dove of summertime, a verandah shaded by an old vine, a terrace overlooking the river, another terrace reached by a spiral staircase, sunny places, shady places and families of wild geese sailing by.

Brian Lovrey has the tenancy and he and Dale Neil, his manager, guard the old pub's character. No music. No gaming machines. Neil's wife, Janya, comes from Thailand which accounts for the delicious Thai food they serve there in the evening.

The river is never as threatening as in the days before the Thames Barrier and the London Pride, the ESB and the two draught lagers stay safely dry and cool in the old tavern's deep cellars. The Dove has been a Fuller's house since 1796.

OPEN: Mon-Sun. **HOURS:** 11.00am-11.00pm (12.00-3.00pm and 7.00-10.30pm Sun). **CREDIT CARDS ACCEPTED:** None. **BAR FOOD AVAILABLE:** 12.00-3.00pm and 6.00-10.30pm Sun-Fri (12.00-5.00pm and 6.00-10.30pm Sat). Wheelchair access (but not lavatory). Tables outside seat 125. **BEERS AVAILABLE:** London Pride, ESB, Grolsch, Heineken, Guinness. **NEAREST TUBE STATION:** Hammersmith.

The Drayton Arms

72

153 Old Brompton Road, SW5 **071-373 0385**

'High Victoriana in full flower'

For grandeur and self-confidence it is hard to beat the Drayton Arms. It is high Victoriana, all buff terracotta and purple brick. You may feel impelled to give it a round of applause as you pass.

The interior is almost as grand as the exterior with beautiful art-nouveau lanterns and a wonderful mahogany bar with marble columns. There is a much less attractive back room but that's back rooms for you. It is in all other regards a most distinguished pub and I congratulate Miss Day, the owner, on her choice of forebears.

Miss Day, a single lady of a certain age, lives in Brighton and does not intervene in the running of the pub. The manager has never met her. Her family though has owned the land on which a lot of Old Brompton Road stands for more than 200 years.

The first pub on the site went up in 1847 and contained the largest single household in the area – the publican, his wife, their seven children and five servants. It was demolished in 1891 and up went this one, infinitely grander. Thankfully it has survived the thousand natural shocks that pubs are heir to. It is a listed building now.

The Drayton Arms is half way between South Kensington and Earls Court so you might expect it to lead, as it does, two lives. At 9pm each day from Wednesday to Saturday the well-bred murmur of the rest of the week abruptly disappears and you are in a lively venue for folk, heavy rock, blue grass, jazz and assorted entertainers. An Elvis impersonator regularly packs the place.

It does well with an all-day menu called Goodbye Mr Chips – no chips – and there is a loyal following for the Caffreys Irish Ale. This takes four minutes to settle.

The Webber-Douglas Academy has a small theatre for its student productions on the first floor – capacity houses every time I'm told. It seats thirty-three.

OPEN: Mon-Sun. **HOURS:** 8.00am-11.00pm (9.00am-3.00pm and 7.00-10.30pm Sun). **CREDIT CARDS ACCEPTED:** All major cards except AmEx. **BAR FOOD AVAILABLE:** 8.00am-11.00pm. **SET BREAKFAST:** £3.50. No smoking area. Wheelchair access (but not lavatory). Tables outside seat 48. **BEERS AVAILABLE:** Caffreys, Grolsch, Bass, Worthington, Carling Black Label, Tennent's Extra, Tennent's Pilsner, Beamish. **NEAREST TUBE STATIONS:** Gloucester Road, South Kensington. **MAP REF:** 2, B/3

Dublin Castle

73

94 Parkway, NW1 — **071-485 1773**

'Rap, ska, R&B and every customer a critic'

A small Victorian local in Camden Town making its way in a competitive new world with a music room behind the bar. It's rap, ska, R&B, and every customer a critic at the Dublin Castle nowadays.

A roving rapper writes: 'Long established on the rock scene. Madness got their first break here. Smallish venue means you're close to the band but music room lacks atmosphere so ennui if band not up to much. Different bands on pub circuit seven days a week, some MoR. So pick your night.'

MoR: *derog. middle of the road.*

OPEN: Mon-Sun. **HOURS:** 12.00pm-12.00am (12.00-3.00pm and 7.00-10.30pm Sun). **CLOSED:** Christmas Day. **CREDIT CARDS ACCEPTED:** None. Wheelchair access (but not lavatory). Tables outside seat 12. Private room seats 70. **BEERS AVAILABLE:** John Smith's, Budweiser, Sol, Molsten Dry, Holsten. **NEAREST TUBE STATION:** Camden Town.

The Duke of Cumberland

74

235 New King's Road, SW6 — **071-736 2777**

'A man of broad and varied interests'

There was a tremendous pub boom in the 1890s. Potential profits seemed limitless and old pubs were being sold and extravagantly remodelled all over London. As prices spiralled heavenwards Young's rebuilt its comparatively modest Duke's Head in the splendid style of the times.

This is the pub we now know as the Duke of Cumberland, the big, swanky four-storey pub looking across New King's Road to Parson's Green, balusters, arched windows and soaring chimneys and superbly fitted inside. The cost of such a display of mahogany, engraved glass and so on was perhaps well spent. Quite a lot of it is still in daily use 100 years on.

The pub kept its original name until 1971 when it was thoroughly renovated. It reopened as the Duke of Cumberland and won the *Evening Standard* Pub of the Year Competition the same year. It has had another refurbishment since then, getting a new public bar at the back where the beer is 4d a pint cheaper and the darts board is in constant use.

It is the quiet, well-groomed, and spacious saloon bar that addresses the character and achievements of the man whose name the pub now bears. He murdered his valet, declares a large board prominently displayed. He committed adultery, sodomy and incest, blackmailed his brother, indecently assaulted the wife of the Lord Chamberlain and plotted the assassination of his neice, the future Queen Victoria. A man, in short, of broad and varied interests, most suited to the role of King of Hanover which is what he became.

OPEN: Mon-Sun. **HOURS:** 11.00am-11.00pm (12.00-3.00pm and 7.00-10.30pm Sun). **CREDIT CARDS ACCEPTED:** None. **BAR FOOD AVAILABLE:** 12.00-3.00pm (hot) and 6.00-9.00pm (cold). Wheelchair access. Tables outside seat 20. **BEERS AVAILABLE:** All Young's bitters, Tennent's, Castlemaine, Premium Lager, London Lager, Beamish, Guinness, Oatmeal Stout. **NEAREST TUBE STATION:** Parsons Green.

Duke of Somerset

75

14 Little Somerset Street, E1 **071-481 0785**

'Office gossip and office romance are the driving forces'

Cheerful youthful pubs like this one are now a standard part of modern office developments. Like its siblings the Duke of Somerset occupies the ground floor of a new block and gets packed at lunchtimes and early evenings. Office gossip and office romance are the driving forces.

Most have useful forecourts. This has a particularly good one with trees and benches and it gets crowded with junior staff in shirt sleeves when the sun shines. The young chef manning the barbecue here has no time to draw breath. On winter days the same young crowd packs the big bar with its quick food counter, music and gaming machines.

The drink is lager. Straight from the bottle.

OPEN: Mon-Fri. **HOURS:** 11.00am-10.00pm (11.00am-11.00pm Thur-Fri). **CLOSED:** Bank Holidays. **CREDIT CARDS ACCEPTED:** All major cards. **RESTAURANT FOOD AVAILABLE:** 11.00am-3.00pm. Wheelchair access. Tables outside seat 100. **BEERS AVAILABLE:** Bass, London Pride, Tennent's, Grolsch, Carling Black Label, Guinness, Caffreys. **NEAREST TUBE STATION:** Aldgate.

Duke of Wellington

76

77 Wardour Street, W1 **071-439 1274**

'once very rough but now a reformed character'

The gateway to Soho, some say, a dark mock-Tudor pub with coats of arms and leaded lights, once very rough but now a reformed character with sofas, small tables and anodyne music on the laser disc machine – Abba, Simon and Garfunkel, Van Morrison, Eric Clapton. Open all day. Live jazz on Sunday nights.

OPEN: Mon-Sun. **HOURS:** 11.00am-11.00pm Mon-Fri; 12.00-11.00pm Sat; 12.00-3.00pm and 7.00-10.30pm Sun. **CREDIT CARDS ACCEPTED:** None. **BAR FOOD AVAILABLE:** 12.00-4.00pm (12.00-3.00pm Sun). Wheelchair access (but not lavatory). Tables outside seat 12. **BEERS AVAILABLE:** Theakston Best, Marstons Pedigree, Becks, Coors, Guinness. **NEAREST TUBE STATION:** Piccadilly Circus. **MAP REF:** 1, D/2

The Duke of Wellington

77

179 Portobello Road, W11 **071-727 6727**

'A lot remaining of the great gin palace'

Stallholders in the Portobello Road still call the Duke of Wellington Finches, which would have pleased the late Mr H H Finch who owned so many pubs in central London and unofficially lent his name to them all.

It is a busy pub with a lot remaining of the great gin palace it must have been – the ornate mahogany of the island bar, the brass candelabra and etched-glass windows. Low partitions form booths for drinkers around the walls and in the summer customers spill out onto the pavement with their drinks and are forbidden to take their bar stools with them. Summer or winter, the world's best known antique market guarantees hectic Saturdays.

The Duke, in his Goya mode, looking just like Michael Wilding, looks haughtily down from the inn sign and the windows on the side seem permanently open at the bottom. Note to burglars. Don't bother. They are trompe l'oiel, just painted on.

OPEN: Mon-Sun. **HOURS:** 11.00am-3.30pm and 5.30-11.00pm (11.00am-11.00pm Sat; 12.00-3.00pm and 7.00-10.30pm Sun). **CREDIT CARDS ACCEPTED:** None. **BAR FOOD AVAILABLE:** 12.00-3.00pm. Wheelchair access. Tables outside seat 3. **BEERS AVAILABLE:** Young's Special, Young's Bitter, London Lager, Oatmeal Stout, Tennent's, Castlemaine, Guinness, Rolling Rock, Becks, Stein. **NEAREST TUBE STATION:** Notting Hill Gate.

The Duke's Head

78

8 Lower Richmond Road, SW15 **081-788 2552**

'A lot of plastic glasses'

The 1994 University Boat Race beat at least one record. The twenty barmen assembled for the day by the Duke's Head sold 15,000 pints of beer. Can this be right? That's what they say: 15,000 pints of beer.

If you stand on Putney Bridge and look up river the first pub on the left is the massive Star and Garter which also had a gala boat race day. The Duke's Head is the next pub along, an elegant Georgian building painted cream. After that it's all rowing club boathouses shoulder to shoulder.

The Duke's Head has always been deeply involved in rowing. At one time a boat builder built boats on the top floor, lowering the finished ones down on the hoist which is still there. For years Putney Town Boat Club used the front part of the pub's cellars as its boathouse and oarsmen and -women still drink in the Duke's Head as a matter of course.

It is a good-looking pub, well-preserved, lots of carved mahogany and fine etched glass. Some of this was lost in the war. A bomb in Fulham put a lot of windows out but they have all been carefully and expensively replaced.

It is a peaceable place. Norman Golding, the landlord, has known only one fight in the bar in seventeen years. He is very much in control. There's no children or dogs, no pool tables, or jukeboxes. Plastic glasses only if you take your drink outside. They get through a lot of plastic glasses at the Duke's Head on a sunny day – 15,000 on boat race day in 1994.

OPEN: Mon-Sun. **HOURS:** 11.30am-3.00pm and 7.00-11.00pm (11.00am-11.00pm Sat; 12.00-3.00pm and 7.00-10.30pm Sun). **CREDIT CARDS ACCEPTED:** None. **BAR AND RESTAURANT FOOD AVAILABLE:** 12.00-2.30pm. Wheelchair access. **BEERS AVAILABLE:** Young's Special, Castlemaine, Red Stripe, Tennent's Extra. **NEAREST TUBE STATION:** Putney Bridge.

The Eagle

79

159 Farringdon Road, EC1 **071-837 1353**

'Why shouldn't a pub have good food'

The *Good Pub Guide* which, unlike this guide, concerns itself only with good pubs, says that the Eagle has the best food it can remember having in any London pub. Fay Maschler says this is the way forward for pubs and puts it in her *London Restaurant Guide* and Egon Ronay gives it a star.

So you might suppose that this was more a restaurant than a pub in which case you would hurt the feelings of Michael Belben and David Eyre who took the old pub over in January 1991 and like to think that it is still every inch a pub. Why shouldn't a pub have good food is what they say.

They liked it when *Harpers* called their food pleb Med and day after day they produce delicious, simple things from Spain and Portugal, the South of France, Italy and the Eastern Mediterranean at very reasonable prices. There's no booking, no quiet little table anywhere, no one buttering you up. People in the know get in either early or late. That way four people can sometimes get a table for four. Otherwise you often have to share someone else's.

The menu is chalked up and changes often. You see and smell what is being cooked, order your food from the bar and have a drink at your table. The Italian sausages sizzling on the grill will be with you soon. Nothing takes more than ten minutes.

All these people tucking into the fish and chic pea soup, the grilled squid and the lovely pasta, *Guardian* journos, fashion photographers, advertising people, are in and out in no time, a drink, a shared bottle of wine, lots of chat. Hardly anyone has more than one course. Puddings don't seem right, somehow, in a pub.

There are Spanish cheeses though and excellent coffee and then it's back to the office, darkroom or studio so you'll get a seat before long and this is food worth waiting for. People quite often thank the two chefs as they go out. This hardly ever happened says David Eyre, when he worked in restaurants.

Nothing matches at the Eagle, it is all odd chairs and strange tables, nothing smart, nothing designed. They do good cask beers and get through a lot of wine and in the afternoon when it empties you can see what a nice old pub it is.

It opens at midday and stays open until 11pm and on Saturdays and Sundays they close it and recover from the week.

There is an art gallery upstairs, a light, white, dazzling space.

OPEN: Mon-Fri. **HOURS:** 12.00-11.00pm. **CLOSED:** Bank Holidays. **CREDIT CARDS ACCEPTED:** None. **RESTAURANT FOOD AVAILABLE:** 12.30-2.30pm and 6.30-10.30pm. Wheelchair access. Tables outside seat 15. **BEERS AVAILABLE:** Shefford, Eagle IPA, Carlsberg, Kronenbourg. **NEAREST TUBE STATION:** Farringdon.

The Eagle Tavern (80)

2 Shepherdess Walk, N1 **071-253 4715**

'"Up and down the City Road/In and out the Eagle . . ."'

The words of the song that still makes this pub a household name are high on the side wall so that all who turn into Shepherdess Walk from the City Road can read them.

Up and down the City Road
In and out the Eagle
That's the way the money goes
Pop goes the weasel!

The Eagle of the song was not this pub actually. It was the Royal Eagle Music Hall, the place where Marie Lloyd first appeared at the age of fifteen. It had extensive pleasure grounds with fountains, gas devices, illuminations, cosmoramas, magic mirrors and the famous Grecian Saloon. This became so notorious that General Booth of the Salvation Army took it over to close it down. The whole lot was demolished in 1901 and this pub went up instead.

It is looking very well just now, confident Edwardian frontage all spruced up, handsome eagle on the cupola brightly gilded, big saloon bar with its pictures of music hall stars, public bar with its pool table and TV sport and the big beer garden at the back. You have to get there early on summer lunchtimes or you don't get a table.

The Eagle is part of local life of course and there is always the 'Pop Goes the Weasel' bonus. It brings in the most unexpected people. The Brits know all the words of course. We learned this song about pawning our tailor's iron or whatever at our mothers' knee. Weird really.

Half a pound of twopenny rice
Half a pound of treacle
That's the way the money goes
Pop goes the weasel!

OPEN: Mon-Sun. **HOURS:** 11.00am-11.00pm (5.00-11.00pm Sat; 12.00-3.00pm and 7.00-10.30pm Sun). **CLOSED:** 4 days at Christmas. **CREDIT CARDS ACCEPTED:** Access, Visa. **BAR FOOD AVAILABLE:** 12.00-3.00pm and 6.00-10.00pm. Wheelchair access (but not lavatory). Beer garden seats 100. **BEERS AVAILABLE:** Bass, Carling Black Label, Tennent's Extra, Grolsch, Caffreys, Guinness. **NEAREST TUBE STATION:** Old Street.

The Edgar Wallace

81

40 Essex Street, WC2 **071-353 3120**

'The Edgar who?'

In 1975 the Essex Arms, a small pub in a little street off Fleet Street, was renovated and given a new name. Whitbreads decreed that to mark the 100th anniversary of the birth of Edgar Wallace it would henceforth be called the Edgar Wallace. 'Edgar who?' people said.

The great man's daughter Penny loaned the pub a collection of memorabilia, handsomely framed. It was distributed over the walls of the saloon bar, photographs, letters, newspaper cuttings, playbills, interesting stuff. The Edgar Wallace society descended on the pub's first floor restaurant, once for lunch, once for dinner. Miss Wallace went too. This pleasing custom has continued every year since.

An account of his life, on a large high board in the entrance to the Edgar Wallace is difficult to read and goes unread. The pub regulars drink their London Pride and Boddingtons, busy themselves with the fruit machine, watch sport on satellite TV. 'Not many know who Edgar Wallace WAS,' murmurs the licensee's wife.

Edgar Wallace was a great journalist. He wrote more than 170 novels and plays, among them *The Four Just Men*, *Sanders of the River*, *The Ringer* and *The Squealer*. When he died in Hollywood in 1932 they brought his body home in the Berengaria. He was a household name. Now he's on an inn-sign, smoking a cigarette.

It was time we had a pub named after a journalist.

OPEN: Mon-Sat. **HOURS:** 11.00am-11.00pm (11.00am-6.00pm Sat). **CLOSED:** Christmas Day. **BAR AND RESTAURANT FOOD AVAILABLE:** 12.00-2.30pm. Wheelchair access (but not lavatory). Private room seats 40. **BEERS AVAILABLE:** Boddingtons, London Pride, Castle Eden, Heineken, Stella Artois, Murphy's. **NEAREST TUBE STATION:** Temple.

The Elephant and Castle

82

Newington Causeway, SE1 **071-357 9134**

'Hard lines on the poor pub'

A number of Elephant and Castles have flourished in London and one became seriously famous. It gave its name to a road junction, a tube station, a bus route and a vast pink shopping centre and it stood more or less where this one does.

It had had the sense to pick a site where three major roads met. As time went by two more big roads joined in and the pub became known all over London, first as a terminus for stage coaches, then as a terminus for trams. When it became a stop on the Northern Line and the south London terminus of the Bakerloo, well . . .

Planners promised to replace the pub when they redeveloped the Elephant and Castle and in the early 1960s the work began – a vast new traffic system, two huge roundabouts and a network of pedestrian underpasses, a gargantuan shopping centre of hideous aspect and Erno Goldfinger's Alexander Fleming House. The pub had not been forgotten. Alexander Fleming House appeared to have pupped. A smaller version stood in the lee of the big one and a peculiarly uninteresting public house occupied the ground floor. It was called, of course, the Elephant and Castle.

Goldfinger's building, 'one of London's most hated carbuncles' wrote Mira Bar-Hillel, stands empty and dire, its unhappy occupant, the Department of the Environment having fled. It has supporters. Some want it to be listed – 'unhinged' breathed art critic Brian Sewell when he heard – but there seems little chance of that now. Years of increasing dilapidation and eventual demolition seem most likely.

All this is hard lines on the poor pub. Its fate seems bound to that of the hulk behind it. In the meantime it soldiers on. It has a pool table, a dartsboard, a darts team. It sells elephant and castle lighters for £1 each and has a clear view of the Elephant and Castle electricity substation, the nice one that looks like a square chrome waffle.

Quiz programmes like to ask why the Elephant and Castle and you are meant to say that it was really the Infanta of Castile but the Brits of the day got it wrong. The boring answer has to do with the sign of the Cutlers' Company and alas, this is probably it.

OPEN: Mon-Sun. **HOURS:** 11.00am-11.00pm (12.00-3.00pm and 7.00-10.30pm Sun). **CREDIT CARDS ACCEPTED:** None. **BAR FOOD AVAILABLE:** 12.00-10.00pm. Wheelchair access. Tables outside seat 30. **BEERS AVAILABLE:** Ruddells, Kronenbourg, Budweiser, Foster's, Carlsberg. **NEAREST TUBE STATION:** Elephant and Castle. **MAP REF:** 7, B/1

The Elgin

83

96 Ladbroke Grove W11 **071-229 5663**

'Boisterous jollity rules'

Once a glittering Victorian beauty, the Elgin is a game old girl though I'm afraid more than her slip is showing. Remnants of sumptuous Victoriana are overlaid by the pressing needs of the moment, notices, menus, ads. Four pool tables bring customers in, the music is loud and the Sky TV ever present, screens everywhere, three of them in a row. Boisterous jollity rules. Not a place to take your aunt.

On the pub sign outside is a portrait of the long-departed Lord Elgin. We still have his marbles.

OPEN: Mon-Sun. **HOURS:** 12.00-11.00pm (12.00-3.00pm and 7.00-10.30pm Sun). **CREDIT CARDS ACCEPTED:** None. **BAR FOOD AVAILABLE:** 12.00-8.00pm (12.00-3.00pm and 7.00-8.00pm Sun). Wheelchair access. **BEERS AVAILABLE:** Carlsberg, Castlemaine, Lowenbrau, Sol, Becks, Labatts Ice, Molsen, Tetley, John Bull, Guinness. **NEAREST TUBE STATION:** Ladbroke Grove.

The Enterprise

84

35 Walton Street, SW3 **071-584 3148**

'It has indeed become so upmarket that it is hardly recognisably a pub at all.'

Something very remarkable has happened to the Enterprise. Three years ago it was a slightly gloomy pub doing its best but any of the old regulars looking in for pint today are dazzled by the change.

It is now a haunt of the Princess of Wales and other ladies who lunch, of Tom Conti, of Nigel Havers. Gone the shades of nicotine brown and instead pale walls, great looped tapestried curtains, blue jugs of fresh flowers, designer baskets of lemons, lots of white tablecloths and magnums of champagne on the bar counter.

It has indeed become so upmarket that it is hardly recognizably a pub at all. A pub, though, it remains. It has a pub licence. It has pub hours and one or two residual pub ways. You can look in at llam, have a beer and go your way. Pubs come in many forms. This is one of them.

My top-drawer pub inspector reports: 'When Tim Kemp took over the Enterprise his wife Kit did the decor. The Kemps have three small pretty London hotels, Durley House, the Pelham Hotel and Dorset Square Hotel so in no time the old Enterprise was expertly swagged and distressed. Kemp likes things to look generous and hates any hint of meanness.

'The beer on offer is Grolsch lager, a half is £1.50. No crisps. No toasted sandwiches or shepherd's pie. Instead there is green tomato and basil tart or a robust Toulouse sausage with mashed potato. The atmosphere is fizzy but not Hooray noisy. It is rather like a club bar and appeals to a large number of brokers and estate agents; in

Wimbledon week the place was packed. You can eat outside but these tables cannot be booked. A polished Algerian waiter called Freddie brought roasted peppers with garlic, thyme and rosemary and warm goats cheese (£4.50) and an entrecôte steak with juniper butter (£9.75) with the speed of a skater. A bottle of Grenache Blanc Resplandy was £9.75.

'You do not have to eat – indeed it is possible to spend an economical evening at the bar as many of the locals do. There are lots of books scattered about. One is *Pitman's Shorthand*; never mind, they add a pleasing decorative touch carelessly strewn along the window sills.

'The manager is Jenny Collins, a 27-year-old engaging blonde. Formerly a cardio-thoracic nurse at Guy's Hospital, she says, "Happily I have never had to resuscitate any of our customers yet." Though many of them might wish . . .'

OPEN: Mon-Sun. **HOURS:** 12.00-3.30pm and 5.30-11.00pm (12.00-3.00pm and 7.00-10.30pm Sun). **CLOSED:** Christmas Day, Boxing Day. **CREDIT CARDS ACCEPTED:** All major cards except Diner's Club. **RESTAURANT FOOD AVAILABLE:** 12.30-2.30pm and 7.30-10.30pm. Wheelchair access. Tables outside seat 10. **BEERS AVAILABLE:** Grolsch, Rolling Rock, Sol, Becks, Budweiser. **NEAREST TUBE STATIONS:** South Kensington, Knightsbridge.

MAP REF: 2, D/3

Ferret and Firkin

85

114 Lots Road, SW10 **071-352 6645**

'The longest pub name in London'

This semi-circular old pub is the semi-circular corner where Lots Road heading for the river turns left and becomes Lots Road heading for Cheyne Walk. It now has the towers of the new Chelsea Harbour against the skyline. On a fine day you can see Michael Caine's penthouse. These grand new neighbours suit the Ferret and Firkin well. It is one of the original Firkins and the most profitable of them all. It is distinctly up-market and would be obliged if you would give it its full name, which is the Ferret and Firkin in the Balloon up the Creek. This is the longest pub name in London. The ferret and the balloon appear on the pub sign, a rather cliquey set of regulars call themselves the Balloonatics and the brewhouse in the cellar produces copious quantities of a bitter called Balloonastic. The best bitter is Ferret ale and they make Dogbolter and Full Mash Mild, too.

The Ferret shows how well the classic Firkin style wears. The brass chandeliers, the ceiling fans, the wooden floor, the church pews, they will last, you feel, for ever. The pews are unexpectedly roomy and comfortable. They come from a firm in the Midlands called Pew Corner.

All Firkins have music, usually several times a week. There is in fact a Firkin circuit of entertainers. Some appear at a different Firkin every night. The star of the circuit, by general consent, is Jamie Borer, known just as Jamie, sometimes as Jamie and his Organ. He arrives with his electronic keyboard and he is a sensation at the Ferret. On Fridays, his night at the Ferret, you can hardly move.

OPEN: Mon-Sun. **HOURS:** 11.00am-11.00pm (12.00-3.00pm and 7.00-10.30pm Sun). **CREDIT CARDS ACCEPTED:** None. **BAR FOOD AVAILABLE:** 12.00-2.30pm. **SET PRICE LUNCH:** £3.50. Wheelchair access. **BEERS AVAILABLE:** Ferret Ale, Dogbolter, Balloon, Golden Glory, Castlemaine, Carlsberg. **NEAREST TUBE STATION:** Fulham Broadway. **MAP REF:** 2, A/1

Finch's

86

190 Fulham Road, SW10 **071-351 5043**

'A large, feisty-looking finch'

The public houses of Mr Henry Hobson Finch all had proper names of their own but almost all of them were known as Finch's. This one, the Finch's in Chelsea, was really called the King's Arms. The name appears, rather small but very permanently in wrought iron, above the entrance but it has been Finch's to anyone who ever drank there since, oh, probably 1897, which is when Mr Finch bought it.

Young's bought all the Finches in 1991 and in this case at least it has accepted the reality of the situation. This Finch's really is Finch's now. FINCH'S declares the fascia and a new pub sign has gone up. On it is a large, feisty-looking finch. Old Mr Finch would surely be pleased. He would be pleased, too, to see that his handsome Victorian pub, once considered so Bohemian, has kept so much of its splendid mahogany and brass, so many of its decorated mirrors and etched glass screens and that it remains as popular as ever.

This spring the assistant manager, Alex Langlands Pearse, and the Australian barman, Matt Silvester, stood aghast in the bar while their heads were totally shaved for charity. Their hair has grown again now.

OPEN: Mon-Sun. **HOURS:** 11.00am-11.00pm (12.00-3.00pm and 7.00-10.30pm Sun). **CREDIT CARDS ACCEPTED:** None. **BAR FOOD AVAILABLE:** all open hours. Wheelchair access. Tables outside seat 8. **BEERS AVAILABLE:** Young's Ordinary, Young's Special, Winter Warmer, Oatmeal Stout, Castlemaine, London Lager, Tennent's Extra, Red Stripe, Guinness, Beamish. **NEAREST TUBE STATION:** Gloucester Road. **MAP REF:** 2, B/3

The Fitzroy Tavern

87

16 Charlotte Street, W1 **071-580 3714**

'Still where the action is'

This famous bohemian pub seems to have settled down to a respectable middle age now, looking nostalgically back at scandalous days gone by.

Those were the days – the 1930s when free spirits gathered round Augustus John and Nina Hamnet in the boozy, high-spirited saloon bar; the war years when the Fitzroy Tavern adopted HMS *Fitzroy* and wore a banner saying 'We're Here for the Duration We Hope'; the fifties with an all-star cast as the photographs on every wall show, George Orwell, Dylan and Caitlin Thomas, Tommy Cooper, a very pretty Barbara Castle, a very young Richard Attenborough . . .

The regulars today are every bit as sparky of course, who can doubt it? Their time will come to be photographed, glass in hand and hung on the wall. Meanwhile the Fitzroy has been greatly smartened up by the new owners, Sam Smith, a smart new carpet and modern wallpaper, swagged curtains, new comfortably upholstered seats.

What would Augustus John have made of the piped music and the gaming machines? Well, he could always have gone downstairs to the panelled Writers and Artists Bar. No music or machines in there. This is where local writers' groups and historical societies meet.

But I think he would have been back in the saloon bar quite soon. It may not be what it was but it is still where the action is.

OPEN: Mon-Sun. **HOURS:** 11.00am-11.00pm (12.00-3.00pm and 7.00-10.30pm Sun). **CLOSED:** Christmas Day. **CREDIT CARDS ACCEPTED:** All major cards. **BAR FOOD AVAILABLE:** 12.00-9.30pm. **SET PRICE LUNCH:** £3.95. **SET PRICE DINNER:** £4.75. Wheelchair access (but not lavatory). Beer garden seats 10. Private room seats 30. **BEERS AVAILABLE:** Samuel Smith variants, Museum Ale, Old Brewery. **NEAREST TUBE STATION:** Goodge Street, Tottenham Court Road.

The Flask

88

77 Highgate West Hill, N6 **081-340 7260**

'You then get the Freedom of Highgate and can kiss the prettiest girl in the room'

The Flask in Highgate is one of London's best loved pubs. People like it for its age, for its character, for where it is. This is a lovely bit of London, the church, the trees, the comely houses. John Betjeman was born up the road. 'Deeply I loved you, 31 West Hill!' he wrote.

The Flask, the archetypal village pub, was built in 1663, rebuilt in 1767, done over in 1910 and again three years ago, a thorough renovation that closed the old pub for three months. People feared the worst but were relieved by what they found. The Flask now had the plumbing and the kitchens of a three-year-old but it wandered along as always, up steps here, down steps there, ceilings still low, oak panelling and floorboards, doors and windows as they were.

It got its name from the flasks it sold to be filled with water from Hampstead's mineral springs but it was its strong ale that attracted the villagers, Hogarth among them. He is glimpsed down the years sketching in the bar after a particularly nasty brawl. Brawls are out at the Flask now but other old customs survive. There is, for instance, the annual Swearing on the Horns. This is one of those Merrie England things like morris dancing and involves kissing an ancient set of antlers and swearing strange oaths. You then get to kiss the prettiest girl in the room.

A beautiful white wisteria covers the frontage with foliage and, more briefly, with blossom and the picnic tables on the forecourt fill with people at the smallest glimpse of the sun. There is food all day at the Flask and, such are the crowds, customers are to be seen eating their lunch on the road island in high summer.

The Flask was the *Evening Standard* Pub of the Year in 1974.

OPEN: Mon-Sun. **HOURS:** 11.00am-11.00pm (12.00-3.00pm and 7.00-10.30pm Sun). **CREDIT CARDS ACCEPTED:** Access, Visa, Mastercard, Eurocard. **BAR FOOD AVAILABLE:** 12.00-9.00pm. Beer garden seats 150. **BEERS AVAILABLE:** Tetley, Burton, Young's IPA, Young's Special, Winter Warmer. **NEAREST TUBE STATION:** Highgate.

The Flask

89

14 Flask Walk, NW3 **071-435 4580**

'rather glum waters for 3d a flask'

The current passion for bottled water is not new. It was a hot item in the 18th century too, much to the advantage of Hampstead where a mineral spring was found that cured idleness, dissipation and frivolity. These rather glum waters were bottled in The Thatched House and sold to the public for 3d a flask. The Thatched House became the Lower Flask and got a place in Eng.Lit. In his novel *Clarissa* Samuel Richardson described the Lower Flask as a place where second-rate characters were to be found in swinish conditions.

Never mind, the Lower Flask did well with its flasks of water, and in 1874 the old thatched building was replaced by the tiled and distinctly unswinish one we see today. It has been the Flask ever since. Nothing is now heard of Hampstead's spring and idleness, dissipation and frivolity flourish.

The Flask, made of Hampstead's nice yellow brick with big gas lanterns to guide you to the door, has always been a popular local. It has kept its separate public and saloon bars and they are divided by a fine listed Victorian screen. A big conservatory was recently added and is used for food, music hall nights and whatever else comes to mind. It sells Young's ale and was CAMRA's pub of the year in 1993.

OPEN: Mon-Sun. **HOURS:** 11.00am-11.00pm (12.00-3.00pm and 7.00-10.30pm Sun). **CREDIT CARDS ACCEPTED:** All major cards. **BAR FOOD AVAILABLE:** 12.00-3.00pm and 6.00-10.00pm Mon-Fri; 11.00am-11.00pm Sat; 12.00-3.00pm and 7.00-10.00pm Sun. **AVERAGE COST:** £6.50. Wheelchair access (disabled lavatory). Tables outside seat 25. Private room seats 30. Live music occasionally. **BEERS AVAILABLE:** Young's Bitter,Young's Special, Young's Oatmeal Stout, Young's Premium Lager, Young's London Lager, Tennents Extra, Red Stripe, Castlemaine. **NEAREST TUBE STATION:** Hampstead.

The Flower and Firkin

90

Kew Gardens Station **081-332 1162**

'A pub where once the buffet was'

A sight as welcome as flowers that bloom in the spring, tra la, a Firkin on the District Line, a pub where once the British Rail buffet was. It does very well in the spring and summer with thousands taking the tube to Kew to see the botanical gardens and stopping off for a drink and a snack. It stays open all Sunday afternoon, does good salads and on sunny days you can pick up a picnic there and have it on the grass.

It is proud of its conservatory but in this department I rather think Kew Gardens has the edge.

OPEN: Mon-Sun. **HOURS:** 12.00-11.00pm (12.00-3.00pm and 7.00-10.30pm Sun). **CLOSED:** Christmas Day. **CREDIT CARDS ACCEPTED:** None. **BAR FOOD AVAILABLE:** 12.00-8.00pm. Wheelchair access (but not lavatory). Tables outside seat 30. **BEERS AVAILABLE:** Dogbolter, Murphy's, Guinness, Lowenbrau, Castlemaine, Carlsberg. **Nearest tube station:** Kew Gardens.

49 Gresham Street

91

49 Gresham Street, EC2 **071-606 0399**

'Observe the name and the address. The same. Will this work?'

A brand new pub in the city, a very smart pub at that and a great relief to people who had started to think that no one would ever do anything with this prime corner site. It had been an empty concrete shell for years and now look at it, a most superior Fuller's pub with a wine bar underneath.

Is this a sign of better times? Yes it is and should you wish to celebrate, the landlord, Mark Noble-Campbell, can offer you real ales, 24 wines and a house champagne at £17.99 a bottle.

Observe the name and the address. The same. Will this work? My bet is that 49 Gresham Street will be known as Fuller's. It has made a good start. Note: it keeps City hours. That is to say it closes at 9.30pm on weekdays and doesn't open at all at weekends.

OPEN: Mon-Fri. **HOURS:** 11.00am-9.30pm (11.00am-10.30pm Fri). **CLOSED:** Bank Holidays. **CREDIT CARDS ACCEPTED:** All major cards. **BAR FOOD AVAILABLE:** 12.00-3.00pm. Wheelchair access (disabled lavatory). Private room seats 60. **BEERS AVAILABLE:** Chiswick Bitter, London Pride, ESB, Hock, Lummer Ale, Guinness. **NEAREST TUBE STATIONS:** St Paul's, Bank.

MAP REF: 6, C/2

The Founders Arms

92

52 Hopton Street, SE1 **071-928 1899**

'One of the great views'

This fine modern pub stands boldly on the river bank on the south side of Blackfriar's Bridge. It is hard to find the first time but the Dean of St Paul's managed all right. He formally opened it in 1979.

When you get there you have Young's beer, a glass-walled bar, a pleasant restaurant and a big riverside terrace, wonderful on a sunny day. Bar and terrace give you one of the great views of St Paul's.

OPEN: Mon-Sun. **HOURS:** 11.00am-11.00pm (12.00-3.00pm and 7.00-10.30pm Sun). **CREDIT CARDS ACCEPTED:** AmEx, Visa, Access, Mastercard. **BAR FOOD AVAILABLE:** 11.00am-9.30pm. **RESTAURANT FOOD AVAILABLE:** 12.00-2.30pm and 6.30-9.30pm. Wheelchair access. Beer garden seats 80. **BEERS AVAILABLE:** All Young's variants. **NEAREST TUBE STATION:** Blackfriars.

The Fox and Anchor

93

115 Charterhouse Street, EC1 **071-253 4838**

'Few white coats . . . none bloodstained'

After a night's work in Smithfield market generations of bummarees, porters, pitchers and butchers would stream into the Fox and Anchor at the dot of 6am, white coats often streaked with blood, for a pint of porter and a hearty breakfast. The market is a shadow of its old self now, its very survival is in the balance. Most remarkably, though, the Fox and Anchor is busier than ever. It still has its all-day licence and at 7am, an hour later than in the old days, it opens its doors and in come the customers. There are few white coats among them, none bloodstained. Instead there are men in suits on their way to the office, business women having business breakfasts. They come in such numbers that they have to book the day before. It is nothing for the Fox and Anchor to have 90 for breakfast and to turn another 20 away.

Such a breakfast it is – two sausages, two rashers of bacon, a fried egg, black pudding, fried bread, baked beans, tomatoes, toast. This is known as the English breakfast and it costs £6.50. With it they drink pints of Guinness, pints of Tetley. A pint of champagne is not unknown. There's not much call for the coffee.

The Fox and Anchor has been serving this breakfast virtually unchanged since 1898. Its lunches are pretty hearty too, the steak and kidney pie is recommended, and the pub itself does not seem to have changed much. It was decorated quite recently but so carefully you would hardly know. Look at the old snugs at the back. Surely they have always been here? They are, in fact, two years old. They replaced the loos, now upstairs.

OPEN: Mon-Sat. **HOURS:** 7.00am-10.00pm (8.00am-12.00pm Sat). **CLOSED:** Bank holidays. **CREDIT CARDS ACCEPTED:** All major cards. **BAR FOOD AVAILABLE:** 7.00-10.30am and 12.00-2.15pm. **SET PRICE BREAKFAST:** £6.50. **SET PRICE LUNCH:** £7.50. Private room seats 20. **BEERS AVAILABLE:** Tetley, Nicholson's, Carlsberg, Castlemaine. **NEAREST TUBE STATIONS:** Farringdon, Barbican. **MAP REF:** 6, B/2

The Fox and Grapes

94

Camp Road, SW19 **081-946 5599**

'At busy times people will perch their plates on any available surface'

Camp Road potters along on the west side of Wimbledon Common where the golf courses are and an attractive low black and white pub overflows onto the narrow pavement. This is the Fox and Grapes which has been there, part of it anyway, since 1787.

It was a tea and gin shop then. Now the tea and gin bit is a cosy comfortable bar with a low wooden ceiling supported by huge oak pillars – Caesar's Bar they call it after a certain J Caesar who built the Roman fort up the road.

It is not known if Jules called in on some distant forebear of the Fox and Grapes before marching on London, nor if Dick Turpin really stabled Black Bess here, but people like to think so. The stables now form the lounge bar, a large, high room with a gas log fire, wood panelling and a beamed and raftered roof. An old wooden propeller adorns one wall. This may or again may not be connected with the World War II bomber pilot who, having just crashed on the Common, staggered in for a little something to steady the nerves.

The Fox and Grapes is renowned for its home-cooked food, served all day. At busy times people will perch their plates on any available surface – radiators, the floor, cars parked outside. Special occasions like Christmas Eve and Hallowe'en are huge thrashes, when all the tables and chairs are cleared out of the lounge to make room.

The Fox and Grapes is popular with most ages, shapes and sizes. Plastic glasses are provided for younger drinkers heading for the common, golfers stock up here after their morning rounds and dog-walkers particularly like to pop in. Dogs, unusually, are welcome.

Oliver Reed no longer drinks here.

OPEN: Mon-Sun. **HOURS:** 11.00am-11.00pm (12.00-3.00pm and 7.00-10.30pm Sun). **CREDIT CARDS ACCEPTED:** AmEx, Mastercard, Visa. **RESTAURANT FOOD AVAILABLE:** 12.00-9.30pm (12.00-3.00pm and 7.00-9.30pm Sun). Wheelchair access (but not lavatory). **BEERS AVAILABLE:** Wadworth, Courage Directors, John Smith's, Young's Special, Young's Best, Courage Best, Kronenbourg, Foster's, Miller. **NEAREST TUBE STATION:** Wimbledon.

The Fox and Hounds 95

29 Passmore Street, SW1 **071-730 6367**

'Safer than gin for the working man'

The Fox and Hounds is sorry but you can't have a gin and something or a whisky and anything. They are, they will explain for the millionth time, only licensed to sell beer.

There used to be lots of pubs like this, beer houses, a Victorian notion. Beer, thought the licensing authorities of the time, was safer than gin for the working man. The Fox and Hounds may be the only one left and Diane Harvey, the licensee, doesn't mind at all.

The Fox and Hounds started out in the 1860s, the archetypal beer house. The street door opened onto a small room with a wooden floor, settles round the walls and a couple of tables. The landlady would hand your beer through a flap in her living-room door. Things hardly changed for 100 years. One room for the pub, three for the licensees and their children. Family and customers shared one outside loo.

The outside lav stayed right up to 1980 by which time the whole character of the district had changed. What had been terraces of working men's cottages had become fashionable and expensive and got steadily more so. In Passmore Street today the modish new shop on the corner is Lord Linley's and if one of the small houses comes up for sale nowadays they ask around £400,000 for perhaps a 50-year lease.

The pub has changed too of course but thankfully it has not been spoiled. It is actually quite nice to have inside loos, a bar counter and more room and it remains a period piece with nice Mrs Harvey still running the show in the old way.

She has been at the Fox and Hounds for 26 years, has survived successive attempts to pull it down, endured building work that lasted a year and that closed the pub altogether for five months. Her customers have an agreeable diversity. It is not unusual on a Sunday night to see a white-cassocked priest standing outside the pub with a beer, surrounded by acolytes and members of the choir. They are regulars from St Mary's, Bourne Street and the Fox is regularly discovered by successive casts at the Royal Court hence the occasional presence of Peter O'Toole, Harrison Ford and Pierce Brosnan.

OPEN: Mon-Sun. **HOURS:** 11.00-3.00pm and 5.30-11.00pm (11.00-3.00pm and 6.00-11.00pm Sat; 12.00-2.00pm and 7.00-10.30 Sun). **CLOSED:** Christmas Day. **CREDIT CARDS ACCEPTED:** None. Wheelchair access (but not lavatory). **BEERS AVAILABLE:** Real ales. **NEAREST TUBE STATION:** Sloane Square. **MAP REF:** 2, F/2

The Fox and Pheasant

96

1 Billing Road, SW10 **071-352 2943**

'A minor drawback, you may think, is its nearness to Chelsea Football Ground. You can hear them score'

There is a smart little enclave off Fulham Road known to estate agents as The Billings. This is where the Fox and Pheasant stands. It is worth seeking out, a little country pub created 200 years ago by knocking two small houses into one and it cheers you up just to look at it.

Inside it is quite unmodernized with exposed beams, leaded windows, basic hardwood tables and chairs and a big log fireplace. The two rooms are separated by a central bar and both have lots of sporting prints. Foxes feature. Also pheasants.

There is an excellent walled beer garden at the back, very popular in the summer. They don't go in for food much but there are sandwiches.

A minor drawback, you may think, is its nearness to Chelsea Football Ground. You can hear them score. Chelsea fans can be Fox and Pheasant fans, too. Best keep away on match days.

OPEN: Mon-Sun. **HOURS:** 12.00-3.00pm and 5.30-11.00pm (7.00-10.30pm Sun). **CLOSED:** Christmas Day and New Year's Day. **CREDIT CARDS ACCEPTED:** None. Beer garden seats 24. **BEERS AVAILABLE:** Greene King IPA, Rayments Special, Abbot Ale, Bass, Carling Black Label, Kronenbourg, Harp, Guinness, Brewers Bitter, Steinlager, Budweiser, Becks, Pale Ale, Gold Label. **NEAREST TUBE STATION:** Fulham Broadway.

‸e Freemasons Arms

97

‸2 Downshire Hill, NW3 **071-435 4498**

'This game, known as London skittles, was once played in pubs all over the South of England'

What's with these Freemasons Arms? Do Freemasons meet in them, exchanging coded handshakes and doing good works? Apparently they used to but not especially now.

London has at least four Freemasons Arms. There's one in Long Acre, others in Stepney and Wood Green and this one in Hampstead near the heath. It is a big prosperous modern pub, built in 1932 to replace an earlier Freemasons Arms that was having trouble standing up.

There can be few bigger pubs in North London. The garden is vast, full of roses and picnic tables. It also has a sunken courtyard with a fountain and more tables and a flagged terrace overlooking the fountain with yet more tables.

Inside the pub a well turned-out saloon bar merges with the public bar which has a pool table and darts board. There is another sitting room and a large comfortable dining room and down a flight of stairs and you are in a skittle alley, a 21-foot pitch with big hornbeam skittles awaiting Tuesday, Thursday and Saturday nights when the skittles club arrives and tries to knock them over. You do this by throwing massive cheeses made from lignum vitae at them. They can weigh up to 12lbs, these cheeses, and take some throwing.

This game, known as London skittles, was once played in pubs all over the south of England. It is an endangered species now but it is alive and well in the Freemasons Arms.

OPEN: Mon-Sun. **HOURS:** 11.00am-11.00pm (12.00-3.00pm and 7.00-10.30pm Sun). **CREDIT CARDS ACCEPTED:** Visa, Mastercard. **BAR FOOD AVAILABLE:** 12.00-10.00pm. No smoking area. Wheelchair access. Beer garden seats 200. Private room seats 50. **BEERS AVAILABLE:** Bass, London Pride, Carling Black Label, Tennent's Pilsner, Tennent's Extra, Grolsch. **NEAREST TUBE STATION:** Hampstead.

The French House

98

49 Dean Street, W1 **071-437 2799**

'Maurice Chevalier . . . Georges Carpentier . . . General de Gaulle'

Ah the French pub, still a favourite watering hole of the chattering classes. It is officially the French House now. It used to be officially the York Minister but no one ever called it that either. The French pub is what it is.

Its Frenchness began with a Belgian, the splendidly moustachioed Victor Berlemont who bought the pub just before the First World War and through the 20s and 30s filled it with singers and actors and boxers. Maurice Chevalier came. So did Georges Carpentier. Then came the war and the Free French and General de Gaulle who wrote his historic declaration of defiance to the Nazis in the room above the bar.

The war over, Victor's son, Gaston, took charge. He had the stylish moustaches and strong personality of his father and life at the French pub got more bohemian than ever. Dylan Thomas left the only manuscript of *Under Milk Wood* there, Brendan Behan sang and danced, Francis Bacon, Lucien Freud, Dan Farson *et al* got agreeably tanked up and Gaston opened yet another crate of champagne. He retired on Bastille Day, 1989, and happily ideal new owners were at hand. Noel Botham and Lesley Lewis had been drinking in the French pub for years and, apart from reopening the restaurant which Gaston had closed, they changed nothing that mattered. The restaurant has proved an outstanding success and the pub remains uniquely itself, tricolours flying, photographs of regulars, famous and not, plastering the walls. The regulars chat in carrying tones, newcomers feel a bit out of it but it was ever thus.

The French pub still sells more champagne across the bar than the Savoy Grill, is still the country's largest single retail outlet of Ricard. Pernod sales can't be far behind. Fifteen wines are sold by the glass and beer is sold in half-pint glasses only. Coca Cola, resisted by Gaston, is sold now but not crisps, or, *mon Dieu*, pork crackling. There is no music, no television, no fruit machine. *Vive la* French pub.

OPEN: Mon-Sun. **HOURS:** 12.00-11.00pm (12.00-3.00pm and 7.00-10.30pm Sun). **CREDIT CARDS ACCEPTED:** All major cards. **BAR FOOD AVAILABLE:** 12.30-3.00pm and 6.30-10.00pm. **RESTAURANT FOOD AVAILABLE:** 12.30pm-12.00am. Wheelchair access to pub (but not lavatory or restaurant). Private room seats 35. **BEERS AVAILABLE:** Adelscott, Carlsberg, Websters. **NEAREST TUBE STATION:** Leicester Square. **MAP REF:** 1, E/2

Friar and Firkin 99

120 Euston Road, NW1 **071-387 2419**

'Impeccably firkinised'

David Bruce, founder of the Firkins, sold his idiosyncratic chain of pubs in 1978 and was soon regretting it. He missed them, tried to get them back but by then Allied Lyons had taken to them, indeed was adding to them. Many of us held our breath . . .

This was the first of the new Firkins, the Rising Sun, an unexceptional Victorian pub in Euston Road. In 1992 Allied Lyons closed it. Four weeks later it reopened as the Friar and Firkin and firkin fans breathed again. It had been impeccably firkinized.

It it is a long, wandering pub with all the well-tried Firkin features, the bare floorboards, the pews, the barrel tables, the brass chandeliers, the Firkin food and the firkin notices – the Firkin Loos, Mind the Firkin Step. It has the essential dais and piano and a late license for Thursday, Friday and Saturday nights with entertainers from the Firkin circuit and, alleluia, as the friar might say, it has a five-barrel brewhouse underneath.

So the Friar and Firkin makes its own ale right there in the Euston

Confessionale, Friar, full mash mild and the redoubtable Dogbolter. You can see it happening by way of a carefully placed mirror on the cellar steps while outside the Friar, astride a barrel on the new pub sign, beams sunnily down on impassable traffic.

OPEN: Mon-Sun. **HOURS:** 11.00am-11.00pm Mon-Wed; 11.00-12.00am Thur-Sat; 12.00-3.00pm and 7.00-10.30 Sun. **CLOSED:** Christmas Day. **CREDIT CARDS ACCEPTED:** None. **BAR FOOD AVAILABLE:** 12.00-7.30pm. **SET PRICE LUNCH AND DINNER:** £3.75. No smoking area. Wheelchair access (but not lavatory). Tables outside seat 16. **BEERS AVAILABLE:** Dogbolter, Friar Ale, Confessional Ale, Firkin Full Mash Mild, Tetley, Becks, Carlsberg, Castlemaine, Tuborg Gold, Weston's Scrumpy, Budweiser, Lowenbrau, Rolling Rock, Oranjeboom, Newcastle Brown Ale. **NEAREST TUBE STATIONS:** Euston, King's Cross. **MAP REF:** 1, F/4

The Front Page

100

35 Old Church Street, SW3 **071-352 2908**

'Reflects the old bohemian quarter as no other does just now'

Some say that this is now *the* Chelsea pub. It's the social mix. The Front Page reflects the old bohemian quarter as no other does just now. Its patrons include the local vicar and the rag-and-bone man, the dustmen on collection days and several peers, writers and actors rehearsing at the parish hall down the street. Dustin Hoffman and Sharon Gless, for instance. After 9pm crowds of young Chelsea arrive.

The Front Page used to be the Black Lion but when the Phillips and the Fowlers took it over in 1986 they changed the name. There had been a Black Lion on this spot for 300 years so not everyone was pleased.

But theirs has been a popular regime. The Front Page is a plain pub without piped music, fruit machine or fitted carpets. Its big windows make it light and airy and the food is original and substantial The locals go for lunch; audiences of the Cannon cinema up the street go for pre- or post-movie supper; there is a private dining-room upstairs.

The staff is young and cheerful, the regulars are all ages and cheerful and everyone gets on well.

OPEN: Mon-Sun. **HOURS:** 11.00am-3.00pm and 5.30-11.00pm. (11.00am-3.00pm, 6:00-11.00pm Sat; 12.00-3.00pm, 7.00-10.30pm Sun). **CLOSED:** Christmas. **CREDIT CARDS ACCEPTED:** Visa, Mastercard, Eurocard, but not AmEx. **BAR FOOD AVAILABLE:** 12.30-2.30pm and 7.00-10.00pm (12.30-2.30pm and 7.00-9.30pm Sun). Wheelchair access. Private room seats 22. **BEERS AVAILABLE:** Boddingtons, Webster's, John Smith's, Ruddells County, Foster's, Holsten, Kronenbourg, Beamish. **NEAREST TUBE STATION:** Sloane Square. **MAP REF:** 2, B/2

Fulmar and Firkin

101

51 Parker Street, WC2 **071-405 0590**

'Class of '93'

Here we have a Firkin, class of '93, just off the Kingsway, formerly, indeed, the Kingsway Tavern and much bigger than it looks.

It is popular with students and tutors from various local groves of academe including the LSE and the St Martin's School of Art, who can make Friday evenings very far out indeed.

In its previous life the pub was so quiet on Saturday night that it stopped opening. The Fulmar has found the answer. Every Saturday it now has free alternative comedy, four, five, even six alternative comedians one after the other, and it is packed. The Fulmar is considered a good audience. This means it does not actually throw things. Exhausted, it closes on Sundays.

Fulmars are large handsome sea birds. Three of them, stuffed, are in evidence, one in a tie, one in dark glasses, one sitting on eggs. Others appear on T-shirts and one soars high on the inn sign. Fulmars, though! Are the Firkins running out of Fs?

OPEN: Mon-Sat. **HOURS:** 11.00am-11.00pm. **CLOSED:** Bank holidays. **CREDIT CARDS ACCEPTED:** All major cards. **BAR FOOD AVAILABLE:** 11.30am-6.00pm. **SET PRICE LUNCH:** £3.50. Wheelchair access (but not lavatory). **BEERS AVAILABLE:** Dogbolter, Fulmar, Wingspan, Golden Glory, Firkin Mild, Ridley ESX, Tetley, Flowers IPA, Castlemaine, Lowenbrau, Kronenbourg. **NEAREST TUBE STATION:** Holborn. **MAP REF:** 1, F/2

…usilier and Firkin
102

…halk Farm Road, NW1 **071-485 7858**

…g business with ozzie steak baps'

A rather drunken-looking redcoat on the new pub sign welcomes you to another of the Firkin class of '92, the one-time Carnarvon Castle with a new name and a whole new personality. This cavernous old pub stands directly opposite Camden Market, which is thick with people every week from Thursday onwards. The Fusilier, big as it is, gets packed. Stall-holders, bargain hunters, tourists, they all crowd in. It has a little platform and piano as all Firkins do but alone among them it has live music every Saturday afternoon, dragging in the crowds by their ears. There's live music on Friday evenings too. In its Carnarvon Castle days it had pool tables at the back. Now there is bar billiards pleasantly lit by the bell vault, a superior sky light they discovered behind the old false ceiling.

The Fusilier does big business with Ozzie steak baps – hot steak in a bap with a fried egg added or mushrooms or cheese or whatever. The espresso coffee machine is in demand and the firkin phonograph much used.

OPEN: Mon-Sun. **HOURS:** 12.00-11.00pm Mon-Thur; 12.00pm-12.00am Fri; 11.00-12.00am Sat; 11.00am-3.00pm and 4.00-10.30pm Sun. **CLOSED:** Christmas Day. **CREDIT CARDS ACCEPTED:** None. **BAR FOOD AVAILABLE:** 12.00-4.00pm; 12.00-5.30pm in winter (11.00am-2.30pm Sat; 12.00-6.00pm Sun). **SET PRICE LUNCH AND DINNER:** £3.95. Wheelchair access (but not lavatory). **BEERS AVAILABLE:** The Firkin brews, Lowenbrau, Carlsberg, Castlemaine, Guinness, Mersey's, Scrumpy, Old English. **NEAREST TUBE STATIONS:** Camden Town.

The Gallery
103

1 Lupus Street, SW1 **071-821 7573**

'The yobs departed'

It is surprising how often pubs change their names. This one, for instance, originally the Queen of Denmark, became the Perseverance, went back to the Queen of Denmark, then became the Perseverance again. What about the Dither?

It was having its second go at the Perseverance when Edward and Patricia Burke saw it two years ago. They already had a pub in Chelmsford and another in Ashford, Middlesex, but two isn't many. Bass has 7,190. A third would be nice, thought Mr and Mrs Burke and the Perserverance, very run down, Christmas decorations still up in March, did seem in need of a little TLC. So they bought it, refurbished it from top to bottom, changed its name for the fifth time and put their nephew Paul Corcoran in to manage it. It was now the Gallery.

Now Lupus Street is well-behaved Pimlico. The Tate is near – hence the Gallery – and Dolphin Square is nearer still, so young Mr Corcoran was surprised to find it so, well, rough. 'Unbelievable,' he says.

So his first job was to lose some very regular customers. They bowled in to the newly furbished pub, prints of famous paintings all round the walls, and resumed the yobbish tenor of their ways.

Confrontation. Verbals. Threats. A full can of lager through one of the costly etched windows. New manager stands ground. Mona Lisa, tight-lipped in lobby, makes her position plain. 'After five or six weeks they got the message that they weren't going to get a drink,' says Corcoran. The yobs departed – an even better name for the pub.

It is pleasant and peaceful now and I wouldn't be surprised if the Burkes were not looking for a fourth pub. They seem to have the bit between their teeth.

OPEN: Mon-Sun. **HOURS:** 11.00am-11.00pm (12.00-3.00pm and 7.00-11.00 Sat-Sun). **CREDIT CARDS ACCEPTED:** None. **BAR FOOD AVAILABLE:** 12.00-2.30pm (12.00-3.00pm and 7.00-9.30 Sat-Sun). **SET PRICE LUNCH:** £4.25. **SET PRICE DINNER:** £5.25. Wheelchair access (but not lavatory). **BEERS AVAILABLE:** Webster's Yorkshire Bitter, Marston's Pedigree, John Smith's, Thomas Hardy Country Bitter, Wadworth, Moorlands Old Speckled Hen. **NEAREST TUBE STATION:** Pimlico.

The Gatehouse

104

North Road, N6 **081-340 8054**

'Consternation in the well-established old pubs round about'

In Elizabethan times the Bishop of London built a toll house on the top of the hill, a high gate spanning the road. It gave the place its name, Highgate. There was an old tavern up there too and when they pulled the toll gate down it stayed put.

Its successor is the Gatehouse, still there after many ups and downs. It was on a major down in 1993, empty and disconsolate when Wetherspoons took it over and it seems to be enjoying life again.

There it is on its hilltop glossily repainted from top to toe and totally changed inside. Ithas no music, gives non-smokers a big non-smoking bit, serves good quick food all day and its cask ales include the great Wetherspoon bargain, a pint of Youngers Scotch Bitter for only 99p. This caused consternation in the well-established old pubs round about.

Traffic grinds past, bumper to bumper. That Bishop of London who put the toll house up had his head screwed on. Get stuck on the other side of the road and it might take you half an hour to reach the refurbed bar.

OPEN: Mon-Sun. **HOURS:** 11.00am-11.00pm (12.00-3.00pm and 7.00-10.30pm Sun). **CREDIT CARDS ACCEPTED:** Access, Visa, Delta, Switch. **BAR FOOD AVAILABLE:** 11.00am-11.00pm (12.00-3.00pm and 7.00-10.30pm Sun). **SET PRICE LUNCH AND DINNER:** £3.95. No smoking area. Wheelchair access. Beer garden seats 30. **BEERS AVAILABLE:** Theakston Best, Theakston XB, Younger Scotch Bitter, Courage Directors, Wadworth 6X, Becks, Foster's, McEwans. **NEAREST TUBE STATION:** Highgate.

? ...zebo 105

...assage, Kingston **081-546 4495**

'...n wooden gazebos flank the frontage'

...he Gazebo is currently the extreme tip of Sam Smith's Southern colonisation which started a few miles downriver at the Rose of York at Richmond and proceeds apace.

It is an attractive modern pub less than ten years old in a lovely spot on the Thames, right next door to Young's Bishop out of Residence. Twin wooden gazebos flank the frontage and steps lead down to moorings for customers who have come by boat. Downstairs the public bar, wooden floors, a pinball machine and a pool table; upstairs the saloon bar with a big verandah overlooking the river and the green vistas beyond.

Very impressive choice of salads, a carvery on Sundays, a children's menu and some good old-fashioned puds.

OPEN: Mon-Sun. **HOURS:** 11.00am-11.00pm (12.00-3.00pm and 7.00-10.30pm Sun). **CLOSED:** Christmas Day. **CREDIT CARDS ACCEPTED:** Visa, Access, Mastercard. **BAR FOOD AVAILABLE:** 11.30am-2.45pm and 7.30-9.30pm. Wheelchair access (disabled lavatory). Tables outside seat 100. Private room seats 100. **BEERS AVAILABLE:** Samuel Smith Old Brewery Ale, Museum Ale, Ayingerbrau, Pils, Prinz, Samuel Smith's Extra Strong Stout. **NEAREST BR STATION:** Kingston.

The George Canning 106

95 Effra Road, SW2 **071-738 4959**

'Quality bands playing ska, soul, r&b, funk'

Irish-run funky pub in Brixton, cosmopolitan and laid back. There's a bar, a music room and a cheerful crowd nearer thirty than twenty. The bar's a bar, you don't pay to get in. The music room's a music room, you pay at the door.

A funk-freak writes: 'At the start of the week it's football with Sky soccer on Mondays and European games on Tuesdays and Wednesdays and on Thursday it's stand-up comedy. Then it's music. Friday night is country rock, a new nineties country and western with line dancing, the American craze. Saturday is funky night, quality bands playing ska, soul, r&b, funk.

'The music is played in a beautiful and airy room with a table you can sit at. You can usually watch the band from your seat. No bouncers. They actually seem pleased to see you at the Canning.'

OPEN: Mon-Sun. **HOURS:** 11.00am-12.00am (12.00-10.30pm Sun). **CREDIT CARDS ACCEPTED:** All major cards. **BAR FOOD AVAILABLE:** All opening hours. Wheelchair access. Tables ouside seat 65. Private room seats 180. **BEERS AVAILABLE:** Courage Best, Budweiser, Sol, Newcastle Brown, Grolsch, Michelob, Foster's Ice, Carlsberg, Holsten Pils. **NEAREST TUBE STATION:** Brixton.

The George Inn

77 Borough High Street, SE1 **071-407 205**

'You should really arrive in a stage coach'

The George Inn at Southwark is perhaps the most famous pub in London. To come across it for the first time is to meet an old friend. You feel you know it already from Christmas cards, Dickens, and old movies. It is the all-time coaching inn, you should really arrive in a stage coach. Instead you park where you can and walk through the wrought iron gateway on Borough High Street and there it is, the cobbled yard, the overhanging galleries, the south front, all still in daily use. It is a moving sight.

We know a lot about it. We know it was going strong in 1542, the year Henry VIII executed his fifth wife. We know it was rebuilt three times, emerging splendidly intact into the railway age, the same three-sided galleried building, one big courtyard and a smaller one beyond it surrounded by stables.

Then, humiliatingly, the George became a depot of the Great Northern Railway which pulled down two of the fronts and built warehousing in their place. Luckily the south front survived and the railway buildings did not. They were bombed in the war and what replaces them is pretty awful, two dreadful modern blocks, but you can keep your back to them as you sit at one of the picnic tables in the courtyard. With only the George in view you are in another age.

The old floorboards creak loudly as you pass from bar to bar in the old inn, twice as loudly as you go upstairs to the dark panelled restaurant and various function rooms. These upper storeys were of course bedchambers in the George's great days. You can't find a bed there now but the food is good, the ale is better, old settles and chimney corners beckon and in the summer there's the courtyard where Shakespeare, they say, once performed. It is a romantic place. The George Inn, safely in the hands of the National Trust, does not disappoint you.

OPEN: Mon-Sun. **HOURS:** 11.00am-11.00pm (12.00-3.00pm and 7.00-10.30pm Sun). **CLOSED:** Christmas Day. **CREDIT CARDS ACCEPTED:** AmEx, Diner's Club, Access, Visa. **BAR AND RESTAURANT FOOD AVAILABLE:** 12.00-2.30pm. Courtyard seats 80. Private room seats 60. **BEERS AVAILABLE:** Abbot Ale, Boddingtons, London Pride, Castle Eden, Flowers IPA. **NEAREST TUBE STATION:** London Bridge. **MAP REF:** 7, D/1

The Gipsy Moth

108

60 Greenwich Church Street, SE10 **081-858 0786**

'It is hard work looking at famous ships'

The magnificent Cutty Sark and the gallant little Gipsy Moth, both enjoying new careers as tourist attractions at Greenwich get perhaps 300,000 visitors every year. It is hard work looking at famous ships g two of them the whole family needs a drink and a oo. This large efficient pub is right on the spot. A bit of nd really.

to be, unmemorably, the Wheatsheaf but changed its name Gipsy Moth when Sir Francis Chichester's little boat, having round the world with only him on board, settled on its doorstep. now every summer tourists arrive in a never-ending stream, have a neal and a drink, go to the loo and move on, letting someone else have the table.

The Gipsy Moth has no complaints about the turnover. All the same it would like to have an open-air barbecue, live music, something for the children in its garden. It's whole instinct is to be jollier. It's neighbours, however, take a different view. You see the problem. Pubs do not make the quietest neighbours of course. At the same time neighbours can give pubs a bad time too. By long tradition people have been able to drink on the pavement outside many London pubs. This summer, I'm sorry to say, a lot of this was stopped.

OPEN: Mon-Sun. **HOURS:** 11.00am-11.00pm (12.00-3.00pm and 7.00-10.30pm Sun). **CREDIT CARDS ACCEPTED:** All major cards. **BAR FOOD AVAILABLE:** 11.30am-4.00pm (12.00-3.00pm Sun). **SET PRICE LUNCH:** £4.50. Wheelchair access. Beer garden seats 100. **BEERS AVAILABLE:** Tetley, Burton Ale, Young's Special, Lowenbrau, Tuborg, Carlsberg, Castlemaine. **NEAREST BR STATION:** Greenwich.

The Glassblower 109

Glasshouse Street, W1 **071-734 8547**

'Blokish is the word that comes to mind'

An everyday sort of pub five minutes from Piccadilly Circus. Blokish is the word that comes to mind, cigarette smoke, gaming machines, jukebox, Sky TV. There is an upturned table on the ceiling complete with beer glass, ash-tray, beer bottles and playing cards.

It used to be the Bodega. It was sort of Spanish in those days. Then Youngers got it and called it the Kilt and Celt and it became Celtic. Sort of. Now Scottish and Newcastle has gone for the Glassblower. Still that's easier to say after a few pints than Kilt and Celt.

There's quite a nice room upstairs.

OPEN: Mon-Sun. **HOURS:** 11.00am-11.00pm (12.00-3.00pm and 7.00-10.30pm Sun). **CLOSED:** Christmas Day. **CREDIT CARDS ACCEPTED:** All major cards. **BAR FOOD AVAILABLE:** 11.30am-9.00pm. **SET PRICE LUNCH AND DINNER:** £4.85. **RESTAURANT FOOD AVAILABLE:** 12.00-2.00pm. Wheelchair access (but not lavatory). Private room seats 60. **BEERS AVAILABLE:** Theakston, Courage Best, Courage Directors, John Smith's, Carlsberg, Foster's, Coors, Kronenbourg, Budweiser. **NEAREST TUBE STATION:** Piccadilly Circus. **MAP REF:** 1, D/2

The Gloucester

110

187 Sloane Street, SW1 **071-235 0298**

'A famous victory'

The Battle of Alexandria, 1801, is celebrated on the sign outside the Gloucester, a famous victory against Napoleon which earned the Gloucestershire Regiment the unique distinction of being permitted to wear a badge at the back of their headdress as well as the front.

The Gloucester has been loyally marking this noted feat of arms ever since it was built 150 years ago and the Gloucestershire Vets still meet in the back room there on the first Friday of the month.

It is a small, comfortable pub which opens at 8am for breakfast – the full fandango for £5.50. Food is then served all day until 8.30pm, rather dashing sort of food. There are good reports of its beef and Stilton pie, also £5.50.

OPEN: Mon-Sun. **HOURS:** 11.00am-11.00pm (12.00-3.00 and 7.00-10.30pm). **CLOSED:** Christmas Day. **CREDIT CARDS ACCEPTED:** All major cards. **BAR FOOD AVAILABLE:** 11.00am-11.00pm. **RESTAURANT FOOD AVAILABLE:** 8.00am-9.30pm. Wheelchair access (but not lavatory). Private room seats 25. **BEERS AVAILABLE:** Molsen, Grolsch, Budweiser, Becks, Holsten Pils, Wadworth, John Smith's, Courage, Theakston. **NEAREST TUBE STATION:** Knightsbridge. **MAP REF:** 2, F/4

Golden Lion

111

51 Dean Street, W1 **071-434 0661**

'Female-friendly'

For years the Golden Lion in Dean Street was one of London's best-known gay pubs. Its customers did well to take care. It was one of the haunts of Dennis Nilsen, the serial killer.

A new bar policy has changed it radically. The aim, say managers John Sandiland and Jo Passby, is to make it more female-friendly. It is comparatively sedate now.

OPEN: Mon-Sun. **HOURS:** 11.00am-11.30pm (12.00-3.00pm and 7.00-10.30pm Sun). **CLOSED:** Christmas Day. **CREDIT CARDS ACCEPTED:** Visa. **BAR FOOD AVAILABLE:** 12.00-3.00pm and 5.00-7.00pm. Wheelchair access (but not lavatory). Private room seats 15. **BEERS AVAILABLE:** Theakston Best, Theakston XB, McEwans, Coors Extra Gold, Budweiser, Guinness. **NEAREST TUBE STATION:** Piccadilly Circus. **MAP REF:** 1, E/2

The Golden Lion (112)

25 King Street, W1 **071-930 7227**

'furious objections'

The Golden Lion, or Golden Lyon Tavern as it was in 1732, is a striking sight in this rather uneventful street. Five storeys and a roof garret of imitation Jacobean baroque, black marble columns, projecting windows and stucco balustrade, hemmed in by flat modern office buildings – you certainly can't miss it.

Something is missing though. The lovely old St James's Theatre, its old friend which stood next to it for more than 100 years was pulled down by developers in 1959. There were furious objections. Sir Laurence Olivier and Vivien Leigh actually led demonstrations but the demolition men went in anyway. One of those office blocks replaced it. The one on the right . . .

Theatre and pub were unusually close. A door led directly from the circle to the Golden Lion's upstairs bar which became the official theatre bar with warning bells for the start of performances and ordered drinks waiting at the interval. The Golden Lion went into rather a depression when the theatre was demolished but it has had a necessary face lift now and seems to be feeling a lot better.

Programmes and photographs from its theatrical past have started appearing in the upstairs bar. Not very many, a bit disappointing really. But more are promised and it is a nice old pub.

Did I mention that Nell Gwynne was often here when she wasn't at the Red Lion round the corner? And that in 1822 one of the customers murdered the landlady?

OPEN: Mon-Sat. **HOURS:** 11.00am-11.00pm (12.00-4.00pm Sat). **CLOSED:** Sun and all bank holidays. **CREDIT CARDS ACCEPTED:** Visa, Mastercard, AmEx. **BAR FOOD AVAILABLE:** 12.00-2.30pm. Private room seats 40. **BEERS AVAILABLE:** Nicholson's Best, Tetley, Greene King IPA, Brakspear. **NEAREST TUBE STATION:** Green Park.

The Goose and Firkin (113)

47-48 Borough Road, SE1 **071-403 3590**

'Bold revival of an ancient tradition'

The first-ever Firkin, fifteen years old this year, is still as wholesome and welcome as home-made brown bread. David Bruce and his wife started the Firkin chain with this old Southwark pub, then the Duke of York, in 1979. What they did here set the pattern for all the Firkins to come – particularly the brewhouse in the cellar.

This bold revival of an ancient tradition is still the heart of the Firkin philosophy though the brewing technique has been improved. So, sadly, the Goose and Firkin's original brewhouse has been mothballed. The equipment may be replaced but this is one of the smaller Firkins so it may not. Meanwhile it takes its beer from the big brewhouse in the Falcon and Firkin at Hackney which delivers regular supplies of Firkin Borough, Firkin Goose and Dogbolter.

All Firkins have Dogbolter, all Firkins have live music at some time in the week – at the Goose it is every Wednesday and Saturday. This is much enjoyed, it is thought, by the perky goose flying overhead in scuba gear, though perhaps less by the rather regal one behind the bar.

Very little changes at Firkin pubs though, with its 15th birthday approaching, the Goose and Firkin did have a bit of a facelift last year. A new bar counter was being installed and the pub was astonished to hear that the producers of *EastEnders* wanted to buy the old one. They had a starring role for it, they said. They did. When the Vic caught fire it was the old bar from the Goose and Firkin that blazed on the nation's television screens.

OPEN: Mon-Sun. **HOURS:** 12.00-11.00pm (12.00-3.00pm, 7.00-11.00pm Sat; 12.00-3.00 and 7.00-10.30pm Sun). **CLOSED:** Good Friday, Easter Sunday, Christmas Day, Boxing Day. **BAR FOOD AVAILABLE:** 12.00-7.00pm Mon-Fri (12.00-3.00pm Sat). Wheelchair access (but not lavatory). Tables outside seat 18. **BEERS AVAILABLE:** Goose, Borough Bitter, Dogbolter, Winter Warmer, Firkin's Golden Glory, Castlemaine, Lowenbrau, Carlsberg. **NEAREST TUBE STATIONS:** Elephant and Castle, Borough.

The Grafton Arms

114

72 Grafton Way, W1 **071-387 7923**

'Walls recently painted to look as if they had been through years of heavy smoking'

The Grafton Arms is an agreeable little pub in what they call Fitzrovia now, the bit round Fitzroy Square. The Dukes of Grafton are FitzRoys. The name means that the first duke was the bastard son of the king, Charles II in this case.

If the dukes ever had any doings with the Grafton Arms they don't now. It's a Whitbread pub, one of their new Hogshead ale houses. This one has eight cask ales ready at all times. It will sell you a lager or a stout but doesn't go on about it. It has the usual Hogshead features – a bare board floor, walls recently painted to look as if they had been through years of heavy smoking. The food counter is upstairs and there's a small roof garden with a view of other roofs.

A hogshead is a very big barrel. It holds 54 gallons. The Grafton Arms had one on the pavement outside until lately but someone pinched it.

OPEN: Mon-Sun. **HOURS:** 11.00am-11.00pm (12.00-3.00pm and 7.00-10.30pm Sun). **CREDIT CARDS ACCEPTED:** All major cards except AmEx, Switch, Diner's Club. **BAR FOOD AVAILABLE:** 12.00-9.00pm (12.00-2.30pm and 7.00-9.00pm Sun). Wheelchair access (but not lavatory). Tables outside seat 30. Private room seats 28. **BEERS AVAILABLE:** Boddington, Pedigree, Wadworth, London Pride, Old Speckled Hen, Pigswill, Heineken, Stella Artois, Guinness, Murphy's. **NEAREST TUBE STATION:** Warren Street, Goodge Street. **MAP REF:** 1, E/4

Graftons

115

2 Strutton Ground, SW1 **071-222 7310**

'That was all of 46 years ago and people still go to Graftons to ask about the Goons'

Graftons is famous for the Goons. They started there upstairs in the front room, Harry Secombe, Spike Milligan, Peter Sellers and Michael Bentine, young comic hopefuls brought together by aspiring scriptwriter Jimmy Grafton, son of the house, and whoosh, up, up and away they went, all of them but Jimmy. That was all of 46 years ago and people still go to Graftons to ask about the Goons.

The pub stands at the Victoria Street end of Strutton Ground where there has been a daily market since 1718. Its panelled wooden front at street level is painted a pleasing red, there are fine latticed windows, three gas lamps and above them the name spelled out in gold: Graftons.

The long saloon bar is bisected by a thick pillar of brick which has been getting in the way of generations of drinkers making their way to the fireplace at the back. Some of these are noticeably sporting size eleven footwear. This is one of Scotland Yard's locals. It is also the regular meeting place of the Goons' appreciation society and a place of pilgrimage for other fans from all over. Alcoves facing the bar display Goons memorabilia which they like but the fans are not invited upstairs. What might have been a hallowed temple is now the living room of manager Paddy Rice and his wife Joanna who had not heard of the Goons before they took over at Graftons. It's their young age you see.

Still, they have heard of them now all right and give out leaflets at the bar telling more of the story.

OPEN: Mon-Sat. **HOURS:** 11.00am-11.00pm (12.00-3.00pm Sat). **CREDIT CARDS ACCEPTED:** All major cards. **BAR FOOD AVAILABLE:** 11.00am-9.00pm. **SET PRICE LUNCH AND DINNER:** £3.95. Wheelchair access. **BEERS AVAILABLE:** John Smith's, Courage Best, Courage Directors, Foster's, Carlsberg, Holsten, Guinness, Beamish. **NEAREST TUBE STATION:** St James's Park. **MAP REF:** 8, B/1

The Grapes

116

76 Narrow Street, E14 **071-987 4396**

'Press gangs and dark doings'

The Six Jolly Fellowship-Porters, a tavern of a dropsical appearance, had long settled down into a state of hale infirmity,' wrote Charles Dickens in *Our Mutual Friend*. 'In its whole constitution it had not a straight floor and hardly a straight line; but it had outlasted and would yet outlast many a better-trimmed building, many a sprucer public house.'

The real name of the Six Jolly Fellowship-Porters was, and is, the Grapes. Dickens knew it well, described it perfectly and it is still there on the river at Limehouse. It hasn't changed all that much.

It was old when Dickens knew it, with a history of press gangs and dark doings. It is 100 years older now and, not surprisingly, there is still not a straight floor, hardly a straight line. The bar and tap of

Dickens' day have somehow come together and it's up a shallow step to what used to be the parlour and cosy.

A deck at the back hangs over the river in the old dropsical way, old bottles apparently long forgotten sleep on a high shelf and up narrow creaking stairs there is a tiny room where fresh fish is served daily, Dover soles, plaice, skate, scallops. If you want the lobster or a dressed crab you have to order it the day before.

The present agreeable licensees resemble in no way the battleaxe who reigned in *Our Mutual Friend*. That is a change for the better but I hope you notice how exactly Dickens hit the nail on the head about the shape of things to come. The Grapes, aka the Six Jolly Fellowship-Porters, has indeed outlasted many a better-trimmed building, many a sprucer public house.

OPEN: Mon-Sun. **HOURS:** 12.00-3.00pm and 5.30-11.00pm (12.00-3.00pm and 7.00-11.00pm Sat; 12.00-3.00 and 7.00-10.30 Sun). **CLOSED:** Boxing Day, New Year's Day. **CREDIT CARDS ACCEPTED:** All major cards. **BAR FOOD AVAILABLE:** 12.00-2.00pm Mon-Fri; 7.00-10.00pm Tue-Sat. **SET PRICE LUNCH AND DINNER:** £4.50. **RESTAURANT FOOD AVAILABLE:** 12.00-1.45pm Mon-Fri; 7.00-9.30pm Tue-Sat. Wheelchair access (but not lavatory). Private room seats 28. **BEERS AVAILABLE:** Burton, Tetley, Friary Mieux, Guinness, Becks, Castlemaine, Carlsberg. **NEAREST TUBE STATION:** Mile End.

Ye Grapes 117

16 Shepherd Market, W1 **071-499 1563**

'The contents of a grand country house attic'

Shepherd Market is not what it was. It used to have girls smiling at you from every doorway and when Ye Grapes was built in 1882 one of its five bars was called the cattle bar because it was exclusively used by the ladies of the night, not to mention the afternoon. Today the girls rely on tasteful advertisements and you could take your maiden aunt to Ye Grapes provided she doesn't mind a crush. It is a popular pub on the corner of the market square and gets very crowded on occasion.

Ye Grape is a privately owned pub, a true Free House, not too many of them around. The owner is Anthony Wigram who has a lot of property, property being his thing, but only one pub, this one. He has a tenant, Eric Lewis, who runs it but Wigram pops in every now and then, as does George Best. Best is fond of Ye Grapes.

It is hard to see the walls of Ye Grapes for the profusion of objects. You might suppose that the contents of a grand country house attic had been scattered on it, the heads of horned beasts, a pair of oars, a pair of guns, fish in glass cases, birds in glass cases.

It takes its beer seriously. Seven real ales are on offer. There are two gambling machines and a jukebox tucked away at the back.

OPEN: Mon-Sun. **HOURS:** 11.00am-11.00pm (12.00-3.00pm and 7.00-10.30pm Sun). **CLOSED:** Christmas Day. **CREDIT CARDS ACCEPTED:** None. **RESTAURANT FOOD AVAILABLE:** 11.30am-10.30pm. **SET PRICE LUNCH:** £8.50. **SET PRICE DINNER:** £10.95. Wheelchair access. **BEERS AVAILABLE:** Boddingtons, Wadworth, Old Speckled Hen, Flowers Original, Flowers IPA, Wethered, Brakspear, Murphy's, Newquay Steam Lager, Guinness, Heineken, Stella Artois. **NEAREST TUBE STATION:** Green Park. **MAP REF:1, B/1**

The Green Man

118

Putney Heath, SW15 **081-788 8096**

'The talk of the Green Man . . .'

In May 1798 , the Prime Minister, William Pitt, rather fell out with the MP for Southwark so they rode to Putney Heath and fought a duel. Each fired twice, missed and rode home again. It was the talk of the Green Man I can tell.

The Green Man was then a remote country inn on the edge of a notoriously dangerous bit of London. Putney had become a fashionable suburb, 'well inhabited by gentry' it was said at the time, but the Heath was not a place to walk at night. Highwaymen prospered, footpads abounded and rough justice was dispensed. Dick Turpin hid his guns in the Green Man and lived to rob another day but Jerry Abbershaw was hanged on a gibbet outside it.

The Victorians took to Putney which spread and prospered and respectable citizens enjoyed a walk to the Green Man. Algernon Charles Swinburne, living with his friend Theodore Watts-Dunton at The Pines, 11 Putney Hill, always called in for a drink on his way to the Rose and Crown in Wimbledon Village. It was a warren of private bars and snugs then but Swinburne would still know the pub today. It now has two bars, a public bar on the left, the saloon bar on the right, linked by the counter. They are light on summer days with large windows overlooking the heath and the garden, snug and cosy after dark.

Outside the old pub is flanked by two pretty courtyards with tables and benches and a big garden at the back has just been newly landscaped to its great advantage. It is a lovely place to eat and drink on a fine summer evening.

OPEN: Mon-Sun. **HOURS:** 11.00am-11.00pm (12.00-3.00pm and 7.00-10.30pm Sun). **CREDIT CARDS ACCEPTED:** None. **BAR FOOD AVAILABLE:** 12.00-2.30pm and 7.00-9.30pm. Beer garden seats 100. **BEERS AVAILABLE:** Young's Bitter, Young's Special, Young's Premium, London Lager, Castlemaine, Tennent's Extra, Red Stripe, Oatmeal Stout, Guinness. **NEAREST TUBE STATION:** Putney Bridge.

The Grenadier

119

18 Wilton Row, SW1 **071-235 3074**

'The ghost seems to be lying low'

A smart little pub, a Richard Burton and Elizabeth Taylor little pub, tucked away in a quiet Knightsbridge mews and keeping up its standards. 'It is house policy,' says the notice on the door, 'that customers should be suitably dressed . . .' 'Gentlemen, 'tis my desire that everyone should see the fire' begins a poem over the fireplace. Mine too.

The Duke of Wellington is the presiding spirit in the Grenadier. His officers used it as their mess, he is said to have played cards here himself, his mounting block is outside and his patrician features look scornfully down at you from the walls.

Did I mention it was small? There is a tiny bar and a little restaurant, candlelit at night, that seats twenty-one at the back but happily every summer customers can spill out onto the mews and there always seems to be room.

It is the most patriotic of pubs, red, white and blue outside, with a sentry box, pillarbox red, by the steps to the front door. The pewter bar counter has been scrubbed and polished daily since 1827 when the pub was built and military memorabilia has steadily accumulated. They used to send a chap from Wellington Barracks every week to groom the Guardsman's bearskin in the bar. It is made from the pelt of a female Canadian bear which, they say, like fingernails, goes on growing.

They are proud of their food at the Grenadier and of their beer and they are known for their Bloody Marys. These are made from a secret recipe passed from licensee to licensee and Peter Martin, who has run the pub for six years, sets up a special Bloody Mary bar every Sunday lunchtime. The record for a single session, he says, is 276.

OPEN: Mon-Sun. **HOURS:** 12.00-3.00pm and 5.00-11.00pm (12.00-3.00pm and 7.00-10.30pm Sun). **CLOSED:** Christmas Day, Boxing Day, New Year's Day. **CREDIT CARDS ACCEPTED:** Access, Visa, AmEx. **BAR AND RESTAURANT FOOD AVAILABLE:** 12.00-2.30pm and 6.00-10.00pm (7.00-10.00pm Sun). Wheelchair access. **BEERS AVAILABLE:** Courage Best, Courage Directors, John Smith's, Carlsberg, Foster's, Holsten, Guinness. **NEAREST TUBE STATION:** Hyde Park Corner. **MAP REF:** 2, F/4

The Greyhound 120

1 Kensington Square, W8 **071-937 7140**

'The billiard tables were blown to smithereens'

Thackeray lived opposite the Greyhound. He mentioned it in his novel *Henry Esmond*. His elegant regency house it still there with one of the early LCC brown plaques and the Greyhound is still there too. Or rather a Greyhound is – the Greyhound Thackeray knew was the Greyhound Mark I but this did not survive him long. In 1899 it was replaced by the Greyhound Mark II, much smarter.

This was a fine pub. The *Evening Standard* thought a lot of it, particularly admired its glass-fronted billiard room. It contained two full-size billiard tables and took up a lot of the bar. Most leading players had played there, Joe Davis often.

In 1975 we made it *Evening Standard* Pub of the year and in 1979 it blew up. There was a gas leak and the explosion it caused was quite spectacular in its way. It took the pub out as in a surgical strike. Happily it was at night, the landlord and his wife were on holiday and the relief managers weren't in either. The billiard tables were blown to smithereens though as, indeed, was the pub.

There was a neat gap in the row of offices and shops and houses for a short time, then they built the Greyhound Mark III. That is the one that is there now. It looks exactly the same from the outside but the pub itself...

Well, these things sometimes take time.

OPEN: Mon-Sun. **HOURS:** 11.00am-11.00pm (12.00-3.30pm and 7.00-10.30pm Sun). **CREDIT CARDS ACCEPTED:** Access, AmEx. **BAR FOOD AVAILABLE:** 12.00-3.00pm and 6.00-9.00pm. Wheelchair access (but not lavatory). Tables outside seat 12. **BEERS AVAILABLE:** Theakston Best, Theakston XB, Courage Best, Courage Directors, Foster's, Carlsberg, Holsten Export, Kronenbourg, Guinness. **NEAREST TUBE STATION:** High Street Kensington. **MAP REF:** 3, D/2

Grosvenor's 121

52 Cambridge Street, SW1 **071-834 5281**

'The name was the gift of the Hon. William Grosvenor'

It seems that these three men, well-connected, well-heeled and rather hard to please, decided they didn't like any London pubs. The solution was clear. They would open one they did like. So they did and this is it. Grosvenor's in Pimlico.

Until it got its new name and new identity Grosvenor's was an ordinary sort of pub called the Clarendon Arms, a town pub. Its new owners set about changing it to their idea of a country pub. They lowered the ceiling, shortened the bar counter, put in a second open fire, fitted olde beams and covered them in horse brasses, brought in dark oak tables, chairs and bar stools, hung up a hunting horn, a saddle, old prints and old copper pans and masked the windows so once inside you could not tell the time of day or season of the year. The final change was the new board outside. Grosvenor's, it said. The Country Pub in London.

The name was the gift of the Hon. William Grosvenor, one of the three founding fathers, recreations: shooting, fishing, golf. He approved of the food – simple country fare, you understand, asparagus, lobster, pheasant casserole, guinea fowl stew . . .

OPEN: Mon-Sun. **HOURS:** 12.00-11.00pm (12.00-3.00pm and 7.00-10.30pm Sun). **CREDIT CARDS ACCEPTED:** Visa, Mastercard, AmEx. **BAR FOOD AVAILABLE:** 12.00-3.00pm and 6.00-10.00pm (7.00-10.00pm Sun). **BEERS AVAILABLE:** Boddingtons, Flowers Original, Black Sheep Best, Black Sheep Special, Stella Artois, Heineken, Konig Pilsner, Guinness, Murphy's, Strongbow, Addlestones Cask Cider. **NEAREST TUBE STATION:** Pimlico.

The Ground Floor Bar

122

Portobello Road, W11 **071-243 8701**

'If anyone's rolling anything up or lining anything up out they go'

The Colville Arms the Pub Most Likely to Succeed. It was the one nearly opposite the Electric Cinema in the busiest bit of Portobello Road. It started rough and got rougher. Why did Inspector Knacker and his men look in so often? Could it be they had heard whispers of exotic substances? Perish the thought.

The Colville Arms closed down, changed hands, re-opened as the Colville, changed hands again, became the Colville Arms again. Then a whole new chapter . . . The first floor became the First Floor, a most respectable and respected restaurant, visited and approvingly reviewed by Fay Maschler no less. The ground floor struck out anew as the Ground Floor Bar, music from morning till night, jazz, blues, soul, rap, 'An evening bar,' says Marjorie Davis who runs it, 'a young bar, DJs Monday, Tuesday, Thursday, Friday and Saturday nights in here like nothing else, Saturday afternoons pretty crazy and pretty great, we've got a good reputation now, security walking up and down and I walk up and down, check the toilets and if anyone's rolling anything up or lining anything up out they go . . . We've never been raided since we took over,' says streetwise, plain-talking Ms Davis.

Then there's Pearlettes. Every Saturday morning Pearlettes, known as Lady P, arrives with the lunch she's been cooking, and such a lunch. Try her spare ribs says the barman, they're to die for says Ms Davis. The food's so good, says Lady P, it will take your mind off the music.

Noted for its parties. Very big at Carnival. That's what's become of the Colville Arms.

OPEN: Mon-Sun. **HOURS:** 11.00am-11.00pm Mon-Fri; 10.00am-11.00pm Sat; 7.00-10.30pm Sun. **CLOSED:** Christmas Day. **CREDIT CARDS ACCEPTED:** All major cards. **BAR FOOD AVAILABLE:** 12.00-4.00pm Sat. **SET PRICE LUNCH:** £5.00. Wheelchair access. Private room seats 40. **BEERS AVAILABLE:** Becks, Holsten, Stella Artois, Sol, Flowers IPA, Guinness. **NEAREST TUBE STATIONS:** Ladbroke Grove, Notting Hill Gate.

The Grove

123

39 Oldridge Road, SW12 **081-673 6531**

'Ambitious ceilings'

People have been known to go to the Grove to see the ceiling in the saloon bar. It is certainly wonderfully ornate. They went in for ambitious ceilings in the 1870s when the Grove was built.

This is a big, pleasant local on a quiet one-way street in Balham and nothing much has changed there in 100 years except perhaps the recent arrival of the fruit machine. It has a separate darts room, does good toasted sandwiches at lunchtime and has seats outside.

OPEN: Mon-Sun. **HOURS:** 11.00am-11.00pm (12.00-3.00pm and 7.00-10.30pm). **CLOSED:** Christmas Day. **CREDIT CARDS ACCEPTED:** None. **BAR FOOD AVAILABLE:** 11.30am-3.00pm. Wheelchair access. Tables outside seat 5. **BEERS AVAILABLE:** Young's, Castlemaine, Tennent's Extra, Guinness. **NEAREST TUBE STATIONS:** Clapham South.

The Guinea

124

30 Bruton Place, W1 **071-409 1728**

'Jack Nicklaus . . . Charlton Heston . . . King Hussein . . .'

This exclusive little pub tucked down a Mayfair mews is of astonishing antiquity. It goes back to 1423 when the infant King Henry VI had just had his first birthday and all round here was fields. The bar is small and dark and richly accoutred and gets packed at lunchtimes. Well the beer is Young's and the bar food is so good. Its steak, kidney and mushroom pie is the current national champion and even the sandwiches win national prizes.

It was not the sandwiches I think that brought Princess Margaret here or Richard Burton and Elizabeth Taylor or Frank Sinatra. They came for the restaurant, one of the classiest pub restaurants in town, known for its grills. Its steaks are aristos, certified as genuine Aberdeen Angus by the Aberdeen Angus Society, laid out raw for you to select and then grilled before your eyes. This is serious steak fancying. They do a two-course set lunch at the Guineas for £15.50 which includes a rump steak if you like. Stray to the à la carte side of the menu though and the price rises like a soufflé. It was ever thus.

Did I mention that Jack Nicklaus ate here? And Charlton Heston? And King Hussein? You meet a superior class of person eating steak in Mayfair mewses.

OPEN: Mon-Sat. **HOURS:** 11.00am-11.00pm. **CLOSED:** Bank holidays. **CREDIT CARDS ACCEPTED:** All major cards. **BAR FOOD AVAILABLE:** 11.30am-2.30pm and 6.30-10.30pm. **RESTAURANT FOOD AVAILABLE:** 12.30-2.30pm (Mon-Fri) and 6.30-11.00pm (Mon-Sat). **SET PRICE LUNCH:** £18.50. No smoking area. Wheelchair access (but not lavatory). Private room seats 30. **BEERS AVAILABLE:** Young's Ordinary, Young's Special, Oatmeal Stout, Beamish, London Lager, Tennent's Extra, Castlemaine. **NEAREST TUBE STATIONS:** Green Park, Bond Street. **MAP REF:** 1, C/2

Hamilton Hall 125

Liverpool Street Station, EC2 **071-247 3579**

'Unless you use Liverpool Street Station you may never have heard of it'

Which, do you suppose, is London's most successful pub? It is almost certainly Hamilton Hall. Unless you use Liverpool Street Station though you may never have heard of it.

Hamilton Hall was built in 1901 as the ballroom of the Great Eastern Hotel. Railway companies of the day were given to *folies de grandeur* but this surely beat everything. It put everyone's eye out. It was three storeys high inside and decorated with astonishing sumptuousness. The scheme derived, we are told, from an apartment in the Palais Soubise in Paris so it was plaster nudes, garlands and cornucopias, palatial mirrors, paintings, chandeliers.

Finding occasions grand enough for such a room must have been a problem for a railway hotel at the best of times and when war broke out in 1939 it was closed for the duration. It stayed closed until the recent renovation of Liverpool Street Station when J D Wetherspoon won the contract to take it over. The priceless fittings and decorations were found in a storeroom and two years ago Hamilton Hall reopened as London's newest pub. It astonished everyone all over again.

Wetherspoons had to make one major alteration. A pub needs kitchens, lavatories, space to store beer and staff rooms so a utilities block was built in the far corner of the ballroom, a handsome staircase leading to its flat roof. This became a mezzanine bar bigger than most pubs. It is now a no smoking area and does well but lean over the parapet and look down. Sometimes you can't see an inch of carpet, such is the crush.

If Hamilton Hall is a phenomenon so is Wetherspoons. In 15 years Tim Martin, the founder, has built up a chain of 87 pubs, with 100 in immediate prospect. These pubs have some things in common. No music. Big no smoking areas. Cut price beer. A 99p pint. Hamilton Hall has these too. It is a remarkable pub.

OPEN: Mon-Sun. **HOURS:** 11.00am-11.00pm (12.00-3.00pm and 7.00-10.30pm Sun). **CREDIT CARDS ACCEPTED:** Access, Visa, Delta, Switch. **BAR FOOD AVAILABLE:** 11.00am-10.00pm (12.00-3.00pm and 7.00-9.30pm Sun). **SET PRICE LUNCH AND DINNER:** £3.95. No smoking area. Wheelchair access (disabled lavatory). Tables outside seat 60. **BEERS AVAILABLE:** Theakston Best, Theakston XB, Younger Scotch Bitter, Courage Directors, Wadworth 6X, Becks, Foster's, McEwans. **NEAREST TUBE STATION:** Liverpool Street.

Hand and Shears 126

1 Middle Street, EC1 **071-600 0257**

'In the Middle Ages . . . it was absolutely buzzing'

How nice to see this seemly old pub enjoying the autumn of its days in its placid little backwater off Smithfield. John Betjeman, who lived along the way in Cloth Fair, used to pop in sometimes and overworked doctors and nurses from nearby Barts like it. There is no music or machines. It has kept its snug, the fire burns at the far end, the service is friendly, you can get doorstep sandwiches at the bar and a pubby lunch upstairs quite cheaply. It gets quite busy at lunchtime but a man may nod off there over his Director's bitter in the afternoon.

In the Middle Ages, though, it was absolutely buzzing. Cloth Fair was the centre of the tailoring trade and cloth merchants from all over Europe used to join the London drapers and country clothiers at the Hand and Shears. The Lord Mayor proclaimed Bartholomew Fair open from the inn doorway every year and the court of Pie Poudre (*Pieds Poudres*, dusty feet) met in the room above the bar to grant licences, redress grievances and pursue fraud. Life swirled round it. For the Hand and Shears those were the days.

OPEN: Mon-Fri. **HOURS:** 11.00am-11.00pm. **CLOSED:** Bank holidays. **CREDIT CARDS ACCEPTED:** All major cards except AmEx. **RESTAURANT FOOD AVAILABLE:** 12.00-3.00pm. Wheelchair access. Private room seats 36. **BEERS AVAILABLE:** Courage Best, Courage Directors, Theakston, Foster's, Kronenbourg, Holsten. **NEAREST TUBE STATION:** Barbican.

MAP REF: 6, B/2

The Hand in Hand 127

6 Crooked Billet, SW19 **081-946 5720**

'Four cottages run together'

A few doors along from the Crooked Billet, facing the same small green where customers from both pubs lounge on the grass on long summer evenings, is the Hand in Hand, the *Evening Standard*'s Pub of the Year in 1982. We said then that it was a lovely village pub. It still is.

What you see is four cottages run together with a pretty south-facing courtyard in front. There is a prize-winning riot of hanging baskets and window boxes, a horse chestnut gives shade to the tables, a vine crawls over one wall and a wooden porch leads into the pub.

You find yourself in a popular, busy inn, plainly decorated and simply furnished with carved wooden benches, simple stools and solid old tables. There's a smoke-free family room for children, games machines and darts and people are very keen on the home-made pasta, the pizzas and the burgers, but the Hand in Hand's great achievement is having kept the atmosphere of the simple beer house it was for 100 years before Young's took it over in 1974.

There have been changes but most are hard to spot. The general feeling is that this exceptionally nice cottagey pub is much as it always has been.

OPEN: Mon-Sun. **HOURS:** 11.00am-11.00pm (12.00-3.00pm and 7.00-10.30pm Sun). **CREDIT CARDS ACCEPTED:** Visa, Mastercard, Access. **BAR FOOD AVAILABLE:** 12.00-2.30pm and 7.00-10.00pm. No smoking area. Wheelchair access (but not lavatory). Beer garden seats 30. Private room seats 20. **BEERS AVAILABLE:** Young's IPA, Young's Special, Young's Winter Warmer, Red Stripe, Tennent's Extra, Castlemaine. **NEAREST TUBE STATION:** Wimbledon.

The Hare and Hounds

128

216 Upper Richmond Road West,
SW14 **081-876 4304**

'The finest pub in East Sheen'

The Hare and Hounds is a fine Georgian house of red brick on the Upper Richmond Road in East Sheen. My East Sheen correspondent says quite flatly that this is the finest pub in East Sheen and makes the following observation: 'Sadly the pub's faded, rather dingy charm has been swept away in a major renovation just completed. The pub is now lighter, sprucer, more comfortable, more intimate and consequently much busier.

'Fortunately some good bits remain, the old bar, the panelling, the huge garden with its vast lawn and, most important of all, the Hare and Hounds' most distinguished feature, the full-sized snooker table.'

OPEN: Mon-Sun. **HOURS:** 11.00am-11.00pm (12.00-3.00pm and 7.00-10.30pm Sun). **CREDIT CARDS ACCEPTED:** All major cards. **BAR FOOD AVAILABLE:** 11.00am-9.30pm. No smoking area. Wheelchair access. Beer garden seats 100. **BEERS AVAILABLE:** All Young's variants, Tennent's Extra, Castlemaine. **NEAREST BR STATION:** Mortlake.

The Henry Addington

129

20-28 Mackenzie Walk,
London E14 **071-512 9022**

'Bass spent £1 million on it'

Two contrasting new water-holes have been provided for the sometimes hard-pressed toilers on Canary Wharf. This is the light and airy one. For olde atmosphere see the Cat and Canary.

You reach it by going down the Docklands Light Railway escalator and taking the South Colonnade exit. 'It is like being on the deck of a luxury liner,' say the Henry Addington licensees Colin and Phyl Swallow in lyrical mood.

Bass spent £1 million on it. It seems a lot but, as it points out, it was aiming for environmental friendliness. This is daily reflected in the demeanour of journalists plotting and financiers computing. Its bar is 97-feet long and the extrovert landlord would like to add a yard or so and make it the longest in Europe.

The Swallows have been in the business for 30 years and pride themselves on their real ale weeks – some of the beers have a gravity that is downright alarming – and on an above-average wine list. The food includes justly-famed salt-beef sandwiches and Swallow's own pickled onions, a specialité of the maison.

Henry Addington, as of course you know, was Prime Minister from 1801 to 1804. In the course of time he became Viscount Sidmouth and gave the go-ahead for a wharf to be built on the Isle of Dogs to receive goodies from the Canary Isles. Hence Canary Wharf. Canning wrote of him 'Pitt is to Addington as London is to Paddington.' Conservatives could be unkind to each other even in those days.

OPEN: Mon-Sun. **HOURS:** 11.00am-11.00pm (12.00-3.00pm and 7.00-10.30pm Sun). **CREDIT CARDS ACCEPTED:** All major cards. **BAR FOOD AVAILABLE:** All day. **RESTAURANT FOOD AVAILABLE:** 12.00-3.00pm. Wheelchair access. Beer garden seats 40. Private area seats 50. **BEERS AVAILABLE:** Bass, London Pride, Stones, Speckled Hen Brew II, Exmoor Beast, Young's, Tennent's Extra and Pilsner, Grolsch, Carling Black Label. **NEAREST DOCKLANDS STATION:** Canary Wharf.

The Henry Holland

130

39 Duke Street, W1 **071-629 4426**

'This Henry Holland was quite a goer'

This pleasant old pub is sometimes taken for a mirage by persons shopping till they drop in Oxford Street. There it is down a side street with a good looking bar downstairs and a fine panelled dining room upstairs and a general air of having actually been built by the great 18th-century architect Henry Holland. Actually it was built, or anyway rebuilt, by Whitbreads in 1956. It was called the Red Lion before that.

This Henry Holland was quite a goer. He had his setbacks. His new Drury Lane Theatre incorporated all the latest safety devices but burned down all the same. By then though he had designed the first version of the Brighton Pavilion, quite a lot of Knightsbridge and, rather a stroke of luck, Southill Park in Beds for Mr Samuel Whitbread, the brewer. The present Samuel Whitbread, great-great-great-great-grandson of the founder, lives there still. Furthermore Henry Holland designed Brooks's, Mr Whitbread's club.

So now his name is on a Whitbread pub whether he built it or not. Quite right.

OPEN: Mon-Sun. **HOURS:** 11.00am-11.00pm (12.00-3.00pm Sun). **CLOSED:** Christmas Day, Boxing Day. **CREDIT CARDS ACCEPTED:** Mastercard, Visa. **BAR FOOD AVAILABLE:** 12.00-3.00pm. Wheelchair access (but not lavatory). Tables outside seat 30. Private room seats 50. **BEERS AVAILABLE:** Flowers Original, Wadworth, Marston's Pedigree, Brakspear, Boddingtons, Heineken, Stella Artois. **NEAREST TUBE STATIONS:** Marble Arch, Bond Street.

MAP REF: 1, B/3

Henry J Beans

131

195 King's Road, SW3 **071-352 9255**

'An American vision of a London pub'

In the swinging sixties this was the swinging Six Bells. It has certainly swung some since then.

Henry J Beans is an American vision of a London pub. About an acre of floor space. High pedestal tables with swivel-top stools. Wallfuls of enamelled ads. A vast paved garden with rows of picnic tables and benches. Jokey young barmen, their names pinned to their chests, wall-to-wall music, a high-speed kitchen producing Tex-Mex specials, burgers and French fries and the like, a bar that serves frozen daiquiris, Slow Comfortable Screws, Long Island Iced Tea. They charge £2.40 for a pint of Websters. Is this the most expensive pint in London? 'In ENGLAND,' says the young barman disarmingly.

The Kings Road brat pack loves it, doesn't drink bitter anyway and keeps the place buzzing. It may not sound like a pub but the hours at least are familiar: 11.45am-11pm.

Long Island Iced tea, by the way, is gin, rum, vodka, tequila, triple sec, lemon and Coca-Cola.

OPEN: 11.45am-11.00pm (12.00-3.00 and 7.00-10.30pm Sun). **CLOSED:** Christmas Day, Boxing Day. **CREDIT CARDS ACCEPTED:** All major cards except Diner's Club. **BAR FOOD AVAILABLE:** 11.45am-10.45pm (12.00-3.00pm and 7.00-10.15pm Sun). Beer garden seats 300. **BEERS AVAILABLE:** Large selection of bitters and lagers. **NEAREST TUBE STATIONS:** Sloane Square, South Kensington. **MAP REF:** 2, C/2

The Hercules Tavern

132

2 Kennington Road, SE1 **071-928 6816**

'As good as a Dublin pub now, says the manager'

On the wall of this much-improved Lambeth pub is a picture of two chaps of a certain age chatting. One is Frank Sinatra. The other is Paddy Maddigan.

Paddy Maddigan is a household name in Dublin. His family firm, Maddigan's, own some of the best-known pubs there. They have some pubs in London too and this is one of them.

In Dublin Maddigan pubs are mostly called Maddigan's, in London only sometimes. This is the Hercules Tavern. The one down the road is the Pineapple. The Pimlico one, on the other hand, is Maddigan's. You just don't know where you are.

Maddigan's started buying pubs in London in the 1980s when pubs were doing well and had fourteen when the recession started biting. Now they have only four left. They have certainly made a difference here though, reshaping the bar entirely, pushing the counter right back, recarpeting, recovering the banquettes, bringing an artist over from Ireland to paint Hercules murals.

It is as good as a Dublin pub now, says the manager.

OPEN: Mon-Sun. **HOURS:** 11.00am-11.00pm (12.00-3.00pm and 7.00-10.30pm Sun). **CREDIT CARDS ACCEPTED:** None. **BAR FOOD AVAILABLE:** 12.00-3.00pm. **SET PRICE LUNCH:** £2.65. Wheelchair access. Tables outside seat 36. **BEERS AVAILABLE:** Boddingtons, Flowers, Abbot Ale, John Smith's, Foster's, Carlsberg, Stella Artois. **NEAREST TUBE STATION:** Lambeth North. **MAP REF:** 7, B/2

The Hereford Arms
133

127 Gloucester Road, SW7 **071-370 4988**

'Miss Haversham comes to mind'

There have been any number of possible Jack the Rippers and one of them, the real one, used to drink in the Hereford Arms. I don't know how they know but this is what they say.

During the war the Hereford Arms was used by waves of American GIs who became devoted to it. The attractive garden of Hereford Square is just opposite and it was turned into a baseball diamond for them. The outstanding bill for broken windows has yet to be settled.

The Hereford Arms is extremely smart outside, a low William and Mary building painted black with gold lettering. Inside it is, well, dark. Dark panelled walls, dark beams, dark pillars and a low dark ceiling made lower and darker with sagging dark rope netting containing hops. Miss Haversham comes to mind.

I think I know why it is so dark. Not much light gets in, that may be it. There is a sweep of windows the full length of the bar but most of the small square panes are tinted yellow and putting the lights on doesn't seem to make much difference. The effect is deliberate and seems to work. This is a very popular upmarket pub.

OPEN: Mon-Sun. **HOURS:** 12.00-11.00pm (12.00-3.00pm and 7.00-11.00pm Sat; 12.00-3.00pm and 7.00-10.30pm Sun). **CLOSED:** Christmas Day. **CREDIT CARDS ACCEPTED:** AmEx, Mastercard, Visa. **BAR FOOD AVAILABLE:** 12.00-2.00pm and 5.00-9.00pm. Wheelchair access. Beer garden seats 30. **BEERS AVAILABLE:** Holsten Pils, Budweiser, Foster's, Newcastle Brown Ale, Molsen, Becks. **NEAREST TUBE STATION:** Gloucester Road.

Hillgate Arms
134

24 Hillgate Street, W8 **071-727 8543**

'A quiet backwater'

There are times in the summer when you can hardly see the pub for the flowers. They cascade from window boxes and hanging baskets, overflow tubs and urns. Shrubs, even small trees, flourish in the narrow strip between pub and pavement and, inside, certificates the Hillgate has won with this display cover a wall.

This is a very pleasant upmarket pub in a quiet backwater off Notting Hill Gate. There is just room for tables and small benches along one outside wall and there they are, basking in whatever sun is about, but I won't mention this. It is hard enough getting a seat there in summer as it is.

OPEN: Mon-Sun. **HOURS:** 11.00am-11.00pm (12.00-3.00pm and 7.00-10.30pm Sun). **CREDIT CARDS ACCEPTED:** All major cards. **BAR FOOD AVAILABLE:** 6.00-9.30pm. **RESTAURANT FOOD AVAILABLE:** 12.00-2.45pm. Wheelchair access (disabled lavatory). Beer garden seats 70. **BEERS AVAILABLE:** Ruddells County, London Pride, Webster's Yorkshire, Wadworth 6X, Carlsberg, Foster's, Holsten, Budweiser. **NEAREST TUBE STATION:** Notting Hill Gate. **MAP REF:** 3, B/2

The Hogshead in St James

135

11 Dering Street, W1 **071-629 0531**

'You could be in an 18th-century taproom'

You may remember this as a small Victorian pub called the Bunch of Grapes. 'Pretty wooden-fronted building,' reported a Nicholson guide. 'Olde worlde red and gold interior . . . A wine-drinker's pub.'

It's nothing like that now. Outside it has a smart glossy black and gold new frontage and inside it seems to have moved back 100 years. You could be in an 18th-century country taproom, plain and spare. Furthermore, it has a new name and a new role. It has become one of Whitbread's specialized real ale pubs, the Hogsheads. There are ten of them now, eight in London, and the idea is to go for real ale in a big way. This one, for instance manages to offer eight real ales, quite a trick with such small cellars. Three of them come direct from 10-gallon barrels in full view behind the bar. They sit there in a chilling unit, enjoying the limelight.

A little dining room upstairs sits twenty people and has busy lunchtimes. People take it for parties and meetings in the evening. There is no charge for this. You pay to get in on Saturday nights, though, if there's alternative comedy. While stand-up comics try to bring the house down a single slender iron pillar tries to keep it up.

OPEN: Mon-Sun. **HOURS:** 11.00am-11.00pm (12.00-3.00pm and 7.00-10.30pm Sun). **CLOSED:** Christmas Day. **CREDIT CARDS ACCEPTED:** None. **BAR AND RESTAURANT FOOD AVAILABLE:** 12.00-2.30pm. Wheelchair access (but not lavatory). Private room seats 20. **BEERS AVAILABLE:** Boddingtons, Flowers IPA, Old Speckled Hen, London Pride, Summer Lightning, Bombadier, Heineken, Stella Artois, Guinness, Scrumpy Jack. **NEAREST TUBE STATIONS:** Bond Street, Oxford Circus. **MAP REF:** 1, C/3

The Holly Bush

136

22 Holly Mount, NW3 **071-435 2892**

'Dr Johnson and Boswell must have caused a stir but nothing to the one caused by Romney'

A long flight of steps up the hill from Heath Street and you reach one of Hampstead's oldest and most picturesque pubs. When it was built in 1643 it stood high and proud on its hill with wonderful views. Now the houses and cottages of old Hampstead crowd round it.

Apart from that it has changed less that anyone could have expected. Well it had seven bars in Victorian times but they must have been exceptionally small. There are four now including one that used to be the landlord's living room and another that was part of the backyard and stables. But the general look of the place can't have been much different in the days they hung a green branch over the door to announce that the beer was ready.

Dr Johnson and Boswell both drank here they say. They must have caused a stir but nothing to the one made by Romney. In 1796 he gave up his grand house in Cavendish Square and bought a house behind the pub. He pulled down the stables, built a gallery for his pictures, enclosed half the garden for a riding house, got very miserable and went back to his wife in Kendal.

Peace returned to the Holly Bush.

OPEN: Mon-Sun. **HOURS:** 11.00am-3.00pm and 5.30-11.00pm (11.00am-4.00pm and 6.00-11.00pm Sat; 12.00-3.00pm and 7.00-10.30pm Sun). **BAR FOOD AVAILABLE:** All opening hours. Wheelchair access. Tables outside seat 20. Private room seats 30. **BEERS AVAILABLE:** Benskins, Tetley, Burton Ale, Lowenbrau, Castlemaine, Carlsberg. **NEAREST TUBE STATION:** Hampstead.

Hollywood Arms

137

Hollywood Road, SW10 **071-351 1031**

'Popular meeting place for young Chelsea'

There must have been times in the last hundred years when this high-Victorian local would have exchanged its neo-Gothic arched windows for a little more passing trade. Life is not always easy so far from the Fulham Road. Happily, good little restaurants have opened on every side and the Hollywood Arms has now become a most popular meeting place for young Chelsea.

The Hollywood Arms has a favourite historical figure, not one you may have come across. Jean-Pierre Blanchard is the one. He was a French balloonist and in 1784 he took off from the field where the pub now stands and became the first man to cross the English Channel by air. This is why he and his balloon appear on the pub sign.

The pub used to have day trips known as Hollywood Outings but they have not survived the years. Possibly the name led to disappointments. Spoof has not survived here either. It was once so popular that regulars founded an International Spoof Club. It is a good old pub game, spoof.

There's a nice beer garden at the back with wooden picnic tables, much enjoyed by families in the summer. Children are allowed, indeed encouraged, until 7pm.

OPEN: Mon-Sun. **HOURS:** 11.00am-11.00pm (12.00-3.00pm and 7.00-10.30pm Sun). **CREDIT CARDS ACCEPTED:** None. **BAR FOOD AVAILABLE:** 12.00-5.00pm Mon-Fri; 12.00-3.00pm Sat. Wheelchair access. Tables outside seat 100. Private room seats 80. **BEERS AVAILABLE:** Theakston, Courage Directors, John Smith's, Holsten, Kronenbourg. **NEAREST TUBE STATIONS:** Fulham Broadway, West Brompton. **MAP REF:** 2, A/3

The Hoop and Grapes

138

47 Aldgate High Street, EC3 **071-480 5739**

'It loooks very old. Well, it is old'

A remarkable thing happened to the Hoop and Grapes in 1666. It was NOT burned down in the Great Fire of London. It escaped by 50 yards and there it still is, the only surviving 17th-century timber-framed building in the City of London. Everyone used brick after the fire.

Until quite recently the Hoop and Grapes was as you might expect so old a pub to be. It leaned, it creaked, its floors sloped to the east. Everyone liked it but it was getting a bit alarming and in the early eighties Bass Charrington called in experts and spent £1.2 million on it.

They stripped the building back to its original softwood frame, replaced timbers when necessary and rebuilt it, keeping as closely as they could to the original design. The building is now totally underpinned, the old frame is supported by steel and the old building is good for another long run. The two courtyards of its coaching inn days are gone, I'm afraid. These are now part of the main bar which is huge, all exposed timbers and brick and changing levels. It looks very old. Well, it is old.

It is managed by Nevio Tedaldi who is Italian and has been in charge of London pubs for nineteen years now. He is hard to please. He looks round a huge lunchtime crowd packing his great bar and knits his brow. He'd hoped for more, he says.

Petticoat Lane is just across the road so the Hoop and Grapes opens on Sundays from 12 to 3pm. It closes, of course, on Saturdays.

OPEN: Sun-Fri. **HOURS:** 11.00am-10.00pm (11.00am-11.00pm Thur-Fri; 12.00-3.00pm Sun). **CLOSED:** Bank Holidays. **CREDIT CARDS ACCEPTED:** All major cards. **BAR FOOD AVAILABLE:** All opening hours. No smoking area. Wheelchair access. Tables outside seat 12. **BEERS AVAILABLE:** Bass, Carling Black Label, Budweiser, Becks. **NEAREST TUBE STATION:** Aldgate.

The Hop Poles

139

17 King Street, W6 **081-748 1411**

'It is huge. Those Victorians must have drunk a lot'

What impresses you most about this Victorian pub is its size. It is huge. There is one immense bar with 20 marble-topped tables lost in one corner, two more bars slightly smaller and a great big room upstairs. Those Victorians must have drunk a lot.

Way back in 1986 brewery, tenant and council all agreed that the best thing to do was pull it down and build a new town on the site. There would still be heaps of room for a brand new pub in the middle. Then they fell out over details and Scheme 2 went into action. They closed it for six months and spent £400,000 on putting the old building right. They saved all the listed bits – the elaborate front, the handsome ceilings, the etched mirrors – put a new roof on and made everything else safe. 'Anything that was falling down got put up again,' says Brendan Hipwell, the tenant. It was formally reopened by Mrs Holloway, a one time hop-picker, 96 and very chipper.

It is a long day at the Hop Picker. It opens at 6.30am for breakfasts – huge fry-ups, as much tea or coffee as you want and the morning papers, £3.50 – and stays open till 11pm.

There's another Hop Pole in Putney Bridge Road and a third in Pitfield Street, Islington. What is this? None of these places were involved with picking hops. However Brendan Hipwell picks hop poles every year. There are two of this year's over the bar with lots of hops and a good few black and white pictures of hop pickers at work, many of them on stilts. A lot of it is done by machines now. Will they open pubs when they are 96?

OPEN: Mon-Sun. **HOURS:** 6.30am-11.00pm (6.30am-3.00pm and 7.00-10.30pm Sun). **CREDIT CARDS ACCEPTED:** Barclaycard. **BAR FOOD AVAILABLE:** 6.30am-3.00pm. **SET PRICE LUNCH:** £2.75. No smoking area. Wheelchair access. Tables outside seat 40. Private room seats 90. **BEERS AVAILABLE:** Guinness, Foster's, Heineken, Carlsberg, Budweiser, Holsten Pils. **NEAREST TUBE STATION:** Hammersmith.

The Horn Tavern

140

29 Knightrider Street, EC4 **071-236 1013**

'Mr Pickwick, languishing in the Fleet Prison, sent to the Horn Tavern for two bottles of good wine'

The Horn Tavern is one of the great survivors. The Great Fire got everything but its cellars in 1666 but it was rebuilt and was still around almost 300 years later when bombs set fire to Ludgate Hill and historic old buildings blazed all round it.

It survived even greater dangers after the war when one rebuilding scheme after another seemed to involve knocking down the Horn Tavern. It is still there, just a step down Sermon Lane to St Paul's and in splendid form. New office buildings hem it in but they provide good customers so that's all right.

There is a reassuring saloon bar, all old panelling and blackened settles, and a corridor of drinking booths stretching almost the full length of little Knightrider Street and down some old stone stairs there is a very cosy bar and a smart little dining room for private parties.

Charles Dickens knew it well of course. In *The Pickwick Papers* Mr Pickwick, languishing in the Fleet Prison, sent to the Horn Tavern for two bottles of good wine and you can picture him in the old pub today, entertaining Mr Tupman, Mr Winkle and Mr Snodgrass.

Eldridge Pope, the Dorchester brewers and wine shippers, took over the Horn Tavern nine years ago and it seems in safe hands with them. It is their only London pub.

OPEN: Mon-Fri. **HOURS:** 11.00am-11.00pm. **CLOSED:** Bank holidays. **BAR FOOD AVAILABLE:** 12.00-3.00pm. **AVERAGE COST:** £7.00. Wheelchair access. Private room seats 30. **BEERS AVAILABLE:** Tetley, Burton, Budweiser, Carlsberg. **NEAREST TUBE STATION:** Mansion House. **MAP REF:6, B/1**

The Horniman at Hays

141

Hays Galleria, Tooley Street, SE1 **071-407 3611**

'The style beer drinkers prefer above all others'

Hay's Galleria with its soaring atrium, its shops and galleries and cafés is a great place for a pub. HMS *Belfast* lies romantically offshore, Tower Bridge with its extraordinary power to cheer you up is just down river and if you have been doing the riverbank walk you will be in need of a drink at just this point.

You will be pleased, then, to find Horniman's waiting, expansive, confident and glossy, the long polished mahogany counter with its choice of five well-kept ales, not to mention all the lagers, turning into a tea bar that also sells coffee and chilled milk. Then there's the big wide-open café, good fast food with children welcome, special portions, special prices. There is a carvery upstairs and a no smoking bit somewhere.

The Horniman in question was Mr F J Horniman, the Victorian tea importer, and this used to be the wharf where his tea was landed. He seems to have been a charismatic character, a great traveller and collector. You can see his collections at the Horniman Museum in Forest Hill where he lived and now there is this pub on his quay with lots of reminders of his life's work and the set of clocks from his office showing the time in foreign parts.

The pub is eight years old, the style Victorian. This is the style, we are told, that beer drinkers prefer above all others.

OPEN: Mon-Sun. **HOURS:** 10.00am-11.00pm (10.00am-4.00pm Sat; 10.00-3.00pm Sun). **CLOSED:** Christmas Day, Boxing Day, New Year's Day. **CREDIT CARDS ACCEPTED:** Visa, Mastercard, AmEx. **BAR FOOD AVAILABLE:** 11.00am-9.00pm. **SET PRICE LUNCH:** £4.95. **RESTAURANT FOOD AVAILABLE:** 12.00-3.00pm and 6.00-10.00pm. No smoking area. Private room seats 60. **BEERS AVAILABLE:** Real ales. **NEAREST TUBE STATION:** London Bridge.

The Horse and Groom

142

68 Heath Street, NW3 **071-435 3140**

'The height of late Victorian taste'

The original Horse and Groom was an 18th-century tavern, all beams and low ceilings, just the kind of old inn we most admire today but it seemed very lumpish to the newly fashionable Hampstead. So in 1899 Young's replaced it with something bang up to date.

This was it, an imposing five-storey public house with a modish striped brick and stone façade and a high decorated gable, the height of late Victorian taste. It was then the tallest building in Heath Street. It still is.

The rich Victorian interior has been largely dismantled over the years though bits of it remain. Today there is one long open room. The front half is where the counter is, the back half where most of the tables are.

It is a friendly local with an industrious landlord and pleasant girls who bring your lunch to your table and chat to regulars spending happy, ruminative afternoons on their bar stools. It remains a genuinely Victorian pub.

Convincing replicas of Charles I's death warrant and the Act of Union, 1707, take in the trusting and the pure in heart.

OPEN: Mon-Sun. **HOURS:** 11.00am-11.00pm (12.00-3.00pm and 7.00-10.30pm Sun). **CLOSED:** Christmas Day. **CREDIT CARDS ACCEPTED:** None. **BAR FOOD AVAILABLE:** 12.00-3.00pm. Wheelchair access (but not lavatory). Private room seats 70. **BEERS AVAILABLE:** Young's Bitter, Young's Special, Young's Oatmeal Stout, Young's Premium Lager, Young's London Lager, Tennents Extra, Red Stripe, Castlemaine. **NEAREST TUBE STATION:** Hampstead.

The House They Left Behind 143

27 Ropemaker's Fields, E14 **071-538 5102**

'It has a new name, one that perfectly describes its curious situation'

Looking at Limehouse now it is hard to imagine it as it used to be, the busy boatyards, the boisterous docks, the maze of tenements . . . One day in 1871 Alexander II, Tsar of Russia, visited a ropeworks here. Could this have been in Ropemaker's Fields where, at No. 27, the Black Horse stood?

The Black Horse was a small, busy inner-city pub built in 1856, part of a terrace in the heart of this teeming bit of the East End. Today it is

still there but not much else is. There is nothing else left of Ropemaker's Fields, not a single house, just this solitary, lonely pub. It has been given a new name, one that perfectly describes its curious situation. It is now called the House They Left Behind.

I called it lonely but that's not quite right. It does not mind standing there on its own. What it does mind is the non-stop public works that have been going on around it for the last five years. As soon as one project is finished another starts. You are advised not to breathe the words Dockland Development anywhere near Mick and Frances Naughton, who have the pub now. It has been a nightmare, they say. It has lost them goodness knows how many customers.

But the crystal starts to clear. The empty space at their front door, once known as the other side of the street, is looking a bit more like the piazza it is meant to be. There are benches, young trees, a large sculpture of a seagull standing on a coil of real rope. People play boules there all summer.

And the pub itself, known to its regulars simply as the House, is getting old customers back and winning new ones. It is an excellent place for lunch and for supper as expats on Canary Dock are discovering with relief. And now the dust has started to settle they can beam across at the tall terrace houses of Narrow Street where David Owen is famously in residence.

OPEN: Mon-Sun. **HOURS:** 11.00am-11.00pm (12.00-3.00pm and 7.00-10.30pm Sun). **CREDIT CARDS ACCEPTED:** AmEx, Visa. **BAR AND RESTAURANT FOOD AVAILABLE:** 11.00am-9.45pm. Wheelchair access (but not lavatory). Tables outside seat 25. **BEERS AVAILABLE:** Bass, Webster's, Courage Directors, Carlsberg, Castlemaine, Tennent's, Stella Artois, Guinness. **NEAREST TUBE STATION:** Mile End.

The Imperial

144

5 Leicester Street, WC2 **071-437 6573**

'An oasis on a fine day'

Leicester Street takes you from the hoopla of Leicester Square to the Chinese restaurants of Lisle Street and halfway up you find this old-fashioned West End local. The street is pedestrianized now like the square itself and the cluster of small tables outside is an oasis on a fine day. Queen Victoria, at her most grandmotherly, gazes down.

OPEN: Mon-Sun. **HOURS:** 12.00-11.00pm (12.00-3.00pm and 7.00-10.30pm Sun). **CLOSED:** Christmas Day, Boxing Day. **CREDIT CARDS ACCEPTED:** All major cards. **BAR FOOD AVAILABLE:** 12.00-11.00pm. Wheelchair access (but not lavatory). Tables outside seat 30. **BEERS AVAILABLE:** Theakston, John Smith's, Courage Best, Courage Directors, Kronenbourg, Holsten, Foster's, Budweiser. **NEAREST TUBE STATION:** Leicester Square. **MAP REF:** 1, E/1

The Intrepid Fox

145

99 Wardour Street W1 **071-287 8359**

'Rock, punk, neo-technic and trash'

The front window of the Intrepid Fox dares you to go in. It reads: 'Is this the definition of you? (in'trepid.) adj: 1. audacious, bold, courageous, daring, fearless, game, heroic, nerveless, plucky, resolute, stout-hearted, undaunted . . . Then this is Your Place.'

Someone has removed the b from bold and the f from fearless.

Undaunted and earless, then, enter. If the music is your music you will want to stay.

Like Soho itself, the Intrepid Fox is old and battered and has seen a thing or two. In its young days its passion was politics, the Whig leader Charles James Fox its hero. It even changed its name for him. It is he who is the Intrepid Fox, he the stout party in the beaver hat on the pub sign. In the 1784 election the pub served free beer to anyone who would vote for him and the management put a relief on the side wall showed Fox waving a banner saying 'Champion of the People'. It (or a copy) is there to this day.

The old pub has hit some rough patches along the way since then but it has a new role, a new passion, a roster of new heroes today. It is now a leading rock, punk, neo-technic and trash pub. At weekends there are queues outside. On any day of the week it is black leather jackets, pony tails and half-shaved heads in the big downstairs bar and the walls are covered with icons of the pub's new heroes, Jimi Hendrix, the Rolling Stones, the Who, David Bowie, Freddie Mercury, the Stranglers. The music of their successors is the current passion in the Intrepid Fox. It plays all day.

OPEN: Mon-Sun. **HOURS:** 12.00-11.00pm (7.00-10.30pm Sun). **CLOSED:** Christmas Day. **CREDIT CARDS ACCEPTED:** None. **BAR FOOD AVAILABLE:** 12.00-11.00pm (7.00-10.30pm Sun). **AVERAGE COST:** £3.25. Wheelchair access. Private room seats 80. **BEERS AVAILABLE:** Castlemaine, Lowenbrau, Carlsberg, Tetley, Burtons, Guinness. **NEAREST TUBE STATION:** Piccadilly Circus. **MAP REF:** 1, D/2

The Island Queen

146

87 Noel Road, N1 **071-359 4037**

'Agreeably eccentric'

Eight-foot wooden puppets, once in Victorian underwear but now gaily painted, hang from the ceiling over the horseshoe bar in this agreeably eccentric Islington local. There's a big wire mesh dragon too. Bare floorboards, ceiling-high Victorian mirrors, a small pool room at the back – people who drink there wouldn't change a thing.

One of the original jukeboxes is generously stocked with music of the Sixties thus assuring a clientele of discrimination and allure. There is a good restaurant upstairs.

OPEN: Mon-Sun. **HOURS:** 12.00-3.00pm and 5.30-11.00pm Mon-Fri; 12.00-11.00pm Sat; 12.00-3.00pm and 7.00-10.30pm Sun. **CLOSED:** Christmas Day. **CREDIT CARDS ACCEPTED:** None. **BAR FOOD AVAILABLE:** 12.00-2.30pm. **RESTAURANT FOOD AVAILABLE:** 6.00-9.00pm Fri-Sat, 12.00-3.00pm Sun. **SET PRICE LUNCH AND DINNER:** £14.95. **BEERS AVAILABLE:** London Pride, Bass, Grolsch, Tennent's Extra, Carling Black Label. **NEAREST TUBE STATION:** Angel.

J J Moon's

147

Terminal Four, Heathrow Airport **081-759 0355**

'In the no-man's land past passport control'

J D Wetherspoon has two pubs in Terminal Four, Wetherspoons and J J Moon's. Wetherspoons is on what they call the landside which means we can all go in. J J Moon's is in the no-man's land past passport control. This is your last chance to get a pint of real beer, possibly for days. They call this airside.

Comfortable, quiet, a no-smoking bit and, for a Wetherspoons, quite small.

OPEN: Mon-Sun. **HOURS:** 11.00am-11.00pm (12.00-3.00om and 7.00-10.30pm Sun). **CREDIT CARDS ACCEPTED:** Access, Visa, Delta, Switch. **BAR FOOD AVAILABLE:** 11.00am-11.00pm (12.00-3.00pm and 7.00-10.30pm Sun). **SET PRICE LUNCH AND DINNER:** £3.95. No smoking area. Wheelchair access. **BEERS AVAILABLE:** Theakston Best, Theakston XB, Younger Scotch Bitter, Courage Directors, Wadworth 6X, Becks, Foster's, McEwans. **NEAREST TUBE STATION:** Heathrow Terminal 4.

Jack Straw's Castle

148

North End Way, NW3 **071-435 8885**

'Georgian Gothic said the architect. Grounded Mississippi river boat said the Evening Standard'

This famous old coaching inn has a swashbuckling past and quite a showy present. Its past first though . . .

Jack Straw was Wat Tyler's right-hand man, a fiery leader of the Peasant's Revolt. He burned down the priory in Clerkenwell, addressed the assembled peasants from a hay waggon on Hampstead Heath and took refuge in the inn. He was caught there and executed outside the front door.

The old inn was known as Jack Straw's Castle after that and kept the name when it was replaced by a coaching inn in 1721 after which it was all coaches arriving and coaches leaving and horses to water and travellers to feed and bustle and drama and ruffians lying in wait. Meanwhile Hampstead grew and got fashionable and Jack Straw's Castle was discovered by literary London. Wilkie Collins started riding over and Thackeray and Dickens (of course) after which nothing much happened until World War Two when it was banged about by a landmine.

It was rebuilt in the early 1960s. A leading architect, Raymond C Erith, was engaged and London got a spectacular new pub. Georgian-Gothic said Mr Erith. Grounded Mississippi Showboat said the *Evening Standard*. It was three storeys high with a long weatherboard frontage, a parade of bay windows, arched Gothic windows from end to end and battlements on top.

It got another major going-over in 1993. Just painting the weatherboarding cream and white took three men six weeks but it is looking very spruce now as do the refurbished bars, function rooms and à la carte restaurant.

There's lots going on. The big L-shaped bar on the ground floor is a home-from-home for Hampstead's rugby, cricket and football clubs, there's a barbecue most summer evenings in the big courtyard at the back, a pleasant place with brick paving and cobbles, a tree with a tree seat and lots of wooden tables and benches. The first floor is receptions and private parties and the top floor is the restaurant.

Jack Straw's Castle occupies one of the highest points in London and the restaurant has panoramic views over the heath. If he had got a good table Jack Straw would have seen them coming.

OPEN: Mon-Sun. **HOURS:** 11.00am-11.00pm (12.00-3.00pm and 7.00-10.30pm Sun) **CREDIT CARDS ACCEPTED:** All major cards. **BAR FOOD AVAILABLE:** 12.00-3.00pm and 6.00-9.00pm. **RESTAURANT FOOD AVAILABLE:** 12.00-3.00pm and 6.00-10.00pm. **SET PRICE LUNCH:** £11.95. Wheelchair access (lift to restaurant). Beer garden seats 70. Private room seats 50. **BEER AVAILABLE:** London Pride, Bass, Hancock's, Carling Black Label, Tennent's, Grolsch, Guinness, Caffreys. **NEAREST TUBE STATION:** Hampstead.

The King of Bohemia

149

10 Hampstead High Street, NW3 **071-435 6513**

'Just the thing for a neo king'

The young Elector Palatine should have left well alone but no, he would become King of Bohemia. You could see what was going to happen, he lost both Bohemia and his Palatinate and Europe got the Thirty Years' War.

What Hampstead got was this pub on the High Street. Not this one exactly you understand but one on the same site, built in 1613, the year the would-be King of Bohemia married James I's daughter. This is more or less the one that replaced it in 1935, bow-fronted, neo-Georgian, just the thing for a neo king.

It got a thorough going-over six years ago. It is now very smart and glossy with shiny black paintwork and glass doors that open the whole frontage to the street in fine weather. New parquet flooring links a series of bars to the distant back wall. It has a games corner, lots of bric-a-brac, a most efficient food operation and no original features. The music really gets going in the evening.

The attractive old brewery next door is now a chic office block.

OPEN: Mon-Sun. **HOURS:** 11.00am-11.00pm (12.00-3.00pm and 7.00-10.30pm Sun). **CLOSED:** Christmas Day. **CREDIT CARDS ACCEPTED:** None. **BAR FOOD AVAILABLE:** 12.00-2.30pm. Wheelchair access (but not lavatory). Tables outside seat 12. **BEERS AVAILABLE:** Boddingtons, Pedigree, Becks, Budweiser, Stella Artois, Grolsch, Tooheys. **NEAREST TUBE STATION:** Hampstead.

The King's Head

150

115 Upper Street, N1 **071-226 1916**

'Brilliant casts and national reviews'

There are now at least a dozen theatre pubs in London. This was the first – the first, that is, since Shakespeare's day or so says Dan Crawford, the licensee. It was Crawford who, to general amazement, turned the big room behind his bar into a theatre in 1970. In spite of regular crises it has been a huge success. Its productions get brilliant casts and national reviews. Many have transferred to the West End; one transferred to Broadway and won four Tony awards.

The pub itself is a substantial Victorian pile with a busy and in some ways eccentric life of its own. When the nation went decimal in 1971 Dan Crawford was reluctant to replace his noble Victorian till so he didn't. The Kings Head, he decreed, would continue with the old currency and it still does. A pint of Benskins, Burtons or Adnams costs £1 16s. A baked potato costs £1 10s, a cup of coffee 12s. Good Lord! A cup of coffee used to cost 6d.

The theatre is at the back. It has seats from the Scala Theatre, Marylebone, velvet curtains from the Theatre Royal, Haymarket and ancient lanterns from the Lyric, Shaftsbury Avenue. There is a fair-sized apron stage and a decent view from just about anywhere.

Supper is served at tables in the theatre before the performance – you don't have to eat there but most people do and there is something very companionable about it. A three-course meal costs £8.50 and you stay on at your table to watch the play. Tickets for this cost £9 during the week and £10 on a Saturday. The capacity is 125 with 80 able to eat.

Meanwhile the pub will have been filling up and, the play over, departing theatregoers have to squeeze through a crowded bar to reach the street. Some stay on for the Adnams and the music which follows the show every night – there is folk, rock or jazz until midnight.

Some good bands have played here, Dire Straits among them, but that is the King's Head. Both halves of it are alive with energy and talent.

OPEN: Mon-Sun. **HOURS:** 11.00-12.00am (12.00-3.00 and 7.00-10.30pm Sun). **CLOSED:** Christmas Day. **CREDIT CARDS ACCEPTED:** None. **BAR FOOD AVAILABLE:** 12.00-3.30pm. Wheelchair access. Private room seats 125. **BEERS AVAILABLE:** Benskins, Adnams, Burton Ale, Castlemaine, Lowenbrau, Guinness. **NEAREST TUBE STATIONS:** Highbury and Islington, Angel.

MAP REF: 5, C/2

The King's Head 151

4 Fulham High Street, SW6 **071-736 1413**

'On a platform in the distance . . . London's most deafening groups perform'

Drive the full length of the New King's Road in a car without brakes without turning right or left and this is what you would eventually hit. It is an enormous five-storey Edwardian pub with a fairytale tower in the middle and, over the imposing main entrance, the words 'London's Premier Live Music Venue'. On Wednesdays and Saturdays you pay £3, get a biro cross on your wrist and are let loose into the semi-darkness of a Gothic ghoularama with flickering lights, massive black fireplace, portcullis, designer cobwebs and ultra violet doing weird things to shirts and teeth. Good lord, it's an Addams family At Home.

On a platform in the distance, surrounded by mega speakers, London's most deafening groups perform. The audience watches in silence then shouts a bit. This is punk and skinhead territory but they are tolerant of strangers wearing the wrong clothes and if this is not your scene you can go through the unlabelled connecting door past the ladies and into the comparatively bright lights of the public bar, also huge.

It has its own clientele, drinking at the massive U-shaped bar, playing pool, keeping an eye on the television screen and actually talking to each other.

OPEN: Mon-Sun. **HOURS:** 11.00am-12.00am (11.00am-11.00pm Mon-Tue; 12.00-3.00pm and 7.00-10.30pm Sun). **CREDIT CARDS ACCEPTED:** None. **BAR FOOD AVAILABLE:** 12.00-3.00pm Mon-Fri. Wheelchair access. Beer garden seats 100. Private room seats 150. **BEERS AVAILABLE:** Budweiser, Sol, Rolling Rock, Molsten, Holsten Pils. **NEAREST TUBE STATION:** Putney Bridge.

The King's Head and Eight Bells 152

50 Cheyne Walk, SW3 **071-352 1820**

'A wealth of modern period features'

For years this much-loved pub was the heart of bohemian Chelsea. Generations of painters, craftsmen and writers drank there, Whistler, Turner, Walter Greaves, Augustus John . . . It is still a pleasant, good-looking pub though successive modern improvements, fruit machines and background music among them, have lessened its old romantic appeal. No doubt they have increased its turnover.

The King's Head and Eight Bells had modest beginnings, starting life as two small 15th-century seamen's pubs side by side on the riverbank. The King's Head was for officers, the Eight Bells for the crews. Eight bells summoned the men back to their ships.

The two pubs merged in 1580 and it became the local river

boatmen's pub, then the artists made it their own and by the 1960s the old stucco building, much changed, had become a tourist attraction. Yet more changes lay ahead.

The tourists still come. What they see may not be the pub that Whistler knew, but it is comfortable and goodness knows it is well-appointed with its big bar at the front and busy dining room at the back, both with a wealth of modern period features.

It is sad but no one's fault that it is no longer on the riverbank. The original riverside Cheyne Walk still passes the door but Chelsea Embankment long since came between river and pub. The Embankment gardens have also intervened. Today customers of the Kings Head and Eight Bells must be content with a glimpse of distant ships and pleasureboats as they slide by above the river wall at high tide while the traffic of modern London thunders past between.

OPEN: Mon-Sun. **HOURS:** 11.00am-11.00pm (12.00-3.00pm and 7.00-10.30pm Sun). **CREDIT CARDS ACCEPTED:** Visa, Mastercard. **BAR FOOD AVAILABLE:** 11.00am-2.30pm and 7.00-10.00pm. Wheelchair access (but not lavatory). **BEERS AVAILABLE:** Boddingtons, Brakspear, Flowers IPA. **NEAREST TUBE STATION:** Sloane Square. **MAP REF:** 2, C/2

The Ladbroke Arms

153

54 Ladbroke Road, W11 **071-727 6648**

'How many pubs have a house dressing?'

Egon Ronay's inspector inspected this pub and wrote thus: 'On the corner of Ladbroke Road and the charming Willby Mews, the Ladbroke Arms is a shining light, hopefully leading other pubs where many fear to tread.'

Mr Ronay's inspector is right in every particular. The Ladbroke Arms is indeed a shining light which will surprise those who remember it as it used to be.

It was a pedestrian sort of pub, noticeably unshining, until Ian MacKenzie took it over. He had already shown what he could do. He had been part of the team that had launched Slug and Lettuces on an alarmed world in the early Eighties. When there were nine of them MacKenzie and his partners sold them and went their several ways.

MacKenzie started his new venture with the Ladbroke Arms. It was built in 1843 and had always been a nice-looking pub. The original mahogany fittings just needed a good polish and the rest of it some papering and carpeting. What needed changing most was the character of the place.

The key to its renaissance has been the bright, friendly new staff and the change in the food. This was dramatic. The Ladbroke Arms, bastion of traditional pub grub, now has an adventurous menu that changes daily. The house dressing is basil and honey. How many pubs have a house dressing?

As for the beer, well, see below and the wine list isn't bad either, classical music or light jazz plays quietly and the raised terrace outside is famously crowded all summer.

OPEN: Mon-Sun. **HOURS:** 11.00am-3.00pm and 5.30-11.00pm (12.00-3.00pm and 7.00-10.30pm Sun). **CREDIT CARDS ACCEPTED:** All major cards. **BAR FOOD AVAILABLE:** 12.00-2.30pm and 7.00-9.30pm. Wheelchair access. **BEERS AVAILABLE:** Webster's Yorkshire, Courage Directors, Eldridge Pope Royal Oak. **NEAREST TUBE STATION:** Holland Park. **MAP REF:** 3, B/1

The Lamb

154

94 Lamb's Conduit Street, WC1 **071-405 0713**

'Brilliant-cut hinged snob screens, the very latest thing in 1894'

The Lamb has long been one of the most admired pubs in London. People like it because, they say, it has not been spoiled which is true. It has been altered quite bit all the same.

It was built in the 1720s, twice improved almost beyond recognition by the Victorians who thought the 18th-century beyond the pale and extensively restored in our own time. Well, 1959. That's it, surely. Who would change anything in this much-loved pub now?

The Lamb is mostly and genuinely Victorian now with its handsome façade, its etched windows, its leather sofas and all that hand-carved mahogany. There are Spy cartoons and an array of Victorian musical comedy stars on the walls and a splendid U-shaped bar counter completely ringed by brilliant-cut hinged snob screens, the very latest thing in 1894. Open them and you are face to face with the barman. Good heavens! Close them and your drink will slide towards you under the screens, despatched by an unseen hand.

What used to be a backyard is now a little patio but whenever they can regulars at the Lamb like to drink outside in Lamb's Conduit Street where, in 1577, a conduit was laid to bring water to the houses there. It was designed and paid for as an act of charity by William Lamb, an Elizabethan engineer with a good heart who also provided 120 pails for poor women to carry the water in. The name of the pub and the name of the street ensure that this good deed is still remembered 400 years later.

OPEN: Mon-Sun. **HOURS:** 11.00am-11.00pm (12,00-3.00pm and 7.00-10.30pm Sun). **CREDIT CARDS ACCEPTED:** Visa, Mastercard, Diner's Club, Access. **BAR FOOD AVAILABLE:** 12.00-2.30pm. **SET PRICE LUNCH:** £3.95. **SET PRICE DINNER:** £4.95. No smoking area. Wheelchair access (but not lavatory). Beer garden seats 30. Private room seats 40. **BEERS AVAILABLE:** Young's IPA Bitter, Special, Porter, Winter Warmer, London Lager, Premium, Castlemaine, Tennent's Extra. **NEAREST TUBE STATIONS:** Russell Square, Holborn.

The Lamb and Flag

155

33 Rose Street, WC2 **071-497 9504**

'Easily the oldest pub in Covent Garden'

This small, charming, much-loved pub is tucked away up an alley between Garrick Street and Floral Street. Half Covent Garden seems to go there for a drink after work. If they can't get in they drink on the pavement. In the summer when everyone drinks outside you can hardly see the pub for people.

It is easily the oldest pub in Covent Garden and it is proud of its hairy youth. The back room was called the Bucket of Blood after the bare-knuckle fights they held there and John Dryden was badly beaten up in the alley in 1679.

They call the upstairs room the Dryden room now. You can get a good straightforward lunch there.

OPEN: Mon-Sun. 11.00am-11.00pm (11.00am-10.45pm Fri-Sat; 12.00-3.00pm and 7.00-10.30pm Sun). **CLOSED:** Christmas Day, Boxing Day. **CREDIT CARDS ACCEPTED:** None. **BAR FOOD AVAILABLE:** 12.00-5.00pm Mon-Sat. **BEERS AVAILABLE:** Courage Best, Courage Directors, John Smith's, Wadworth 6X, Foster's, Kronenbourg, Miller, Carlsberg, Guinness, Beamish. **NEAREST TUBE STATION:** Covent Garden.

The Lamb Tavern 156

Leadenhall Market, EC3 **071-626 2454**

'One of London's truly stately pubs'

Sir Horace Jones, the Victorian architect, gave London three magnificent markets, Smithfield, Billingsgate and Leadenhall. The grandest of these was Leadenhall, the game, fish and poultry market in the heart of the City. It is still a fine sight with its great stone arches, lofty arcades and stunning cast ironwork and it includes one of London's stateliest pubs, the Lamb Tavern.

Every weekday the Lamb fills up with youngish men in suits, energetic, talkative, sometimes exultant, at other times downcast. Many work at Lloyds, taking every opportunity to exchange their spectacular new building for the pubs and wine bars of Sir Horace's market.

I can tell you something about those who pick the Lamb Tavern. In good times and in bad they are great drinkers of draught bitter. This understandable enthusiasm has meant that the recession was not felt at all at the Lamb. Indeed in recent years the pub, always thought rather on the large side with its three floors, all high ceilings and high principles, began to seem a little cramped and Young's slotted in a new mezzanine floor and spiral staircase into the once soaring saloon bar. This reduced its nobility but increased its capacity.

So there are now four floors for the new breed of market trader to populate. It cheerfully does so, arriving around lunchtime. The Lamb is then busy until about nine in the evening when the last City gent makes for home and a dried-up dinner in the oven.

Now that the marble pillars disappear into a ceiling of modest height the main bar is nowhere near as impressive as it was but the cavernous smoking room and wine bar in the basement keeps its old style and so does the top floor with its tall windows and fine view of the market. This is a no smoking bar. It was the City's first and has proved very popular. Each level of the Lamb serves food but this high, elegant room is the place to eat.

At weekends the highly photogenic market closes and quite often film crews move in. John Wayne spent days at the Lamb when scenes for Brannigan were being shot there. Robert Mitchum was there for *The Winds of War* and Tom Selleck for *Magnum*. The BBC shot some of *Bleak House* in the Lamb and the landlord's children both got parts.

OPEN: Mon-Fri. **HOURS:** 11.00am-9.00pm. **CLOSED:** Bank Holidays. **CREDIT CARDS ACCEPTED:** All major cards. **BAR FOOD AVAILABLE:** 11.00am-2.30pm. **SET PRICE LUNCH:** £4. No smoking area. Wheelchair access. Private room seats 50. **BEERS AVAILABLE:** All Young's variants. **NEAREST TUBE STATION:** Bank.

The Leinster Arms

157

17 Leinster Terrace, W2 **071-723 5757**

'The Grand Master Cellarman of the Year'

The Leinster Arms is the home of the Burton Ale Grand Master Cellarman of the Year, a notable personage so watch it that's all. Her name is Olive McCarthy and she is the first woman Grand Master Cellarman ever.

Mrs McCarthy, a disconcertingly youthful-looking mother of two sons both at college, has run the Leinster Arms herself since the departure of her husband four years ago. She took over from him as manager and she has been a conspicuous success. The pub has blossomed and she has been heaped with prizes. Every year it seems there is a new trophy for being puller of the perfect pint and this year she was not only the Grand Master Cellarman of the year, she was Trade Personality of the Year as well.

This has always been an attractive pub. It is an old coaching house in Bayswater with a big, cheerful, comfortable bar, good plain food served all day, Olive herself behind the bar and, you will not be surprised to hear, cask ales that rise from an immaculate cellar in perfect condition.

OPEN: Mon-Sun. **HOURS:** 11.00am-11.00pm (12.00-3.00 and 7.00-10.30pm Sun). **CREDIT CARDS ACCEPTED:** All major cards. **BAR FOOD AVAILABLE:** 11.00am-8.30pm. Wheelchair access. Tables outside seat 30. **BEERS AVAILABLE:** Lowenbrau, Castlemaine, Carlsberg, Tetley, Nicholson's, Burton Ale. **NEAREST TUBE STATIONS:** Queensway, Lancaster Gate.

MAP REF: 4, D/1

The Lyceum Tavern

158

354 Strand, WC2 **071-836 7155**

'Like old times'

In the days when Henry Irving's great Lyceum Theatre was alive and well the little Lyceum Tavern which backed onto it was part of theatrical London.

Alas, the theatre with its great portico in Wellington Street has been empty and abandoned for years, getting more derelict as you looked, and the pub has had to make another life for itself which indeed it has.

Samuel Smith got it with five others when it bought Hennekeys in 1980 and has done it over very nicely with cosy drinking booths in the main bar and a pleasant panelled bar overlooking the Strand upstairs where very reasonable meals are served at lunchtime and in the evening.

Then the summer of 1994 brought news that will surely mean a whole new chapter for the Lyceum Tavern. The ordeal of the old theatre next door is almost over. New owners are spending £15 million on a total restoration and if all goes well it should be open again quite soon. Indeed the idea is that the Royal Opera will come here when the Covent Garden Opera House closes for its major refit.

So the immediate future seems clear: months of builders in the bars and then actors, singers, musicians, theatregoers and opera buffs coming and going. It will be like old times.

OPEN: Mon-Sun. **HOURS:** 11.00am-11.00pm (12.00-3.00pm and 7.00-10.30pm Sun). **CLOSED:** Christmas Day, Boxing Day. **CREDIT CARDS ACCEPTED:** Visa, Mastercard, Eurocard. **BAR FOOD AVAILABLE:** 12.00-2.30pm. **SET PRICE LUNCH:** £3.95. **RESTAURANT FOOD AVAILABLE:** 5.00-9.00pm. Wheelchair access (but not lavatory). **BEERS AVAILABLE:** Samuel Smith variants. **NEAREST TUBE STATION:** Covent Garden. **MAP REF:** 1, F/1

The Magdela Tavern

159

2a South Hill Park, NW3 **071-435 2503**

'Three bullet holes in the cream tile frontage . . .'

There are three bullet holes in the cream tile frontage of the Magdela Tavern in South Hill Park and a notice explaining how they come to be there. It was here, it says, that Ruth Ellis shot and killed her lover David Blakeley on 10 April 1955. This she did, standing over him and putting three more bullets into his body as he lay on the pavement, then quietly waiting for the police to come. She was the last woman to be hanged and she gave this otherwise unmemorable local a sort of macabre glamour that lingers even now.

The pub has a public bar and a saloon bar, each with its own entrance. It was from the saloon bar that David Blakeley emerged that night to find the woman he had fatally offended waiting.

There is a theatrical gloss to it now with photographs of Alan Bates, Richard Attenborough, John Gielgud, Ellen Terry and others and a painting of Oscar Wilde.The star, quite rightly, is Ruth Ellis. She stares bleakly from the frame, blonde, ashen, heavily made-up in an open-neck shirt blouse with a silk scarf and a broad belt tightly fastened. Grouped with the photograph is a letter she wrote from Holloway.

It starts 'Dear Frank' , sends thanks for lovely flowers, is sorry to hear of some accident he had had but she gets to herself in the end. 'No doubt you have heard I do not want to live,' she writes. 'You may find this very hard to believe but that is what I want. I am quite well and happy under the circumstances, I am very well looked after, I have plenty to amuse me. Well Frank this must be all for now. Thanks once again. Yours Ruth Ellis.'

Beneath it are two miniature certificates, one the official declaration that the judgement of death had been executed, the other the death certificate, signed by the prison surgeon on 13 July 1955.

Magdela was the Ethiopian hill fortress taken and destroyed by Sir Robert Napier in 1868. He became Lord Napier of Magdela. There is a painting of the battle on the side of the building.

OPEN: Mon-Sun. **HOURS:** 11.00am-11.00pm (12.00-3.00pm and 7.00-10.30pm Sun). **CREDIT CARDS ACCEPTED:** None. **BAR FOOD AVAILABLE:** 12.30-2.30pm. Tables outside seat 30. **BEERS AVAILABLE:** Young's Special, Bass, Worthington, London Pride, Adnams, Toby, ESB, Carlsberg, Tennent's Extra, Tennent's Pilsner. **NEAREST BR STATION:** Hampstead Heath.

The Magpie and Stump

160

442 King's Road, SW10 **071-352 2543**

'Jukebox rules'

A boisterous, youthful pub where the jukebox rules, gaming machines are rarely still and satelite TV seems always on. Downstairs there's a games room with pool tables and a mini arcade and customers in the main bar get a laugh with the jokily named Canvey Island Iced Tea. This is two pints of any beer or lager for £3.95, consumed from a yard glass.

The Magpie was a good omen in the Middle Ages. Nowadays it is a bad omen if you see only one but all right if you see two. Having seen this one cautious persons may note that there is another Magpie and Stump opposite the Old Bailey.

OPEN: Mon-Sun. **HOURS:** 12.00-11.00pm (12.00-3.00pm and 7.00-10.30pm Sun). **CREDIT CARDS ACCEPTED:** None. **BAR FOOD AVAILABLE:** 12.00-10.00pm. Tables outside seat 25. **BEERS AVAILABLE:** Tetley, Pedigree, Lowenbrau, Castlemaine, Carlsberg. **NEAREST TUBE STATION:** Sloane Square.

The Magpie and Stump

161

18 Old Bailey, EC4 **071-248 5085**

'Nothing, not even the inn sign, was saved from the historic old tavern'

Few London pubs had a more macabre past than this one. It stood facing the gallows of Newgate Jail and would rent out its upper floors for all-night parties before an execution. Vast crowds whooped it up below while the nobs drank, played cards and at dawn watched wretched prisoners slowly strangling on the gibbet while relations hung on their legs to hasten their end. The sight gave them a good appetite for the Magpie and Stump's large execution breakfast.

In time the old pub had a pretty swift coup de grace itself. After being remodelled in 1931 it settled down to a respectable old age as a tourist attraction and all was well until 1988 when it was sold to a developer and demolished. The deal was that a new Magpie and Stump should be part of the new building. This is it.

It would be easy to miss it. The Magpie and Stump keeps its old address but the only hint that there might be a pub in Old Bailey is an inn sign oddly attached to what looks like an office wall. The new pub's fascia and entrance is hidden away round the corner in an alley called Bishop's Court.

The Magpie and Stump is now a large modern pub on three levels, the main bar on what estate agents call the raised ground floor, a wine bar under that, a restaurant under that. Under that are two more floors of kitchens and cellars.

The new pub is spacious, fully air-conditioned and handsomely equipped. There's a lift if you can't manage all the stairs. But nothing, not even the inn sign, was saved from the historic old tavern. Only the name survives.

OPEN: Mon-Fri. **HOURS:** 11.00am-11.00pm. **CLOSED:** Bank holidays. **CREDIT CARDS ACCEPTED:** All major cards except Switch. **BAR FOOD AVAILABLE:** 11.00am-11.00pm. **RESTAURANT FOOD AVAILABLE:** 12.00-3.00pm. Wheelchair access. Private room seats 120. **BEERS AVAILABLE:** Bass, Hancock's Best, Worthington Best, London Pride. **NEAREST TUBE STATION:** St Paul's. **MAP REF:** 6, B/2

The Man in the Moon 162

392 King's Road, SW3 **071-352 5075**

'Fred, a regular for 54 years, is the test'

This big old Georgian pub in the far reaches of the King's Road got a new manager this year. Oisin Rogers moved lock, stock and bar staff from the Magpie and Stump fully 30 yards away. He even brought some of his customers with him.

It is a sociable pub with a massive old oak counter, solid tables and chairs on a plain wooden floor, satellite television, a tireless jukebox the latest in pinball and gambling machines and an unflagging crowd of under-thirties. It gets packed on Friday and Saturday evenings and there's a big demand for fish and chips at £3.15 a time at lunchtime.

The afternoons are more peaceful. This is the time to admire the cornice of beautiful hand-painted tiles by William de Morgan and the huge decorated and devilled mirrors covering the walls. They have been there for 200 years. Spot the one that was installed upside down.

At the back is the Man in the Moon Theatre, a lively part of the London fringe, 60 seats and professional productions throughout the year, mostly new plays from the avant garde. Tickets from the bar.

So how will the new manager do? For Oisin, pronounced Oshin, an extrovert Dublin academic turned publican, the omens seem good. Fred, a regular for 54 years, is the test. He continues to sit in the same position at the bar every day consuming his daily 10 pints of bitter.

OPEN: Mon-Sun. **HOURS:** 11.00am-11.00pm (12.00-3.00pm and 7.00-10.30pm Sun). **CLOSED:** All bank holidays. **CREDIT CARDS ACCEPTED:** None. **BAR FOOD AVAILABLE:** 12.00-2.30pm. **SET PRICE LUNCH:** £4.95. No smoking area. Wheelchair access. **BEERS AVAILABLE:** Moonshine, John Smith's, Theakston, Courage Directors, Wadworth, Carlsberg, Kronenberg, Foster's, Holsten Pils, Guinness. **NEAREST TUBE STATION:** Sloane Square. **MAP REF:** 2, B/2

The Marquess of Granby

163

51-2 Chandos Place, WC2 **071-836 7657**

'The thin end of the wedge'

The Marquess of Granby at the back of the Coliseum has a long imposing frontage that makes you expect a large imposing pub but it is a sliver of a pub really, a wedge, all length and no width. Still, nothing wrong with wedges. At the thin end of the wedge is a very small snug. At the thick end of the wedge is a rather larger bar parlour. The main bar, getting gradually wider, is in between and the whole thing has just been elaborately refitted. Back bar, bar counter, furniture, everything was replaced. It has been carefully done with a Gothic screen rescued from a demolished church put to good use.

The pub's rush hour is the Coliseum interval when opera-goers, cast and orchestra will suddenly erupt in the bar for a very quick one indeed. This is the answer given if anyone asks why there is no music. The orchestra, explains the landlord, won't have it.

There was a pub on this site in Charles II's day, the Hole in the Wall. Was it this shape? It was where Claude Duval the highwayman was caught sleeping it off. After his execution he was buried in St Paul's Church under a stone that reads: 'Here lies Duval, Reader, if male thou art Look to thy purse; if female to thy heart.'

OPEN: Mon-Sun. **HOURS:** 11.00am-11.00pm (12.00-3.00pm and 7.00-10.30pm Sun). **CREDIT CARDS ACCEPTED:** All major cards. **BAR FOOD AVAILABLE:** 11.00am-9.00pm. Private room seats 50. **BEERS AVAILABLE:** Marquess Bitter, Tetley, Burton Ale, Castlemaine, Lowenbrau, Carlsberg. **NEAREST TUBE STATION:** Charing Cross.

The Marquess Tavern

164

32 Canonbury Street, N1 **071-354 2975**

'Restored to its former glory'

See this high-Victorian pub standing proudly by the New River Walk, Corinthian pillars reaching from first floor to balustraded roof, every inch a listed building and a credit to the Marquesses of Northampton whose pub it used to be.

The present Marquess has hung onto a lot of Canonbury, his substantial birthright, but for some reason his father sold the Marquess which must have hurt its feelings. Young's has it now. It bought it in 1979 and, as it says, restored it to its former glory.

It is truly a fine pub and well placed. The New River, originally designed to bring drinking water to the 17th-century City of London, now brings ducks and river walkers to its door. Picnic tables await them. Inside is a big, high-ceilinged saloon bar and the adjoining room is impressive too, a bar-cum-dining room with a high arched ceiling, eating and drinking booths and big mirrors. It was a pool room in its misspent youth.

The Marquess rightly prides itself on its beer and serves hearty traditional food. In keeping with the times it provides unhearty food as well. There's a very good salad bar.

OPEN: Mon-Sun. **HOURS:** 11.00am-11.00pm (12.00-3.00pm and 7.00-10.30pm Sun). **CREDIT CARDS ACCEPTED:** None. **BAR FOOD AVAILABLE:** 11.00am-9.30pm. Wheelchair access. Tables outside seat 50. Private room seats 80. **BEERS AVAILABLE:** Young's, Tennent's Extra, Castlemaine. **NEAREST TUBE STATION:** Highbury and Islington. **MAP REF:** 5, D/1

The Mayflower

165

117 Rotherhithe Street, SE16 — **071-237 4088**

'The little dark bar casts a powerful spell'

In the spring of 1620 the *Mayflower* up-anchored at Rotherhithe and sailed down the Thames on the first lap of her historic journey to the New World. She had been moored next to a riversde tavern called the Shippe. Surely its customers cheered and waved as she started her great adventure.

The *Mayflower* was back at Rotherhithe eight months later, anchoring near the Shippe again. Surely the crew bowled into the bar that night but her glory days were over. Within a year her captain was dead. They buried him in the graveyard of St Mary's Church, hard by the Shippe, and the Mayflower lay rotting at her moorings. The Shippe stood another 100 years or so and was then rebuilt. They called the new pub the Spread Eagle and Crown, a serviceable enough name but the Shippe had been better and its new name is better still. It changed to the Mayflower in the 1960s when, all patched up after the war, it set its cap at American visitors who were understandably thrilled to find it still tucked away by the church among the wharfs and warehouses.

I must say the dark little bar with its old black settles and tables casts a powerful spell. You can buy British and American stamps there under a curious longstanding licensing arrangement and you get a good view of the river from the restaurant upstairs, newly refurbished after a change of owner.

The best view is from the deck at the back of the old pub. It juts out over the river and just over there, where the old Thames barges wallow, is more or less where the Mayflower was anchored. This is the place to drink to a gallant ship, a great voyage and the captain in the graveyard behind you.

OPEN: Mon-Sun. **HOURS:** 11.00am-11.00pm (12.00-3.00pm and 7.00-10.30pm Sun). **CREDIT CARDS ACCEPTED:** Visa, AmEx. **RESTAURANT FOOD AVAILABLE:** 12.00-2.30pm and 6.00-9.30pm. Wheelchair access. Tables outside seat 30. Private room seats 35. **BEERS AVAILABLE:** Greene King, Bass, Stella Artois, Kronenbourg, Carling Black Label, Guinness. **NEAREST TUBE STATION:** Rotherhithe.

The Melton Mowbray

166

18 Holborn, EC1 **071-405 7077**

'Pies rotate behind glass doors and cook in 2 minutes 45 seconds'

For the third of its new Ale and Pie houses Fuller's took over a big sports shop and, after the twelve-week refit costing £170,000, Holborn found it had got itself a spanking new pub.

Its success took everyone aback. It went from nothing to highest trader in the company on Day 1. Middle management from every office in sight converged on it each lunchtime, a highly desirable clientele, good-mannered, good-humoured, free-spending and, as a rule, quick-eating. They all have desks to get back to.

Melton Mowbray's instant popularity has some drawbacks. It can seat 80 people at lunchtime but many more come. 'This is a big problem for us,' says Jimmy Weir, the manager.

There is quite a lot of space even so, well used with different floor and ceiling levels and a gallery at the far end and many a pub would envy the size of the cellars. It is all state of the art down there, with electronic hoists for the beer and amazing computerized ovens in the kitchens. The pies rotate behind glass doors and cook in 2 minutes 45 seconds. It is an arresting piece of kitchen theatre entitled *The Rising and Browning of the Puff Pastry Lid*. They should sell tickets.

OPEN: Mon-Fri. **HOURS:** 11.00am-11.00pm. **CLOSED:** Bank holidays. **CREDIT CARDS ACCEPTED:** All major cards. **BAR FOOD AVAILABLE:** 11.00am-10.30pm. No smoking area. Wheelchair access. Tables outside seat 20. **BEERS AVAILABLE:** Fuller's Ales, ESB, London Pride, Chiswick Bitter, Hock, Mr Harry, Summer Only, Golden Pride. **NEAREST TUBE STATION:** Chancery Lane. **MAP REF:** 6, A/2

The Mitre

167

24 Craven Terrace, W2 **071-262 5240**

'A perfect example of this popular modern pub style'

Whitbreads are great refurbishers of pubs. Each Whitbread pub gets a turn every five years and if it waits long enough it may get a REAL going-over. The Mitre, a much admired pub in Bayswater, a Grade II listed building, has just emerged from one such. It took eleven weeks. It always was Victorian and it is sort of Victorian still, brand new, pastiche Victorian, a perfect example of this popular modern pub style.

There are five bars now, the main saloon bar and four smaller ones, all beautifully decorated and handsomely furnished in the Victorian manner, hung with portraits and pretty clocks. Two have marble fireplaces, one has a stag's head, one a charming skylight formerly boarded up. The smallest at the back has a portrait of Disraeli, the coming man they say, and one is a no smoking bar with its own entrance to the hall and so to the street.

Down worn stone stairs, an original feature, is the Twelve Bar, a jazz bar in the cellar. It is a maze of little drinking areas tucked under low ceilings and arches with flagged floors, big barrels, an old kitchen range and its own entrance to the little cobbled mews at the side. It is full of atmosphere and is thought to have a friendly ghost. There is live jazz down there every night.

OPEN: Mon-Sun. **HOURS:** 11.00am-11.00pm (12.00-3.00pm and 7.00-10.30pm Sun). **CREDIT CARDS ACCEPTED:** All major cards. **BAR FOOD AVAILABLE:** 12.00-9.00pm. No smoking area. Wheelchair access (but not lavatory). Tables outside seat 50. Private room seats 60. **BEERS AVAILABLE:** Boddingtons, Pedigree, Flowers, Brakspear, Abbot Ale, Old Speckled Hen, Heineken, Stella Artois. **NEAREST TUBE STATION:** Lancaster Gate.

MAP REF: 4, D/1

The Monarch

168

49 Chalk Farm Road, NW1 **071-916 1049**

'You just may catch the new Rolling Stones here between 8.30 and 11pm'

This small, intimate and unobtrusive music pub opposite the Roundhouse gets a clued-in crowd which is onto the up-and-coming bands which are the speciality of the maison.

A psychedelic optimist writes: 'Strange objects suspended from the

low-timbered ceiling glow in the half light. One corner is devoted to a psychedelic chill-out zone for those who want to chat until well-known indie-rock acts such as Shed 7, Echobelly and SMASH as well as exciting new pretenders take the small stage.

'You just may catch the new Rolling Stones here between 8.30 and 11pm. A DJ plays from 11pm to 2am on Fridays and Saturdays.

'Recommended.'

OPEN: Mon-Sun. **HOURS:** 8.00pm-12.00am (8.00pm-2.00am Sat-Sun). **CLOSED:** Christmas Day, Boxing Day. **CREDIT CARDS ACCEPTED:** None. **BAR FOOD AVAILABLE:** All opening hours. Tables outside seat 12. **BEERS AVAILABLE:** Lowenbrau, Kronenbourg, Chimay. **NEAREST TUBE STATIONS:** Chalk Farm, Camden Town.

The Monkey Puzzle

169

30 Southwick Street, W2 **071-723 0143**

'A young monkey puzzle tree . . . with its fingers crossed'

A very annoying thing happened to the Monkey Puzzle on the night of 16 October 1987. The great gale blew its monkey puzzle tree down. It was a large, handsome and impossible-to-climb monkey puzzle tree, pride of the garden and the pub had been named after it. Now look.

Well, life in the Monkey Puzzle goes on. It is a modern pub built into the ground floor of an apartment block and lots of cheery red signs guide you in saying 'Welcome' in a dozen different languages.

The Monkey Puzzle gives you a choice of five ales including a house special called Monkey Puzzle bitter. There is bar billiards and satellite TV for all your sporting needs and the garden has picnic tables, strings of coloured lights and regular barbecues in the summer. There is also a young monkey puzzle tree in a sheltered corner with its fingers crossed.

OPEN: Mon-Sun. **HOURS:** 11.00am-11.00pm (12.00-3.00 and 7.00-10.30 Sun). **CLOSED:** Christmas Day. **CREDIT CARDS ACCEPTED:** All major cards. **BAR FOOD AVAILABLE:** 12.00-2.30pm. **RESTAURANT FOOD AVAILABLE:** 12.00-2.30pm and 6.00-9.30pm. Wheelchair access. Beer garden seats 60. **BEERS AVAILABLE:** Monkey Puzzle, Gale HSB, Theakston, Wadworth, Old Speckled Hen, Tennent's Extra, Foster's, Kronenbourg, Stoughton Press. **NEAREST TUBE STATIONS:** Edgware Road, Paddington.

The Moon and Sixpence

170

185 Wardour Street, W1 **071-734 0037**

'Tony Hancock in a ferned grot'

J D Wetherspoon has turned a cinema into a pub in Brent, a Woolworth's into a pub at Ruislip Manor, a post office into a pub in Southend. In Wardour Street it has done the business with a Barclays bank.

This Barclays had beautiful tall arched windows. They are still there but nothing else of the bank remains. Even the massive safe in the vaults has gone though it was a titanic struggle. You don't mention vaults in the Moon and Sixpence. They are cellars now.

It is a roomy pub with busy lunchtimes, three kinds of hologram on the walls and a realistic portrait bust of Tony Hancock in a ferned grot. The manager is called Tadgh, pronounced Tie, Irish for Tim.

OPEN: Mon-Sun. **HOURS:** 11.00am-11.00pm (12.00-3.00pm and 7.00-10.30pm Sun). **CREDIT CARDS ACCEPTED:** Access, Visa, Delta, Switch. **BAR FOOD AVAILABLE:** 11.00am-11.00pm (12.00-3.00pm and 7.00-9.30pm Sun). **SET PRICE LUNCH AND DINNER:** £3.95. No smoking area. Wheelchair access. **BEERS AVAILABLE:** Theakston Best, Theakston XB, Younger Scotch Bitter, Courage Directors, Wadworth 6X, Becks, Foster's, McEwans. **NEAREST TUBE STATIONS:** Tottenham Court Road, Leicester Square.

The Moon under the Water 171

28 Leicester Square, WC2 **071-839 2837**

'It costs £6,000 a week just to open the doors in the morning'

There's only one pub now in Leicester Square. This one. It used to be an Angus Steak House until 1992 when Wetherspoons took it over and from being a long thin restaurant with steaks it became a long thin pub with food all day. It specializes in good cask ales, cheaper than most, but Wetherspoons famous cut-price pint of Youngers Scotch bitter is not quite so cheap here. This being Leicester Square it is £1.30 a pint. 'This is still the cheapest pint in the West End,' says David Shannon, the young manager, 'but it costs £6,000 a week just to open the doors in the morning here.'

Well, when the doors open at 11am there are always people waiting. The Moon under the Water has a lot of friends. It has a strong character, won't have music, has a big no-smoking bit and is full every night, packed at weekends. According to a Capital Radio poll it is the most popular pub in London.

OPEN: Mon-Sun. **HOURS:** 11.00am-11.00pm (12.00-3.00 and 7.00-10.30pm Sun). **CREDIT CARDS ACCEPTED:** Access, Visa, Delta, Switch. **BAR FOOD AVAILABLE:** 11.00am-11.00pm (12.00-3.00pm and 7.00-10.30pm Sun). **SET PRICE LUNCH AND DINNER:** £3.95. No smoking area. Wheelchair access. Tables outside seat 20. **BEERS AVAILABLE:** Theakston Best, Theakston XB, Younger Scotch Bitter, Courage Directors, Wadworth 6X, Becks, Foster's, McEwans. **NEAREST TUBE STATION:** Leicester Square.

The Morpeth Arms 172

58 Millbank, SW1 **071-834 6442**

'Don't venture into the cellars'

The Tate Gallery delights some, sends others reeling down Millbank. They should reel to the right. In minutes they will find comfort and reassurance in this trusty and dependable Victorian pub.

All is traditional and familiar in the Morpeth Arms and will stay so.

It is a listed building now, admired and popular. The summer is particularly busy with stout tables and wooden benches right across the front and down the side. These are regularly filled, particularly at lunchtime. The traffic roars by and you can hardly hear yourself speak, but they do a decent lunch at the Morpeth Arms and it's a Young's pub so the beer is good too.

Don't venture into the cellars though. They say that soon after the pub was built in 1845 a convict on the run hid in the labyrinth of vaults beneath the pub, lost himself and was never seen again. Visitors to the vaults have felt a hand on their shoulder and have been chilled by an unseen presence dripping water. It has sent them dashing back to the Tate.

Stand with your back to the pub and look across the river. The extraordinary building facing you is the new headquarters of MI5.

OPEN: Mon-Sun. **HOURS:** 11.00am-11.00pm (12.00-3.00pm and 7.00-10.30pm Sun). **CREDIT CARDS ACCEPTED:** All major cards. **BAR FOOD AVAILABLE:** 11.00am-9.00pm. **RESTAURANT FOOD AVAILABLE:** 11.00am-8.00pm. **SET PRICE LUNCH AND DINNER:** £3.95. Wheelchair access. Tables outside seat 72. Private room seats 50. **BEERS AVAILABLE:** Young's, Tennent's Extra, Castlemaine. **NEAREST TUBE STATION:** Pimlico.

The Mucky Duck

173

108 Fetter Lane, EC4 **071-242 9518**

'Fat ladies in stripes . . .'

Scene: Two ladies chatting outside a factory bearing the sign 'Sid Brown's Tool Works'. One is saying to the other, 'You're a very lucky woman Mrs Brown.'

Partners Gareth Stones, host, and Tony Crowe, who runs the office, are proud of their display of framed seaside postcards at the Mucky Duck dating back, as the postmarks show, to the 1900s. The characters populating the saloon bar walls, the bathing belles, the landladies, the red-nosed drunks, the vicars and fat ladies in stripes with all their doubles entendres are worth the detour from Holborn or Fleet Street.

Like the Tate Gallery, the Mucky Duck has more in store than on show and Tony Crowe, prowling junk shops in London and Brighton, keeps adding to the collection. As well as the postcards, Donald McGills included, there are 262 pictures on the walls and up the staircase. They come within an inch of looking like a pub decorator's job lot, but have all been picked up by collector Crowe.

The Mucky Duck has been so named only since July 1993 before which it was the Swan, a Fleet Street haunt with a strong presence from the neighbouring and now deserted Daily Mirror building. Gone are the hacks, and also the stuffed swan that used to look down on the assembly at the bar.

Upstairs is Annie's Bar, retaining its name from a previous incumbent, a bright room with banquettes and tables, pink curtains at its several windows, and a busy lunch crowd. Parties are held here. The speciality upstairs as well as down is the Mucky Duck Doorstep, a sandwich measuring two inches thick.

Stones and Crowe have recently set up as The Mucky Pub Co. and are looking for more premises, where the saucy postcard theme will be continued. Punters wandering in to some other pub and spying a hospital scene in which the doctor is crying 'No, no nurse, I said remove his spectacles' can reasonably conclude they're succeeding.

OPEN: Mon-Fri. **HOURS:** 11.00am-11.00pm. **CLOSED:** Bank Holidays. **CREDIT CARDS ACCEPTED:** None. **BAR FOOD AVAILABLE:** All opening hours. **SET PRICE LUNCH:** £3.50. Private room seats 35. **BEERS AVAILABLE:** Bass, Worthington, London Pride, Adnams, Carling Black Label, Tennent's, Beamish, Caffreys. **NEAREST TUBE STATION:** Chancery Lane.

MAP REF: 6, A/2

The Museum Tavern

174

49 Great Russell Street, WC1 **071-242 8987**

'Karl Marx is still suspected by the pub of having broken one of the mirrors . . .'

The pub that first occupied this commanding corner in Bloomsbury was called the Dog and Duck. Well, that wouldn't do once the British Museum opened on the other side of the road and in 1761 it chose a daring new name. It became the British Museum Tavern.

It seems to have been a homely place. You could take your own pork or lamb and have it cooked for a penny. Clearly something grander was required and it was rebuilt in 1798 and again, grander yet and grander, in 1855.

This time William Finch Hill, the theatre architect, was the designer. His building, renamed the Museum Tavern, had four entrances to five bars, with pool and billiards and rooms for lodgers upstairs. He suspended huge globes from ornate iron fittings above the main doors and gas lamps burned in every window. It is this building, the outside hardly changed, that you see today.

Generations of scholars have crossed the road from the British Museum to drink here. Among them was the museum's most famous student Karl Marx who is still suspected by the pub of having broken one of the mirrors in the bar's magnificent back fitting. Marx would presumably have approved of what has happened since, all divisions between public bar, private bar, jug bar and bar parlour abolished.

No jukeboxes or taped music lurks to alarm shy denizens of the British Museum who still come in. It remains a gentlemanly, scholarly pub surrounded by academic bookshops and in nearby Coptic Street is what some people, ie me, consider the best pizza house in London.

OPEN: Mon-Sun. **HOURS:** 11.00am-11.00pm (12.00-3.00pm and 7.00-10.30pm Sun). **CREDIT CARDS ACCEPTED:** All major cards except Diner's Club. **BAR FOOD AVAILABLE:** 11.00am-10.00pm. **SET PRICE LUNCH AND DINNER:** £4.95. Wheelchair access (but not lavatory). **BEERS AVAILABLE:** Real ales, John Smith's, Courage Best, Directors, Brakspear, Greene King, Theakston. **NEAREST TUBE STATIONS:** Tottenham Court Road, Russell Square. **MAP REF:** 1, F/2

The Nag's Head

175

53 Kinnerton Street, SW1 **071-235 1135**

'Full of chat and interest'

The Nag's Head, tucked away in this little mews in the most expensive part of town, is, par excellence, a talking pub.

It is a lot to do with size. It is very small. It also has to do with the height of the bar counter. This is agreeably domestic, as high as your average kitchen table, and the stools around it are the height of ordinary chairs. But above all it has to do with the landlord, Kevin Moran, and his son Peter.

Kevin was a successful stunt man before he hurt his back and Peter describes himself as a jobbing actor though he is mostly at the Nag's Head. Still, he says, a pub is acting and this is an extrovert and entertaining place. Conversation is general, with much laughter, and newcomers are soon part of it.

Kinnerton Street is smart now but it had humble enough beginnings. It started life in the 1820s as a service road for the grand houses in Wilton Place. It was mostly stables and the Nag's Head was the ostlers' pub. It was tiny, a single bar not much bigger than a horse's stall, and this is how it stayed well into the 1960s.

Len Cole, the formidable landlord at that time, would say that the Nag's Head was the smallest pub in London and that was how he liked it. When he left us his successors saw no point in unused space and the place grew. It was not successful with Cole gone though and by the time the Morans arrived in 1979 it had been closed for six months.

It did not take them long to get it on its feet again. Pictures and photographs and mementoes of times past now cover the panelled walls, fires are lit in winter and in the summer people take their drinks into the mews. The front bar is for drinking and, of course, talking, and the back bar is the eating bar with food from noon to 10pm.

It is open every day of the year except Christmas Day and is full of chat and interest.

OPEN: Mon-Sun. **HOURS:** 11.00am-11.00pm (12.00-3.00pm and 7.00-10.30pm Sun). **CLOSED:** Christmas Day. **CREDIT CARDS ACCEPTED:** None. **BAR FOOD AVAILABLE:** 12.00-10.00pm. Wheelchair access. **BEERS AVAILABLE:** Adnams, Young's, Tetley, Benskins, Guinness. **NEAREST TUBE STATION:** Hyde Park Corner. **MAP REF:** 2, F/4

Narrow Boat

176

119 St Peter's Street, N1 **071-226 3906**

'Water on one side . . . St Peter's Street on the other'

This is not, as you may think, a narrow boat made into a pub. It is a pub built to look like a narrow boat. This pretend narrow boat is in Islington on the bank of the Regents Canal, long, low and, you will be surprised to hear, narrow with a hardwood floor and long windows looking down at the towpath and the water on one side and St Peter's Street on the other. Nautical *objets* abound. Sitting at one of the heavy wooden tables you might almost think you were in a narrow boat.

The Narrow Boat attracts a youngish crowd. There's a jukebox and Sky TV and lots of gaming machines and the food is youthful and reasonably priced. Live music fills the bar on Saturday nights, soul, rock 'n' roll, country, a small terrace on the deck is pleasant in the summer and, in the basin beyond, narrow boats gather.

OPEN: Mon-Sun. **HOURS:** 12.00-11.00pm (12.00-3.00pm and 7.00-10.30pm Sun). **CREDIT CARDS ACCEPTED:** None. **BAR FOOD AVAILABLE:** 12.00-3.00pm and 6.00-9.30pm. Wheelchair access. Tables outside seat 35. Private room seats 30. **BEERS AVAILABLE:** Grolsch, Caffreys, London Pride, Bass, Carling Black Label, Tennent's Pilsner. **NEAREST TUBE STATION:** Angel.

MAP REF: 5, C/1

New Moon

177

88 Gracechurch St, EC3 **071-626 3652**

'Lunch in the New Moon costs rather more nowadays'

This handsome dignified city pub occupies a commanding position in lofty Leadenhall Market. Its ornate Victorian hall with its high ceiling and long counter fills with brokers when the markets close.

With offices on all sides the big downstairs bar has busy lunchtimes. This is where the food is served. During the pub's most recent refurbishment John Hall, its veteran licensee, found an old menu dated 18 August 1900. In those days the pub was called the Half Moon and boasted the sort of restaurant that has printed, dated menus. You did well in this one: rump steak ls, fillet steak ls 3d, potatoes (fried) 3d, (boiled) 2d . . .

Lunch in the New Moon costs rather more nowadays.

OPEN: Mon-Sat. **HOURS:** 11.00am-11.00pm (11.30am-3.00pm Sat). **CLOSED:** Bank Holidays. **CREDIT CARDS ACCEPTED:** All major cards except AmEx and Diner's Club. **BAR FOOD AVAILABLE:** 11.30am-2.30pm. Wheelchair access (but not lavatory). **BEERS AVAILABLE:** Boddingtons, London Pride, Wadworth 6X, Flowers IPA, Stella Artois, Heineken. **NEAREST TUBE STATION:** Monument, Liverpool Street.

The Nightingale

178

97 Nightingale Lane, SW12 **081-673 1637**

'Prizes for its flowers'

You aren't likely to hear a nightingale at the Nightingale. Not much woodland left in Balham, not many copses, that is what nightingales like. Still the Nightingale makes a pleasant rural impression and has a delightful and secluded garden the perfect place for a quiet drink on a summer's evening. Its borders, window boxes and hanging baskets are luxuriant. It wins prizes for its flowers.

It has had a prize from Camra for the quality of its beer too and last year it won one for the quality of its customers. The Association of London Brewers and Licensed Retailers had a contest to find which pub inside the M25 had raised most money for charity. It turned out to be the Nightingale. In fourteen years its regulars had raised a whopping £187,000. One year they did a sponsored parachute jump and two of them broke their ankles. Now about 200 of them do an annual 35 miles walk along the Thames Footpath from Windsor to Putney. Last year's raised £22,000.

The pub itself is comfortable and welcoming with home-made soups, cottage pie and real sausages at lunchtime and an impressive wine list, 10 reds, 9 whites, 2 sparkling and a good house claret. It gets packed in the evening.

OPEN: Mon-Sun. **HOURS:** 11.00-3.00pm Mon-Tue; 11.00am-11.00pm Wed-Sat; 12.00-3.00pm and 7.00-10.30pm Sun. **CREDIT CARDS ACCEPTED:** None. **BAR FOOD AVAILABLE:** 12.00-2.30pm and 6.00-9.00pm. Wheelchair access. Beer garden seats over 60. **BEERS AVAILABLE:** All Young's variants. **NEAREST TUBE STATION:** Clapham South.

O-Bar

179

83 Wardour Street, W1 **071-437 3490**

'It never happened to the Round House'

The Round House, built in 1892 on a fine corner site in Soho, was an alderman among pubs, large, dignified and five-storeyed, the personification of Victorian virtues. Ah, those golden carefree days. The sigh of the pumps as the careful pints were drawn. The murmur of conversation from the private bar. If they could see it now!

The Round House has undergone an astonishing transformation. It is now the O Bar, a glittering glam arena fuelled by holiday food and Costa cocktails, strutting its stuff through the nineties with music thudding, disco, acid jazz, funk. And every table taken and outside queues so long they need four tough young doormen with headsets and intercoms to control them. Couples only please.

Queues? Doormen? It never happened to the Round House in all its days.

OPEN: Mon-Sun. **HOURS:** 1.00pm-1.00am Mon-Wed; 1.00pm-2.00am Thurs; 1.00pm-3.00am Fri-Sat; 2.00-10.30pm Sun. **CLOSED:** Christmas Day, New Year's Day. **CREDIT CARDS ACCEPTED:** None. **BAR FOOD AVAILABLE:** 6.00pm to closing time. Wheelchair access. Tables outside seat 28. **BEERS AVAILABLE:** Bottled lagers. **NEAREST TUBE STATIONS:** Leicester Square, Piccadilly Circus.

O'Hanlons (180)

18 Tysoe Street, EC1 **071-837 4112**

'Perhaps the most Irish pub in London'

John O'Hanlon from County Kerry bought a little pub called the Three Crowns three years ago and changed its name. He called it O'Hanlons. What else would he call it?

It is perhaps the most Irish pub in London. It's just a little pub, you understand, it used to be a private house until 1939 but now the ground floor is painted cream and shamrock, the big front window says O'Hanlons in Celtic letters and inside it's all Ireland and rugby. There's a rugby ball signed by the 1982 Irish team, dozens of programmes of Irish Internationals, a bodhran behind the bar and himself getting the crack going and taking infinite care with the Dublin Guinness.

There are only a handful of places in London importing the real stuff and this is one of them. O'Hanlon charges £2 a pint and it takes a while to pour but what's your hurry? Sit at a table and he'll let you know when it's ready. He imports a good draught lager from Czechoslovakia too but that takes less pouring.

There's the one big room with a bare wood floor and a mixture of tables and chairs and a covered beer garden out at the back with whitewashed walls and plants. You can eat out there or in the bar and lots do.

It's real Irish home cooking. John O'Hanlon's mother came over from Ireland to take over the kitchen when he got the pub and she does great food, baked Irish gammon with lots of potatoes, beef and Dublin Guinness pie, and, some say best of all, real Irish soda bread. She gets up at the crack of dawn to make it and it's still warm when the pub opens.

OPEN: Mon-Fri. **HOURS:** 11.00am-11.00pm. **Closed:** Bank Holidays. **CREDIT CARDS ACCEPTED:** None. **RESTAURANT FOOD AVAILABLE:** 12.00-2.30pm and 6.00-9.00pm. Wheelchair access. Patio seats 30. **BEERS AVAILABLE:** Crouch Vale, Bass, Tennent's, Carling Black Label, Guinness. **NEAREST TUBE STATION:** Farringdon. **MAP REF:** 5, A/2

The Old Bell Tavern (181)

95 Fleet Street, EC4 **071-583 0070**

'A senior Fleet Street pub'

What happened to Fleet Street's busy pubs when the newspapers left?

We are nettled to report that this trauma had less effect on them than was expected. One, and only one, closed – the King and Keys, scene of some dramatic confrontations. The rest are looking very well.

Here is the Old Bell Tavern, a senior Fleet Street pub, built in 1678 by Sir Christopher Wren as a hostel for his masons. He was rebuilding St Bride's Church which had been burned out in the Great Fire and he needed somewhere to lodge them so up went the Old Bell. You will know St Bride's. A beautiful church and for all these years the Old Bell has been its nearest neighbour, just a lathe and plaster job but getting steadily more interesting with age. It has been a licensed tavern for 300 years and it, too, is now a listed building.

In the great days of Fleet Street the Old Bell was a printers' pub, small but cosy, its bar tucked away behind its off-licence. With the newspaper diaspora in the late 1980s it had to find an entirely new clientele as did all the pubs in Fleet Street. It is now a lawyers' and bankers' pub and is doing well again.

There have been changes. The off-licence has gone altogether, making the pub a little bigger. In its place is a comfortable snug and a handsome stained-glass window faces the street.

Printers taking a trip down memory lane will notice such things and will be pleased to see that the triangular oak stools, a feature of the pub since its early days, are still there too. These, according to the Old Bell, are unique to the Old Bell.

OPEN: Mon-Fri. **HOURS:** 11.00am-11.00pm. **CLOSED:** Bank holidays. **CREDIT CARDS ACCEPTED:** All major cards. **BAR FOOD AVAILABLE:** 12.00-9.00pm. Wheelchair access. Private room seats 30. **BEERS AVAILABLE:** 6 real ales, Carlsberg, Castlemaine, Guinness. **NEAREST TUBE STATION:** Blackfriars. **MAP REF:** 6, B/1

The Old Bull and Bush

182

North End Road, NW3 **081-455 3685**

'"Come, come, come and make eyes at me..."'

The Old Bull and Bush, declares the Old Bull and Bush, is probably the most famous pub in the world. It probably is.

After years of being altered, extended and refurbished it is a big, sprawly modern pub now but never a month goes by without the saloon bar rocking again to the refrain that made Florrie Forde a fortune and the Old Bull and Bush a household name:

Come, come, come and make eyes at me
Down at the Old Bull and Bush (ta ra ra ra ra)
Come, come, drink some port wine with me
Down at the Old Bull and Bush . . .

The Bull and Bush had a long history before ever Florrie Forde, fifteen stone and swathed in mauve brocade, began belting out her big hit round the halls. Booklets on the bar tell the story. Old farmhouse. Charles I. Medicinal springs. Hogarth, William Pitt, Gainsborough making his helpful remark – 'What a delightful little snuggery is this said Bull and Bush . . .' Then the pleasure garden and the concerts and sing-songs and half the East End heading for a day in the country and a good old knees-up down at the old Bull and Bush. They had the perfect song for it.

The Old Bull and Bush is still going great guns. There were huge changes to it in the Twenties and again in the Eighties when it closed for three and a half months for a major rebuilding job. This cost £400,000 and the pub was changed from top to toe with new bars, new kitchens, new places to eat, a big new car park, a vast new patio. One of the new bars might be a country house library. Another has a classic upright piano around which, on the last Friday of every month, there's Cockney Night. There are no prizes for guessing at least one of the songs . . .

Hear the little German band
Just let me hold your hand
Do do have a little drink or two
Down at the Old Bull and Bush. Bush Bush.

OPEN: Mon-Sun. **HOURS:** 11.00am-11.00pm (12.00-3.00pm and 7.00-10.30pm Sun). **CLOSED:** Christmas Day. **CREDIT CARDS ACCEPTED:** All major cards. **RESTAURANT FOOD AVAILABLE:** 12.00-3.00pm and 6.00-9.00pm. No smoking area. Wheelchair access. Tables outside seat 50. Private room seats 30. **BEERS AVAILABLE:** Burton, Tetley, Lowenbrau, Castlemaine, Labatts, Carlsberg, Guinness. **NEAREST TUBE STATION:** Golders Green.

The Old Coffee House

183

49 Beak Street, W1 **071-437 2197**

'You can still get coffee in the Old Coffee Shop'

The Old Coffee House, people are sometimes bemused to discover, is a pub. It started life as a coffee house, true, but that was in the 18th century. Many a future pub was a coffee house then. The others changed their names when they started selling best bitter but the Old Coffee House saw no reason to. The Old Coffee House it stayed.

Some think it could be called the Old Antique Shop. The bar is filled with stuffed animals, brass things hanging from the ceiling and such rare and curious items as the boxing gloves used by Dave Charnley to knock out David 'Darkie' Hughes when defending his lightweight title in 1961. It was the shortest-ever British title fight. It lasted 40 seconds.

You can still get coffee in the Old Coffee Shop. Filter only.

OPEN: Mon-Sun. **HOURS:** 11.00am-11.00pm (12.00-3.00pm and 7.00-10.30pm Sun). **CLOSED:** Christmas Day and Boxing Day. **CREDIT CARDS ACCEPTED:** None. **BAR FOOD AVAILABLE:** 12.00-3.00pm. **SET PRICE LUNCH:** £3.95. Wheelchair access. Private room seats 30. **BEERS AVAILABLE:** Courage Best, Ruddles, Young's Special, John Smith's, Kronenbourg, Budweiser, Foster's, Holsten. **NEAREST TUBE STATIONS:** Piccadilly Circus, Oxford Circus. **MAP REF:** 1, D/2

The Old Dr Butlers Head

184

Masons Avenue, EC2 **071-606 3504**

'Add piles of horse dung and emptied chamber pots and you could almost be in the London of James I'

Masons Avenue gives you a good idea of how things would have looked in 17th-century London after a miracle clean-up. Add piles of horse dung and emptied chamber pots, don't look too closely and you could almost be in the London of James I.

It is a narrow flagstoned alley, a black and white five-storey half-timbered mansion on one side and the Old Dr Butlers Head a few feet away on the other. The half-timbered mansion is actually an office block built in 1928 and the pub, burned down in the Great Fire and then rebuilt, has been restored and restored again. It has survived, that is the great thing.

There is now one big bar with old timbers, bare floorboards, ancient-looking panelling to the ceiling, old barrels, stout wooden furniture, and every lunchtime the bar is full of smartly dressed City men and City women, drinking and talking ten to the dozen. Up two steps at the back there are tables and chairs and girls making good-looking sandwiches and upstairs two floors of restaurant with roasts and Dr Butler's Daily Specialities. The good doctor's steak and kidney pudding in the Tudor Room or much bigger Balcony Room on the top floor costs £9.85, veg or salad extra.

The doctor himself, neat grey beard, embroidered cap, twinkles down from the inn-sign in the alley. He was a dreadful old fraud, suddenly firing off pistols inches away from the ears of patients to cure epilepsy and dropping poor souls with ague into the river.

The great cure which got him in with King James was his medicinal ale, good for your tum he said. He bought several alehouses to sell it in. He got this one in 1616. It is the last remaining and it hasn't sold the doctor's ale for 300 years.

OPEN: Mon-Fri. **HOURS:** 11.00am-11.00pm. **CLOSED:** Bank Holidays. **CREDIT CARDS ACCEPTED:** All major cards. **BAR AND RESTAURANT FOOD AVAILABLE:** 12.00-2.30pm. Wheelchair access (but not lavatory). Private room seats 120. **BEERS AVAILABLE:** Boddingtons, Flowers, London Pride, Heineken, Stella Artois. **NEAREST TUBE STATION:** Moorgate.

The Old King Lud 185

78 Ludgate Hill, EC4 **071-329 8517**

'The two-pint stein test, have you tried that?'

Some tremendous rebuilding has been going on around Ludgate Hill. Five major new office blocks and a new station have appeared, the old railway bridge has gone, the whole place has changed. So what, you will be asking, has happened to the King Lud?

Well, it disappeared for a while but when the scaffolding and hoardings came down at last there it still was. More or less. Its uninhibited five-storey façade had been saved so hurray for that. The rest of the building had been totally demolished. In its place was a shell for Whitbreads to turn into whatever it had in mind.

What it had in mind was another pub for its Hogshead chain so it was ancient timbers, old flagstones and a great gantry loaded with barrels for the new Old King Lud. Country benches and old wooden tables were brought in and a vast vat labelled Fermenting Vessel No 1 seemed to be wedged into one corner of the bar. This seemed longer, wider and higher and looked, I must say, smashing.

Its character changed too. The King Lud I remember had a disco and did pizzas but it was never as lively or as thirsty as this. A minimum of twenty different cask ales are on tap every day, now, sometimes more, and vast quantities are downed, customers using two-pint tankards and four-pint jugs to save time.

A young and largely antipodean staff throws itself into the spirit of the thing, turning up in nappies, bibs and rattles for the first birthday party and leading all sorts of larks, particularly on Friday nights when the place is jumping. Macho competition is the thing – yards of ale glug-glugging and the two-pint stein test, have you tried that? You stand, arms wide, a two-pint tankard of beer in either hand and stand and stand . . . One drop of beer spilled and that's it. Two minutes is a very good score. The cellarman, described by Danny Andrews, one of the licensees, as a burly young beast, has managed 3.32 minutes.

On Sundays a deep peace descends on the King Lud. Sunday papers are on offer. The four-pint jugs doze behind the bar counter. 'You have the pub to yourself on Sunday mornings,' says Andrews.

OPEN: Mon-Sun. **HOURS:** 11.00am-11.00pm (12.00-3.00pm and 7.00-10.30pm). **CLOSED:** Christmas Day. **CREDIT CARDS ACCEPTED:** Visa, Mastercard. **BAR FOOD AVAILABLE:** All opening hours. No smoking area. Wheelchair access (disabled lavatory). Table outside seats 6. **BEERS AVAILABLE:** Boddingtons, Old Speckled Hen, London Pride, Wadworth 6X, Heineken, Stella Artois, Guinness, Murphy's. **NEAREST TUBE STATION:** Blackfriars. **MAP REF:** 6, B/1

The Old Red Lion

186

72 High Holborn, WC1 **071-405 2892**

'The ghosts of the Lord Protector and his cronies, should they have chosen to hang around, won't know where they are'

This Red Lion has a rather grisly claim to fame. After the restoration of Charles II it was felt necessary to punish the three men considered most responsible for his father's execution – Oliver Cromwell, his son-in-law Henry Ireton and the judge who sentenced Charles I to death, John Bradshaw.

They were dead already as it happened, buried in Westminster Abbey, but they were disinterred, taken to Tyburn and strung up anyway. On their way there the cart stopped off at the Red Lion where the three bodies lay overnight. They can hardly have been very welcome guests. Ireton, the youngest of the three, had been dead ten years.

Well the old pub has been rebuilt, restored and refurbished any number of times since then. The latest renovation closed the pub for six weeks only this year. In the saloon bar they kept the good-looking Victorian back bar but everything else was replaced and the first-floor bar turned into a small restaurant.

The ghosts of the Lord Protector and his cronies, should they have chosen to hang round, won't know where they are.

OPEN: Mon-Fri. **HOURS:** 11.00am-11.00pm. **CLOSED:** Bank holidays. **CREDIT CARDS ACCEPTED:** Visa, Mastercard, AmEx. **BAR FOOD AVAILABLE:** 12.00-10.30pm. **RESTAURANT FOOD AVAILABLE:** 12.00-2.00pm. Wheelchair access (but not lavatory). Tables outside seat 8. Private room seats 25. **BEERS AVAILABLE:** Greene King, Flowers IPA, Rayments, Abbot Ale, Stella Artois, Kronenbourg, Harp, Carling Black Label, Guinness. **NEAREST TUBE STATIONS:** Holborn, Chancery Lane.

Old Red Lion

187

418 St John Street, EC1 **071-837 7816**

'Miracles on a stage the size of an in-tray'

Lively Islington pub with a theatre upstairs that can sit fifty comfortably, sixty if everyone breathes in. Actors, directors and designers perform miracles on a stage the size of an in-tray. Downstairs one set of the original Victorian partitions has survived to give two big bars. Both get packed. Out the back there's a hidden beer garden under high whitewashed walls. Things are usually quieter out there.

OPEN: Mon-Sun. **HOURS:** 11.30am-3.00pm and 5.30-11.00pm (11.00am-3.00pm and 7.00-11.00pm Sat; 12.00-3.00pm and 7.00-10.30pm Sun). **CLOSED:** Christmas Day. **CREDIT CARDS ACCEPTED:** None. **BAR FOOD AVAILABLE:** 11.00am-3.00pm and 5.00-7.00pm. Wheelchair access. Patio seats 18. **BEERS AVAILABLE:** Bass, Flowers IPA, Grolsch, Tennent's, Carling Black Label. **NEAREST TUBE STATION:** Angel. **MAP REF:** 5, B/2

The Old Shades

188

37 Whitehall, SW1 **071-930 4019**

'A Grade II listed building, which means that you get told off if you pull it down'

Walk up Whitehall from Trafalgar Square and you pass three interesting pubs almost next door to each other, the Silver Cross, the Old Shades and the Clarence. The Old Shades is the one in the middle. It is a Grade II listed building which means that you get told off if you pull it down. You wouldn't want to do that. It is Flemish-Gothic, a long thin pub put up in 1898.

Yes, it seems older and there was, in fact, a tavern on the spot long before that. I dare say that the crowd that watched the execution of Charles I just up the road came in for a drink afterwards but the Old Shades believes in letting bygones be bygones and there is a nice portrait of the Queen on a horse over the mantelpiece at the far end.

Old Shades gets a lot of tourists and welcomes events like the marathon which brought in wall-to-wall people this year. Almost any parade down Whitehall does wonders for trade. Riots of the poll tax sort don't. It has had success with real ale festivals lately. At the last one Growler, the strongest real ale on offer, was the first to sell out.

OPEN: Mon-Sun. **HOURS:** 11.00am-11.00pm (12.00-3.00pm and 7.00-10.30pm Sun). **CLOSED:** Christmas Day. **CREDIT CARDS ACCEPTED:** Visa, Mastercard, Delta. **BAR FOOD AVAILABLE:** 12.00-2.30pm and 5.00-9.30pm. No smoking area. Wheelchair access (but not lavatory). Private room seats 40. **BEERS AVAILABLE:** London Pride, Flowers IPA, Bass, Ruddells County, Grolsch, Carling Black Label, Tennent's Extra, Tennent's Pilsner. **NEAREST TUBE STATION:** Embankment. **MAP REF:** 8, D/2

The Old Ship

189

25 Upper Mall, W4 **081-741 2886**

'The new customers are by and large young and like their music loud'

The Old Ship is probably the oldest pub in Hammersmith, a 17th-century riverside hostelery at one time steeped in history and tradition. It was on the sleepy side. No longer, though.

A new lessee, Paul Ball-Murray, arrived recently with plans to perk the old place up a bit and neighbours were soon objecting to the licensing magistrates. 'They were wanting to slap my wrist,' he says. He has pressed on, though, changing the interior, planning a big new kitchen, bringing the main room on the first floor with its wide balcony into the pub. It had been his sitting room. It is now the quarter deck bar.

He is full of plans for change. He will probably have painted the building arcade green by now, one of the new colours he explains, but the biggest change is the music. It was a quiet pub before. Now there is music from opening to closing time.

The new Old Ship has lost some old customers but it has clearly won new ones. It gets packed most evenings and every weekend. The new customers are by and large young and like their music loud and Ball-Murray can't understand why anyone should mind. His customers like what he is doing, he says, and he will go on doing it.

OPEN: Mon-Sun. **HOURS:** 11.00am-11.00pm (12.00-3.00pm and 7.00-10.30pm Sun). **CLOSED:** Christmas Day. **CREDIT CARDS ACCEPTED:** All major cards. **RESTAURANT FOOD AVAILABLE:** 11.00am-11.00pm (12.00-3.00pm and 7.00-10.30pm Sun). Wheelchair access. Tables outside seat 50. Private room seats 30. **BEERS AVAILABLE:** London Pride, Foster's, Kronenbourg, Sol, Budweiser, Molsen, Foster's Ice, Guinness. **NEAREST TUBE STATION:** Hammersmith.

The Old Thameside Inn

190

Clink Street, SE1 **071-403 4243**

'Riverside walkers are pleased to see it'

The Old Thameside Inn is one of London's newer pubs. It opened in 1985. Still, the Thameside bit is right enough. There is just the new riverside walk between it and the river.

Riverside walkers are the more pleased to see it because the stretch of river bank between London Bridge and Cannon Street railway bridge is rather uneventful. There are sandwiches and beer inside, hot food at lunchtime, and the picnic tables along its front have a nice view of Fishmonger's Hall.

The Old Thameside used to be a spice warehouse, busy and prosperous at first, empty and apparently abandoned later on. Then in 1985 it was cleverly converted, the designers keeping what they could, the heavy warehouse timbers, the old flagstone warehouse floor. This has now resumed its working life in what is now the downstairs bar.

An old West Country topsail schooner called the *Kathleen and May* is moored in a small dry dock on the new pub's easterly flank, a pleasant retirement home for a working ship, and follow the road round the back and you will find what remains of the Clink prison. You will come thankfully away.

OPEN: Mon-Sun. **HOURS:** 11.00am-11.00pm (11.00am-5.00pm Sat; 12.00-3.00pm Sun). **CLOSED:** All Bank holidays. **CREDIT CARDS ACCEPTED:** All major cards, except Diner's Club. **BAR FOOD AVAILABLE:** 12.00-2.30pm. Tables outside seating 120. Private room seating 175. **BEERS AVAILABLE:** Carlsberg, Tetley, Tuborg Gold, Castlemaine. **NEAREST TUBE STATION:** London Bridge.

Ye Olde Cheshire Cheese

191

Wine Office Court, EC4 **071-353 6170**

'Six separate bars, three restaurants and a private dining room'

The Cheshire Cheese is one of London's most celebrated taverns, the archetypal 17th-century chop-house, small cosy rooms, black settles, low ceilings, sawdust-covered floors, creaking stairs, open fires and good old boys in the chimney corner. In the Cheshire Cheese's case the old boys happened to be Dr Johnson in the chop room and Charles Dickens in the bar, so its position as a long-running tourist attraction is secure.

The original tavern burned down in the Great Fire of London but was rebuilt the following year, 1667, and there were no major changes for the next 300 years. The Yorkshire brewers Samuel Smith bought it in 1986 and they found it, it must be said, distinctly unsteady on its pins. Also, perhaps, a little small for its commercial possibilities . . .

So in 1990 they did something about both problems. In the next eighteen months the pub was underpinned and tightened up, totally refurbished and effectively extended. By the time it reopened it had just about doubled its size.

The old tavern now has six separate bars, three restaurants – two with annexes – and a private dining room. A modern kitchen on the top floor supplies food to them all. Three sets of new toilets and six staff rooms.

By and large it has been a mannerly restoration. Dr Johnson might have a thing or two to say about the rock music in the cellar bar. Still, you can't hear it anywhere else. He might also want to know why his chair was standing on a table in the chop room with a notice saying Dr Johnson's Chair but I think Dickens would be happy in the ground-floor bar. It seems hardly changed at all, even keeping the faded gilt notice above the door saying 'Gentlemen Only'. The management hope women customers will ignore this.

The building itself has stopped leaning and groaning. The floorboards, still swept and freshly scattered with sawdust twice a day, have lost their creak. 'It is now ready for the next 200 years,' says its cheerful Geordie landlord.

OPEN: Mon-Sun. **HOURS:** 11.30am-11.00pm (12.00-3.00pm Sun). **CLOSED:** Bank holidays. **CREDIT CARDS ACCEPTED:** All major cards. **BAR FOOD AVAILABLE:** 12.00-3.00pm Mon-Sun; 6.00-9.00pm Mon-Thur. **RESTAURANT FOOD AVAILABLE:** 12.00-2.30pm and 6.00-9.30pm Mon-Sat. Private room seats 60. **BEERS AVAILABLE:** Samuel Smith variants, Ayingerbrau variants. **NEAREST TUBE STATION:** Blackfriars.

Ye Olde Cock Tavern

192

22 Fleet Street, EC4 **071-353 8570**

'"Oh plump headwaiter at the Cock to which I most resort . . ."'

Ask not why the chicken crossed the road. Ye Olde Cock crossed the road in 1887 to make way for a bank, uncommonly civil of it.

Ye Olde Cock was, then as now, a famous old tavern. Pepys, Goldsmith, Sheridan and Dickens all knew it well. Tennyson had written a poem about it, not perhaps his best but its first verse is hard to beat:

Oh plump headwaiter at the Cock
To which I most resort
How goes the time?'
'Tis five o'clock'
'Go fetch a pint of port.'

Well, Ye Olde Cock rescued as much as it could from the old building, pictures, furniture, the old fireplace and its overmantel (Grinling Gibbons, they say) and resumed its role in life which was filling poets with port and others with strong ale.

It was comfortably past the 100th anniversary of its great move when, in April 1990, a disastrous fire broke out in the bar and most of the things that had been rescued from the old tavern were destroyed. Still, the building itself, a copy of the old one and a landmark in Fleet Street, was saved. So, happily, was the old fireplace and, after eight months, Ye Olde Cock reopened looking every bit itself again. Some in Fleet Street even reported improvements. The upstairs restaurant was lighter, they said, and in some ways nicer and still had its excellent carvery at lunchtime.

As for the Dickens Room on the second floor with its old panelling and Dickens mementoes, this was untouched by the fire. It is a pleasant period room used for special occasions. Take with a pinch of salt tales of Dickens dining there. He died before the olde cock crossed the road.

OPEN: Mon-Fri. **HOURS:** 11.00am-11.00pm. **CLOSED:** Bank Holidays. **CREDIT CARDS ACCEPTED:** All major cards. **BAR AND RESTAURANT FOOD AVAILABLE:** 12.00-3.00pm. Wheelchair access (but not lavatory). Private room seats 150. **BEERS AVAILABLE:** Courage Best, Courage Directors, Wadworth 6X, Foster's, Holsten, Carlsberg, Budweiser. **NEAREST TUBE STATION:** Aldwych.

Ye Olde Mitre Tavern

193

1 Ely Court, EC1 071-405 4751

'Sometimes a shoehorn would be needed to get one more City businessman in'

Few pubs have had closer brushes with great events than Ye Olde Mitre Tavern. The medieval bishops of Ely were vastly rich and powerful figures. Their palace was hereabouts and in 1547 one of them, the well-named Bishop Goddrich, built this little tavern for his servants.

It was all go in the bishops' palace. The Black Prince stayed there, John of Gaunt died there, Henry VIII feasted there and Elizabeth I danced round its cherry tree and gave most of the estate to her favourite, Sir Christopher Hatton.

Things soured for the bishops and in 1772 their palace was pulled down. The little tavern came down with it but it was speedily rebuilt to the original plan and here it is, one of London's most picturesque pubs with a stone mitre from the bishops' gatehouse in the wall and the trunk of that fateful cherry tree in a glass case in the bar.

The two small dark panelled rooms with their high settles and old prints are as they have always been and sometimes a shoehorn would be needed to get one more City businessman in. Up the narrow winding stairs is a bigger room, the Bishop's Room, they call it. You have a good chance of getting a seat there. Or poke about

outside. There's a narrow yard with barrels for tables if you don't mind standing.

It is well tucked away, this old pub. Ely Court, a narrow covered alley off Hatton Gardens, is the best way to it. Leave by the even narrower alley which will take you to Ely Place and there, turning left, you will find the Mitre's distinguished neighbour, St Etheldreda's, the 13th-century bishops' church. It is a marvel and here is something. By some historical quirk you have sanctuary in both the pub and the church. You can't be arrested in either or so they say.

Note for villains: there's a smartly dressed commissionaire on duty in Ely Place. Before the war he would have been a beadle and would have called out the hour on the hour all night long. The commissionaire assumes you have a watch.

OPEN: Mon-Fri. **HOURS:** 11.00am-11.00pm. **CLOSED:** Bank holidays. **CREDIT CARDS ACCEPTED:** None. **BAR FOOD AVAILABLE:** 11.00am-10.30pm. Private room seats 20. **BEERS AVAILABLE:** Burton, Friary Mieux, Tetley, Carlsberg Export, Carlsberg Pilsner, Guinness, Castlemaine. **NEAREST TUBE STATION:** Chancery Lane. **MAP REF:** 6, A/2

Ye Olde Red Cow

71 Long Lane, EC1 194

'"Ye Olde Red Cowe Gives Good Milk Now"'

This small, plain Smithfield pub was until quite recently the stage for Dick O'Shea, a landlord who relished his role as a local character and filled it with boisterous talk and laughter. His upstairs restaurant, O'Sheas, could be rollicking.

An inscription in large gold letters on the the side of the old pub remembers him. It reads in part: 'Mr Dick O'Shea, a previous host, frequently entertained many personalities of stage and screen such as Bernard Miles and Peter Ustinov and was well known for his hot toddy which consisted of a secret substance together with a ginger wine base.'

Mr O'Shea is, sadly, no longer with us. Nor is O'Sheas, and life in Ye Olde Red Cow seems to be marking time. Things will get better or possibly worse. Meanwhile, Ye Olde Red Cow has two messages for the nation. They are painted above the bar in the corner of the pub's single room. Says one: 'Ye Olde Red Cowe Gives Good Milk Now'. Says the other: 'Gives Such Good Liquor It Would Puzzle The Vicar'.

OPEN: Mon-Sun. **HOURS:** 11.00am-7.00pm (12.00-3.00pm Sun). **CREDIT CARDS ACCEPTED:** None. **BEERS AVAILABLE:** Courage Best, Carlsberg, Foster's, Budweiser. **NEAREST TUBE STATION:** Barbican.

MAP REF: 6, B/2

Ye Olde Surgeon

195

183 Tottenham Court Road, W1 **071-631 3618**

'Cutting bits off and sewing bits on'

A theme pub and what do you suppose the theme is? An operating theatre. Honestly.

It's all Spitting Image-type surgeons and patients at Ye Olde Surgeon, jokes involving cutting bits off and sewing bits on, humorous skulls, funny bandaged bits, real life ads for Ex-Lax, a cocktail called Lop It Off, a bar snack called Double Hernia. The prognosis is not good. Plans are already afoot to wheel in another Ye Olde. Not, I understand, Ye Olde Cadaver.

OPEN: Mon-Sun. **HOURS:** 11.00am-11.00pm (12.00-3.00pm and 7.00-10.30pm Sun). **CLOSED:** Christmas Day. **CREDIT CARDS ACCEPTED:** All major cards. **BAR FOOD AVAILABLE:** 11.00am-11.00pm (12.00-3.00pm and 7.00-10.30pm Sun). Wheelchair access (but not lavatory). Tables outside seat 16. **BEERS AVAILABLE:** Becks, Coors, McEwans Lager, McEwans Export, Younger's IPA, Theakston XB, Theakston Old Peculier, Theakston Best, Guinness, Gillespie's. **NEAREST TUBE STATIONS:** Warren Street, Goodge Street. **MAP REF:** 1, E/3

Ye Olde Wine Shades

196

6 Martin Lane, EC4

'It asks for jackets and ties as it has always done'

A public inquiry at Guildhall pivoted on the merits, architectural, and social, of this small city pub. A major development depended on the outcome. Would developers be allowed to build the new office complex they proposed? It would mean the end of Ye Olde Wine Shades if they did. Architects and lawyers locked in argument. But this was the only city tavern to survive the Great Fire said one side. It had been in continual use since 1663. It was a listed building and it was unique. All right, said the other side. The developers would preserve it. They would put it behind a glass screen as a draught lobby in their new building.

Happily the pub that was mistaken for a lobby is still there so let's drink to that. It is owned by El Vino which also has the famous bar in Fleet Street and it is more of a wine bar itself these days. It asks for jackets and ties as it has always done and keeps its gentlemanly shabbiness, the old carpet runner, the assorted tables and chairs. The City people who eat and drink there find this very agreeable.

Things don't change much at the Old Wine Shades. The wine list is as sound as ever, the food as good and Victor Little who runs it, silver-haired, courteous but an unmistakeable figure of authority, has been there since 1961.

Note the address. People and deliveries often go to the wrong place. It is Martin Lane near Cannon Street, not St Martin's Lane near Trafalgar Square.

OPEN: Mon-Fri. **HOURS:** 11.00am-11.00pm. **BAR FOOD AVAILABLE:** Lunchtimes only. **BEERS AVAILABLE:** Draught and bottled lagers, over 100 wines. **NEAREST TUBE STATION:** Cannon Street.

The Orange Brewery

197

37 Pimlico Road, SW1 **071-730 5984**

'Brewer Jan Musson produces 5,760 pints a week, all for drinking in the premises'

A head of Bacchus looks down from the arch over the corner doorway to the bar of the Orange Brewery, a fine four-storey Victorian pub in the bit of London where Chelsea, Belgravia and Pimlico meet.

Flowers abound in boxes and baskets alongside the hanging gas lamps and in the cellar below Jan Musson, the brewer, produces 5,760 pints of beer a week, all for drinking on the premises. His regular repertoire consists of brews named SW1, a best bitter, SW2, a strong beer for the really serious drinker, Pimlico Porter, his own favourite, Pimlico Light Ale and Victoria Lager, the only lager in the whole of Great Britain to be made in a pub.

That is not all. Five times a year Musson makes what he calls his celebration ales. At Easter the blend is Resurrection Ale, to be drunk reverently, and at Hallowe'en it is Something Wicked. Ditto.

As this guide is being prepared walls are coming down and the blokeish public bar where most of the pints are consumed and the adjoining oak-panelled dining room are being rebuilt as one big bar. The pub part is gas lit. The refurbishment will not change that.

Regulars include City types who make the three-mile plus journey just for the beer as well they might, and visits to the brewery can be made by appointment. Jan Musson will show you the mash tun and copper, the four fermentation vessels and eight conditioning tanks and explain exactly how the magic is worked.

Mozart composed his first symphony round the corner in Ebury Street – No. 180. He was eight years old.

OPEN: Mon-Sun. **HOURS:** 11.00am-11.00pm (12.00-3.00pm and 7.00-10.30pm Sun). **CLOSED:** Christmas Day. **CREDIT CARDS ACCEPTED:** Access, Visa, Diner's Club, AmEx. **BAR FOOD AVAILABLE:** 11.00am-10.00pm. Wheelchair access. Beer garden seats 30. Private room seats 50. **BEERS AVAILABLE:** SW1, SW2, Pimlico Light, Pimlico Porter, Victoria Lager, Theakston. **NEAREST TUBE STATION:** Sloane Square. **MAP REF:** 2, F/2

The Orange Tree

198

45 Kew Road, Richmond **081-940 0944**

'A nice friendly name for this large dignified Victorian public house'

The Orange Tree that stood here in the 18th century got its name from the first orange tree to be brought to Britain, a superstar in Kew

Gardens. It is a nice friendly name for the large dignified Victorian public house that replaced it in the 1890s. A man might raise his hat if he had one to this imposing pub with its fine brick and terracotta façade standing, most obligingly, obliquely opposite Richmond Station.

It is very Victorian inside with red walls covered in pictures, a very large L-shaped bar and big bulbous mahogany pillars but everything is big about this pub. Indeed in 1971 they found there was any amount of room on the first floor for a theatre seating 80 people, the first-ever licensed pub theatre of its kind.

For the next 20 years the Orange Tree Theatre staged plays and sometimes musicals there. Some got transferred to the West End and it became quite famous. It dreamed of more space though and in 1989 converted a little school nearby into a theatre-in-the-round. It still uses the theatre in thepub a lot too.

Meanwhile musicians often perform in the big wine bar in the cellars of the pub. They have jazz there and an opera group sometimes. It is very enterprising, the Orange Tree, as befits a former *Evening Standard* Pub of the Year.

OPEN: Mon-Sun. **HOURS:** 11.00am-11.00pm (12.00-3.00pm and 7.00-10.30pm Sun). **CLOSED:** Christmas Day. **CREDIT CARDS ACCEPTED:** All major cards. **BAR FOOD AVAILABLE:** 12.00-2.30pm and 6.00-11.00pm (6.00-10.30pm Sun). **RESTAURANT FOOD AVAILABLE:** 12.00-3.00pm and 6.00-11.00pm (6.00-10.30pm Sun). No smoking area. Tables outside seat 40. Private room seats 65. **BEERS AVAILABLE:** All Young's variants, Tennent's, Carling Black Label, Labatts, Stella Artois, Rolling Rock, Guinness, Beamish. **NEAREST TUBE STATION:** Richmond.

The Outpost

199

Burdett Road, E3 **081-981 7717**

'The bikes are a magnificent sight'

This is the bikers pub, a pub for bikers run by bikers as they will tell you. The bikes occupy the forecourt, kings of the road from Italy, America, Japan. The bikers line the bar counter inside.

The Outpost sticks out conspicuously on the park side of Burdett Road. It is black with pale blue motorbike murals and if the bikes are a formidable sight so too are the bikers, filling the bar and the pool room, Jack Danielses or bottled lagers in their hands.

Drinks tend to last at the Outpost. Bikers are not, as it happens, big drinkers. Well, the bikes outside can cost a bomb and they are loved with a passion. To ride them needs a strong nerve and a clear head so it's lucky for the Outpost that non-bikers go too sometimes. They get a guarded welcome.

A big spread of snaps on the wall features bikes, bikers' women and bikers at one with nature, bikers getting tattooed, bikers having their nipples pierced. The noticeboard is largely occupied by ads for tattooists and body piercers. The barman is tattooed from shoulder to wrist on both arms, and wears an earring and a nose stud.

OPEN: Mon-Sun. **HOURS:** 11.00am-11.00pm (12.00-3.00pm and 7.00-10.30pm Sun). **CREDIT CARDS ACCEPTED:** None. **BAR FOOD AVAILABLE:** 11.00am-11.00pm Wheelchair access (disabled lavatory). Beer garden seats 15. Private room seats 60. **BEERS AVAILABLE:** Pedigree, Tetley, Grolsch, Budweiser, Newcastle Brown Ale, Holsten, Lowenbrau, Castlemaine. **NEAREST TUBE STATION:** Mile End.

Paddington Stop

200

54 Formosa Street, W9 **071-286 6776**

'A three dartboard pub'

This is a three dartboard pub, built in the 1970s as part of the Amberley Road housing estate. The designer seems to have had a Swiss chalet vaguely in mind. It has one bar, regular blues nights, quizzes on Thursdays and a darts knockout on Sunday evenings.

It does a bitter called Narrow Boat and has one feature which many a better-favoured pub might envy – a terrace overlooking the Grand Union Canal. On sunny days the canal-side patio is a pleasant place, the plain wooden seats, the ducks, the narrow boats slipping by at four miles an hour. From the Paddington Stop to say Leeds or Liverpool takes, oh, a month or two. What's your hurry?

OPEN: Mon-Sun. **HOURS:** 11.00am-11.00pm (12.00-3.00pm and 7.00-10.30pm Sun). **CREDIT CARDS ACCEPTED:** None. **BAR FOOD AVAILABLE:** 12.00-3.00pm and 6.00-9.00pm. Wheelchair access. Tables outside seat 70. **BEERS AVAILABLE:** Real ales, Heineken, Stella Artois, Carlsberg, Guinness, Whitbread Bitter. **NEAREST TUBE STATION:** Warwick Avenue.

MAP REF: 4, A/1

The Park Tavern

201

212 Merton Road, SW18 **081-874 7048**

'When the breathalyser was introduced they bought a horse and carriage and employed a coachman to take customers home'

The Park Tavern is a serious, well-ordered Wandsworth pub. High standards are set by the staff and, you feel, expected of the customers. Bill and Terry Mertis have exercised their benign authority there for twenty-nine years. When Billl Mertis first came here, he says, his job was to teach people how to behave in a pub. This he has done ever since. He is now proud to welcome into his tutelage the sons and daughters of former pupils – boys and girls he had to throw out years ago.

The Park Tavern used to be a coaching inn – the first stage on the Worthing Road. The blacksmith's forge is now the Tavern Room Bar and the stables have become a restaurant. There is a proper public bar with a wooden floor and a bright, comfortable Village Bar at the front of the pub and a large, welcoming lounge at the back.

The main feature of this remarkable room is its dark Victorian panelling, stripped from a country house and installed here by Heals in the 1890s. Good home-cooked food is served at lunchtime and bar snacks in the evening. On special occasionsTerry will lay on one of her medieval feasts with boar's head, suckling pig and a whole salmon.

Behind the servery are photographs of the Mertis's show-business offspring and an old studded leather armchair stands by the door. It is a replica of Dr Johnson's chair that used to have pride of place at the Anchor, Bankside. In 1933 Courage, owners of the Anchor at that time, had 33 replicas made for 33 pubs at a cost of £33 each.

It was typical of the Mertises that when the breathalyser was introduced they bought a horse and carriage and employed a coachman to take customers home. Alas this service is no longer available.

Footnote: I am sorry to report that Dr Johnson's chair is no longer at Bankside. When Fortes bought the Anchor some years ago it discovered that it had unaccountably disappeared. A copy of Dr Johnson's dictionary, another prized possession of the old inn, was also missing.

OPEN: Mon-Sun. **HOURS:** 11.00am-11.00pm (12.00-3.00pm and 7.00-10.30pm Sun). **CREDIT CARDS ACCEPTED:** None. **BAR FOOD AVAILABLE:** 11.00am-2.00pm and 6.00-9.00pm Mon-Fri; 11.00am-4.00pm Sat. **RESTAURANT FOOD AVAILABLE:** 7.00pm-12.00am Mon-Sat; 12.00pm-12.00am Sun. **SET PRICE LUNCH:** £7.95 (Sun only). Wheelchair access (but not lavatory). Tables outside seat 90. Private room seats 60. **BEERS AVAILABLE:** Courage Best, Courage Directors, Wadworth 6X, Kronenbourg, Miller Lite, Foster's, Hoffmeister, Swan Lite. **NEAREST TUBE STATION:** Southfields.

The Paxton's Head

202

153 Knightsbridge, SW1 **071-589 6627**

'It is appropriate that the pub should glitter so splendidly'

Sir Joseph Paxton was the Victorian landscape gardener who designed and built the Crystal Palace. It is appropriate then that the pub that bears his name should glitter so splendidly.

Of course it would have been bigger if he had built it. His conservatory for the Duke of Devonshire was 300 feet long, his Chatsworth fountain 237 feet high. A pub he built would have more like the Albert Hall. He would surely have approved of the brilliant decorated mirrors, though. They cover the walls of the bar. Some have had to be replaced with plain glass but most of the originals have survived and sparkle as they always did. The polished mahogany bar and the listed ceiling are terrific too and as for the huge Victorian mantel clock on the fireplace, that certainly approaches his scale.

The Paxton's Head was a hotel to begin with but the upper floors are offices now. The good news is that the fine room on the first floor is a restaurant again, having reopened this year after standing empty for ages. The original restaurant was quite famous in its day but a murder cast rather a shadow on the silver service. It was out of hours. But all the same . . .

OPEN: Mon-Sat. **HOURS:** 11.00am-11.00pm. **CLOSED:** Christmas Day, Boxing Day and New Year's Day. **CREDIT CARDS ACCEPTED:** AmEx, Visa. **BAR FOOD AVAILABLE:** 12.00-2.30pm. **RESTAURANT FOOD AVAILABLE:** 12.00-4.00pm. No smoking area in dining room. Wheelchair access (but not lavatory). Private room seats 45. **BEERS AVAILABLE:** Nicholson's, Tetley, Brakspear, Bass, Castlemaine, Lowenbrau, Carlsberg, Tennent's Extra. **NEAREST TUBE STATION:** Knightsbridge. **MAP REF:** 2, E/4

The Phene Arms

203

9 Phene Street, SW3 **071-352 3294**

'Thank you, Dr Phene'

Sir John Samuel Phene – it rhymes with meanie – was an eccentric old boy in many ways but he had a lasting claim to fame. He was the first man to plant trees in the streets of large towns. No one seems to have thought of it before. Queen Victoria warmly commended him for it and so do we. Thank you, Dr Phene, and thank you for this nice little pub at the corner of these two leafy Chelsea streets. Dr Phene built the streets and the pub in 1851 and planted lots of acacia saplings around them and I'm pleased to say he lived another 60 years so he saw them grow into mature trees. He also saw his pub pass to Watney's just before he died at a great age in 1912.

The pub is very much as he left it with its tall Victorian bar and its tiny dining room, once the snug. They serve lunch here all week but on Sundays you go upstairs for the roast beef with all the trimmings. There is a much bigger room up there. Sunday lunch is very popular at the Phene and goes on until 4pm.

Three of Dr Phene's acacias still grow in the pub's garden, a lovely place to sit and drink on a sunny day and a great asset to the pub and, indeed, to the streets around. There is a little roof terrace, too. Wesley and Carmen Davis who run the pub now hope to serve supper there on summer evenings if the neighbours will let them. They also hope to see the pub's renowned cricket team, the Phene Philanderers, bestirring itself. It seems to have nodded off in the last few seasons.

OPEN: Mon-Sun. **HOURS:** 11.00am-11.00pm (12.00-2.30pm and 7.00-10.30pm Sun). **CREDIT CARDS ACCEPTED:** All major cards. **BAR AND RESTAURANT FOOD AVAILABLE:** 12.30-2.30pm (12.30-3.00pm Sat; 12.30-4.00pm Sun) and 7.30-10.30pm (7.30-10.00pm Sun). Beer garden seats 100. Private room seats 40. **BEERS AVAILABLE:** Webster's, Adnams, Ruddles County, Ruddles Best, Guinness, Carlsberg, Foster's, Holsten, Budweiser. **NEAREST TUBE STATION:** Sloane Square. **MAP REF:** 2, C/2

The Phoenix and Firkin

204

Windsor Walk, SE15 **071-701 8282**

'He'd rather Mrs Train than Mrs Bovril'

I think we should blow a whistle and wave a flag for this, the flagship of the excellent Firkin chain. It is, as I think you will agree, a remarkable pub. It used to be a railway station. Not many pubs can say that.

You still don't get away from trains at the Phoenix and Firkin. Trains run under it, a model train runs inside it, trains take you almost to the door. You get on at Victoria or London Bridge, get out at Denmark Hill and there it is, straddling all four platforms.

When it was a station it was a good-looking station. The architecture correspondent of *The Times* called it a glorious 1866-vintage Tuscan palazzo. But one night early in 1980 some rotter set fire to it. The palatial ticket hall, the ladies' waiting room, the station master's house, they all went up in smoke and flame. British Rail was going to pull the whole thing down but in view of the local outcry it changed its mind. Instead, Phoenix-like and indeed Firkin-like, the Tuscan palazzo rose from the ashes to start a new chapter as a lively and popular public house.

So have a look at the building before you enter it. Inside it is all classic London, Chatham and Dover, classic Firkin too, everything plain and serviceable and a good view of Platforms 1, 2, 3 and 4. There are some nice old railway posters – 'He'd rather Mrs Train than Mrs Bovril' – and an enormous station clock rescued from Llandudno Junction that has to be wound up every morning.

You'll find live blues and jazz on Mondays and Thursdays in winter and on summer evenings draught scrumpy is the thing and just about everyone sits outside on the steps. Summer or winter the Phoenix does a good trade at lunchtime. It is good plain food there as at any Firkin, nothing fancy. Try one of the big filled baps.

What is really special is the beer. They brew it themselves in a brewhouse in the cellar, the Firkin view being that the old ways are best. So while you drink your ale think of the big vats of English beer coming silently to fruition beneath your feet – the famous Dogbolter, the Firkin Mild and Phoenix Rail Ale which is the pub's best seller.

The Phoenix and Firkin was last year's *Evening Standard* Pub of the Year.

OPEN: Mon-Sun. **HOURS:** 11.00am-11.00pm (12.00-3.00pm and 7.00-10.30pm Sun). **CLOSED:** Christmas Day, Boxing Day, New Year's Day. **CREDIT CARDS ACCEPTED:** None. **BAR FOOD AVAILABLE:** 12.00-11.00pm (12.00-3.00pm and 7.00-10.30pm Sun). No smoking area. Wheelchair access. Beer garden seats 10. Private room seats 30. **BEERS AVAILABLE:** Rail Phoenix, Dogbolter, Castlemaine, Carlsberg, Lownebrau. **NEAREST BR STATION:** Denmark Hill.

The Pineapple (205)

53 Hercules Road, SE1 **071-928 6579**

'A cheerful, workaday Lambeth local'

Look to the right next time your train approaches Waterloo and you may spot a golden pineapple among the rooftops of Lambeth. This is the crowning glory of the Pineapple, a once-ambitious Victorian gin palace, now a cheerful, workaday Lambeth local.

It has imposing marble pillars in pairs, four front doors and a foundation stone laid by Henry Finch in 1870. Maddigan's, the Dublin pub-owners, bought it in 1985 and brought Sean O'Neill over from Ireland to run it. He is still there, cheerily dispensing pints of Murphy's. Lunchtimes are his busy time. 'Basic food,' says Mr O' Neill, 'but cheap.'

William Blake was born along the road.

OPEN: Mon-Sun. **HOURS:** 11.00am-11.00pm (12.00-3.00pm and 7.00-10.30pm Sun). **CREDIT CARDS ACCEPTED:** All major cards. **BAR FOOD AVAILABLE:** 12.00-9.30pm. **SET PRICE LUNCH:** £2.65. Wheelchair access. Beer garden seats 30. **BEERS AVAILABLE:** Greene King, Abbot, Ruddells County, Courage Best, Marstons Pedigree, Whitbread IPA, Foster's, Heineken, Stella Artois, Budweiser, Holsten, Guinness, Murphy's. **NEAREST TUBE STATION:** Lambeth North. **MAP REF:** 7, B/2

Plumbers Arms

206

14 Lower Belgrave Street, SW1 **071-730 4067**

'Belgravia has had its share of horror and mystery'

The Plumbers Arms, despite its robust tradesman's name, is distinctly above stairs. Not too many plumbers live in Lower Belgrave Street though those that do may well commend the house champagne, a very reasonable £14.95.

The Plumbers Arms is said to be so called because of the army of plumbers who helped transform five fields and a stretch of river into Belgravia. The pub itself was one of the first of the new buildings. It was put up in the 1820s to cater for the builders and, of course, the plumbers and when their work was done it served the servants of the grand new houses they had built. Strict class distinctions applied.

Today it is a pleasant single-bar pub with a lincrusta ceiling, a splendid mahogany bar counter, old plates, old prints and smart young barmen in white shirts and grey waistcoats polishing up the gleaming beer pulls. It has well-kept cask ales and denizens of Lower Belgrave Street find it a very good place for lunch.

But it is not its cellar nor its kitchen that has given the Plumber's Arms its celebrity. This stems from the melodramatic events of the cold, rainswept November night in 1974 when, bleeding and soaked to the skin, Lady Lucan stumbled into the pub. She had a shocking story to tell. An intruder had murdered her nanny and had then attacked her. He was still in the house. The police were called and found the nanny dead in the Lucan family home on the other side of the street. Later that night Lord Lucan turned up briefly in a friend's house in Sussex then drove away. He has never been seen since.

The episode has left a lasting mark on the Plumbers Arms which obliquely refers to it in a brief history of Belgravia in its menu. 'In more recent years,' it writes, 'Belgravia has had its share of Horror and Mystery, not only Belgravia but also the Plumbers Arms.'

OPEN: Mon-Sun. **HOURS:** 11.00am-11.00pm Mon-Fri; 12.00-6.00pm Sat; 12.00-3.00pm Sun. **CLOSED:** Christmas Day. **CREDIT CARDS ACCEPTED:** Visa, Mastercard. **BAR FOOD AVAILABLE:** 12.00-10.00pm Mon-Fri; 12.00-

6.00pm Sat; 12.00-3.00pm Sun. Beer garden seats 24. Private room seats 25. **BEERS AVAILABLE:** John Smith's, Wadworth, Courage Best, Courage Directors, Theakston, Foster's, Carlsberg, Heineken, Budweiser, Molsen, Guinness. **NEAREST BR STATION:** Victoria. **MAP REF:** 8, A/2

The Prince Alfred

207

Formosa Street, W9 **071-286 3027**

'A perfect period piece. Well, almost perfect'

The Prince Alfred is a true rarity, a working Victorian pub in full fig. It has hardly changed from the day in 1862 when it first opened its various doors.

It was always a good-looking pub a cut above and still is. It was called after Queen Victoria's second son. He was only 18 but he had already had four years in the Navy and as soon as he could he grew one of those Players cigarette packet naval beards. That was the pub sign problem solved. He was elected King of Greece that year, too. He turned the job down. But back to the pub . . .

It is a remarkable sight. They have kept everything, the beautiful curved and etched glass, the original 15-foot high centrepiece with its shelves and clocks and ornamental flourishes, the massive mahogany counter, best of all the splendid carved and glazed partitions. These divide the space into five separate bars – the public, the gentlemen's, the ladies', the private and the snug.

All but one has its own street entrance. The exception was the snug. Ladies using that had to duck into it through little doors in the partitions, only three-foot-high but once in they had perfect privacy. Rotating snob screens hid them from even the barstaff.

It is a perfect period piece. Well, almost perfect. There has been one change over the years. The stables at the back have been made into a sixth bar, open plan in the modern way and kitted out with a pools table and gaming machines. This is the bar that persons of Prince Alfred's age like. It is the one that gets crowded.

OPEN: Mon-Sun. **HOURS:** 12.00-11.00pm (12.00-3.00pm and 7.00-10.30pm Sun). **CLOSED:** Christmas Day and Boxing Day. **CREDIT CARDS ACCEPTED:** None. **BAR FOOD AVAILABLE:** 12.00-2.30pm and 7.00-10.30pm. Wheelchair access. **BEERS AVAILABLE:** Burton Ale, Tetley, Young's Special, Young's PA, Flowers IPA, Lowenbrau, Castlemaine, Carlsberg. **NEAREST TUBE STATION:** Warwick Avenue. **MAP REF:** 4, A/1

The Prince of Teck

208

161 Earls Court Road, SW5 **071-373 3107**

'Djavagoodweegend?'

Pity homesick Oz expats stranded among the poms in the Earls Court Road. Happily there is an abiding certainty to cheer them. They know that if they stand at the bar in the Prince of Teck long enough they will meet everybody they know.

There are other Oz pubs in London but the Prince of Teck has claimed his kingdom. His is a handsome pub with griffins and gargoyles on the outside not to mention a portrait of the prince, harum-scarum brother of Queen Mary. She would forgive her brother Frank almost anything. When he gave the Cambridge emeralds to his Irish mistress, though . . . but where were we?

Ah Australia! Posters bring it all back. There's a map and boomerangs and Oz roadsigns featuring kangaroos and crocodiles and sitting on the bar is a stuffed and very male kangaroo wearing a short Wallabies Australian Rugby shirt and carrying an empty can of Victoria VB beer and in case you've been away from home too long there's a handy glossary of the language. Gidday. Cow's hoof. Djavagoodweegend?

There are no carpets and very little furniture in the Prince of Teck apart from bar stools along the bar and round the walls. The lager is cold. There is a well-used jukebox. Loos are labelled Sheilas and Bruces and the noticeboard reflects other urgent needs. Some Ozzies want places to live, others want to sell campervans and oh good here's a job offer. A pub wants bar staff. 'Work like slaves for crap wages, crap hours but have a good laugh,' coaxes the ad. 'Live out . . .'

There is a very different room upstairs, the Princess Lounge, where they serve traditional pom pub food. It has a fitted carpet, comfy seats, swagged curtains. Swagged curtains? You're sure this bit isn't for cow's hoofs Bruce?

OPEN: Mon-Sun. **HOURS:** 11.00am-11.00pm (12.00-3.00pm and 7.00-10.30pm Sun). **CLOSED:** Christmas Day. **CREDIT CARDS ACCEPTED:** None. **BAR FOOD AVAILABLE:** 11.00am-3.00pm. Wheelchair access. **BEERS AVAILABLE:** Australian beers, Young's Bitter, Young's Special, Courage Best, Foster's, Kronenbourg. **NEAREST TUBE STATION:** Earls Court.

MAP REF: 3, D/1

The Prince of Wales 209

150 Drury Lane, WC1 **071-240 9935**

'Fruity bottled ale brewed by Trappist monks'

The Prince of Wales rather boasts of its proletarian background. It was, says the potted history on the outside wall, formerly a potato warehouse. In 1852 though it went up in the world, became a pub, a well-appointed pub, good position, heart of theatreland and all that and assumed the rank of the Queen's eldest son.

Time passes: cut to rolling presses, newsboys shouting, and it is 1982. The Prince of Wales, now full of stuffed animals and cobwebs, is looking tired and down at heel. What's this? A gang of revolutionary persons is taking it apart. Farewell Prince of Wales. It reopens as a trendy bar-café with lowered ceilings, red walls, chrome fittings, a jukebox and a new name. It is now Charley's. The kids pour in. It is a big hit.

It does not last. Another decade and Charley's has dated badly too. So this year it got another new personality. It closed for six weeks, reopened and good lord it was the Prince of Wales again. This time though it is one of Scottish and Newcastle's modish T and G Barnard pubs, in the style of the moment: 1990s early ale house. So it is wooden floors and plain wooden furniture, seven English ales on tap and pies with meat, potatoes and veg all under the same puff pastry lid. Also 20 different bottled beers, some quite exotic, in a rack behind the counter. Barbara Fitzgerald, the experienced landlady, thought they would never sell, not at that price, but they go extremely well.

Fruity bottled ale brewed by Trappist monks in a remote monastery is part of 1990s early ale house and, after conventional beginnings, the Prince of Wales is moving with the times.

OPEN: Mon-Sun. **HOURS:** 11.00am-11.00pm (12.00-3.00pm and 7.00-10.30pm Sun). **CLOSED:** Christmas Day, Boxing Day. **CREDIT CARDS ACCEPTED:** All major cards. **BAR FOOD AVAILABLE:** 11.00am-10.00pm (12.00-3.00pm and 7.00-10.00pm Sun). Wheelchair access (but not lavatory). Tables outside seat 20. Private room seats 100. **BEERS AVAILABLE:** Theakston, Courage Directors, Carlsberg, Holsten, Foster's, Guinness, Gillespie's. **NEAREST TUBE STATION:** Covent Garden. **MAP REF:** 1, F/1

The Prince of Wales

210

48 Cleaver Square, SE11 **071-735 9916**

'Where the hard men drank'

Cleaver Square is an agreeable place to live, a backwater of nice houses, Georgian mainly. The middle was once a garden but is now used by the residents to park their cars. The trees remain. A game of boules and you might be in any small French town except, of course, for the pub in the corner.

The Prince of Wales could not be more English. There was a pub here before the square but the original one was rebuilt in 1909 and here it is, a comely Edwardian local named for the Prince who became George IV. It is a small, intimate pub, the public bar at the front and saloon bar behind it knocked into one and still not much room. It seems a peaceful and friendly place but you would hardly believe the troubles it has seen.

For years this pub had a dire reputation. It was where the hard men drank, where the Richardson gang met the Krays for summit meetings and when Kate Emmett, an actress from Australia, arrived as the new tenant eight years ago she found it distinctly unjolly. It had no furniture at all. People sat on the floor and the caretaker manager had a stick with a hook on it behind the bar to protect himself.

Either she had to go or the roughs did so she took them on. She banned them, refused to serve them, stood her ground and she was threatened, bullied and physically attacked.

These battles were followed by legal battles over the freehold and at the time of writing these problems are still unresolved. Still, at least peace has broken out in the pub itself. This must be a relief for Cleaver Square, not to mention the actors, musicians and politicians in the streets roundabout and the ginger tom who rules the bar . . .

OPEN: Mon-Sun. **HOURS:** 12.00-3.00pm Wed-Fri, Sun; 5.00-11.00pm Mon-Sat; 7.00-10.30pm Sun. **CLOSED:** Bank holidays. **CREDIT CARDS ACCEPTED:** None. **BEERS AVAILABLE:** Courage Best, Fuller's, Wadworth, Foster's, Kronenbourg, Holsten Pils, Budweiser, Grolsch. **NEAREST TUBE STATION:** Kennington. **MAP REF:** 7, A/1

The Princess Louise

211

208 High Holborn, WC2 **071-405 8816**

'They are tough old birds, these Princesses Louise'

Princess Louise was the fourth daughter of Queen Victoria. She was the Queen's great-great-aunt. She was unhappily married to the Duke of Argyll. She talked a lot. And in 1891 they named this pub after her.

It was a splendid pub and still is though it has changed a bit of course. Instead of parading round lots of little rooms the massive mahogany bar makes its deep U-turn in the middle of one big open space. But the polished granite pillars, the richly engraved windows, the walls of gilt mirrors, elaborate tiling, fine plaster ceilings and plush banquettes, the polished mahogany and brass have all survived.

It is a miracle really that the Princess Louise is still with us. There was the blitz, of course, but much more dangerous were the redevelopers of the 60s and 70s. The Princess Louise was on the point of coming down to make way for an office block when an outcry from the good guys, cheered on by the *Evening Standard*, saved the day. A preservation order arrived in the nick of time, making it a Listed Building Grade II*. Mark the star, it is important. The regal Victorian gents is separately listed. You don't often meet a listed gents.

The Louise, we'll not stand on ceremony here, has seen various owners come and go. It is now owned by Regent Inns, a lively independent, and it does nine cask ales at last count, a lot of which gets drunk outside on the pavement on sunny days.

To think they almost pulled it down! But then the lady whose name it bears lived to 91. They are tough old birds these Princesses Louise.

It was the *Evening Standard* Pub of the Year in 1986.

OPEN: Mon-Sun. **HOURS:** 11.00am-11.00pm (12.00-3.00pm and 6.00-11.00 Sat; 12.00-2.00pm and 7.30-10.30pm Sun). **CLOSED:** Christmas Day and Boxing Day. **CREDIT CARDS ACCEPTED:** None. **RESTAURANT FOOD AVAILABLE:** 12.00-2.30pm (Mon-Fri only). Wheelchair access (but not lavatory). Private room seats 50. **BEERS AVAILABLE:** Brakspear, Wadworth, Bass, Theakston, Greene King, Thwaites, Charrington IPA. **NEAREST TUBE STATION:** Holborn. **MAP REF:** 1, F/2

The Prospect of Whitby

212

57 Wapping Wall, E1 **071-481 1095**

'Judge Jeffreys came to dine and enjoy the hangings'

The Prospect of Whitby is the oldest riverside pub in London and famous. Its flagstoned bar with its pewter-topped counter sitting on old barrels must have been used by half London in its day. There's a separate section for bar snacks now, a good restaurant up creaking stairs and a jolly riverside terrace with picnic tables under an old weeping willow. It has been the high point of many a day out.

The old inn was built around 1520 and no better than it ought to have been, a haunt of smugglers, thieves and other low lifers. Indeed it boldly called itself the Devil's Tavern. Misbehaving sailors were hanged along the low watermark, a popular entertainment drawing big crowds. Samuel Pepys came to the pub on official business. Judge Jeffreys came to dine and enjoy the hangings.

The pub was burned, rebuilt, changed its name – the Prospect (from Whitby) was a merchant ship which moored nearby – and, slowly, slowly, it started to get respectable.

It is very respectable now, so respectable indeed that two chairs stand side by side at the entrance to the dining room. A notice on one of them reads: 'This chair was occupied by HRH Princess Margaret when dining here on June 26, 1949'. Prince Rainier has had dinner here too, and Kirk Douglas. Where are their chairs?

It was as well the Princess was not dining here on 14 January 1953 when Robert Harrington 'Scarface' Sanders and his red scarf gang raided the Prospect of Whitby. Capt John Cunningham was giving a small dinner party. He and his guests were relieved of their watches, jewellery and money at pistol point. Scarface was caught soon afterwards when, doing another job, he shot at a policeman. He got life. Well, it could have been worse. He could have been hanged at low watermark just below the nice old Prospect of Whitby and left there while the tide rose and fell three times.

OPEN: Mon-Sun. **HOURS:** 11.30am-3.00pm and 5.30-11.00pm (12.00-3.00pm and 7.00-10.30pm). **CLOSED:** Christmas Day and Boxing Day. **CREDIT CARDS ACCEPTED:** Visa, Mastercard, AmEx. **BAR FOOD AVAILABLE:** 12.00-2.30pm and 6.00-9.30pm. **RESTAURANT FOOD AVAILABLE:** 12.00-2.00pm and 7.00-10.00pm (7.00-10.00pm Sat; 12.00-2.00pm Sun). No smoking area. Wheelchair access (but not lavatory). Beer garden seats 80. Private room seats 60. **BEERS AVAILABLE:** Courage Directors, Courage Best, John Smith's, Kronenberg, Foster's, Holsten, Becks, Sol, Molson, Guinness. **NEAREST TUBE STATION:** Wapping.

Punch and Judy

213

40 The Market,
Covent Garden, WC2 **071-379 0923**

'A brilliant place for a pub'

When the famous old flower and vegetable market moved out of Covent Garden in 1974 a miracle happened. Instead of being knocked down the old market was put to wonderful use and when we saw it next there was the Punch and Judy occupying a prime site in Charles's Fowler's elegant market hall.

It was a brilliant place for a pub and the Punch and Judy was a smash hit from the word go. It had a section of the cellars which had once provided overnight storage for vegetables and with its flagged floor and vaulted arches this made a terrific cellar bar, an ideal environment for beer and beer drinkers alike. It led into a courtyard in the glass-roofed arcade, another coup. Customers could sit and drink there whatever the weather and still think they were in the open air . . .

Someone else got the ground floor but the Punch and Judy re-emerges on the floor above with a big light modern bar opening onto a wide balcony of royal proportions, stretching the whole width of the building with a shelf for drinks-in-progress along all its length.

Below is the West Piazza, London's first square, originally designed by Inigo Jones. Now street entertainers perform there to big crowds all summer long and customers of the Punch and Judy, cheerfully crowding the balcony, have the front row in the circle.

The Punch and Judy was one of many prizes in Scottish and Newcastle's purchase of the big Chef and Brewer chain. It was showing distinct signs of wear when it was taken over but the new owners have spent £200,000 on it lately. It is in fine fettle now.

It keeps its well-established character and the devotion of students, British holidaymakers and foreign tourists. The food remains hearty and traditional and it is still a major lager house.

OPEN: Mon-Sun. **HOURS:** 11.30am-11.00pm (12.00-3.00pm and 7.00-10.30pm Sun). **CLOSED:** Christmas Day, Boxing Day. **CREDIT CARDS ACCEPTED:** None. **RESTAURANT FOOD AVAILABLE:** 12.00-5.00pm. No smoking area. Tables outside seat 30. Private room seats 200. **BEERS AVAILABLE:** Courage Best, Courage Directors, John Smith's, Theakston, Foster's, Kronenbourg, Beamish. **NEAREST TUBE STATION:** Covent Garden.

MAP REF: 1, F/1

The Punch Tavern

214

99 Fleet Street, EC4 **071-353 6658**

'Not so much a face lift as timely major surgery'

When *Punch* was young its staff took to a pub in Fleet Street called the Crown and Sugarloaf. It, in turn, took to them, so much so that it changed its name. It became Punch's Tavern. Well, of course, *Punch* is now no more but the Punch Tavern is still there. It has had a slight change of name but is as perky as ever.

It has been helped by not so much a face-lift as timely major surgery. Ten years ago new owners spent £250,000 doing it over so thoroughly that what you have now is a Victorian pub in impeccable condition. The ornately tiled Fleet Street façade might have been put up yesterday and when Alan Coren, penultimate editor of *Punch*, arrived to reopen it, he found a brand new pub sign with a gilded Mr Punch smiling wickedly down. Regular customers were, well, pleased as Punch, particularly when they went to the gents. Before the restoration this was something to be postponed as long as possible. At the Punch Tavern, one guide book had said, a visit to the gents was 'an horrendous and dangerous experience.'

The landlord, Max McSheery, was pleased, too. His takings increased four fold and even without the free-spending journalists his pub does well. He was sorry to see the hacks go all the same. 'They were good drinkers,' he says.

OPEN: Mon-Sun. **HOURS:** 11.30am-11.00pm Mon-Fri; 11.30-3.00pm and 6.00-11.00pm Sat; 12.00-3.00pm and 7.00-10.30pm Sun. **CLOSED:** Christmas Day, Boxing Day, New Year's Day. **CREDIT CARDS ACCEPTED:** None. **BAR FOOD AVAILABLE:** 12.00-3.00pm. Wheelchair access (but not lavatory). **BEERS AVAILABLE:** Tetley, Brakspear, Wadworth, Marstons Pedigree, Bass, Castlemaine, Carling Black Label, Tennent's Extra, Guinness. **NEAREST BR STATION:** Blackfriars. **MAP REF: 6, B/1**

The Queen Mary

215

Victoria Embankment, WC2 **071-240 9404**

'A truly shipshape ship'

The Queen Mary, or the TS *Queen Mary* as she is known on formal occasions, is an extremely pleasant pub some yards offshore between Waterloo and Hungerford bridges. TS stands for Turbine Steamer.

Other working ships retiring to the Thames have sometimes done well as restaurants and the Queen Mary and its immediate upstream neighbour, the Tattershall Castle, have restaurants too. They are true pubs all the same. They have pub licences. They keep pub hours. They

call themselves pubs and operate as pubs. Their saloon bars are populated by persons of distinction sitting at small tables, pints of beer before them. If that's not a pub, what is?

The Queen Mary is a shipshape ship, a child's drawing of a ship with two jaunty red, white and blue funnels and two tiers of square portholes. When she was launched on the Clyde in 1933 she was the most luxurious pleasure steamer the river had ever seen. She went straight into daily service between Glasgow and the Arran Coast and she would have you know that she was the original *Queen Mary*. However, generous to a fault, she loaned her name to the rather larger Cunarder and with good grace became the *Queen Mary* 2. She dropped the 2 the minute the other one was sold to the States.

She was a famous sight criss-crossing the Clyde but in 1977 she was reluctantly retired. The breakers yard loomed but happily Bass stepped in. The old girl was given a £2 million refit in Chatham Docks and started a new life in the Thames.

So there she is with three public bars, all with a marvellous river views, particularly the one on the top deck. The wardroom bar is the smart one with big banquettes and widely spaced tables. The Thames bar has discos twice a week there and attracts a younger crowd. All three are supplied with beer from the tender moored alongside.

There is a good carvery and everything moves gently the while, rising and falling with the tides and rocking just a bit whenever the river police speed by. 'They do it on purpose,' says the Queen Mary, not really minding. The Thames is a millpond compared to the Clyde.

OPEN: Mon-Sun. **HOURS:** 11.00am-11.00pm (12.00-3.00pm and 7.00-10.30pm Sun). **CLOSED:** Bank holidays, Christmas. **CREDIT CARDS ACCEPTED:** All major cards except Diner's Club and Switch. **BAR FOOD AVAILABLE:** 12.00-6.00pm. **RESTAURANT FOOD AVAILABLE:** 6.00-9.00pm (6.00-10.00pm Fri). **SET PRICE DINNER:** £12.95. Tables outside seat 50. Private room seats 150. **BEERS AVAILABLE:** Worthington, Charrington variants, Carling Black Label, Tennent's Extra. **NEAREST TUBE STATION:** Embankment.

The Queens

216

49 Regents Park Road, NW1 **071-586 0408**

'"Kingsley bin in?"'

From my man on Primrose Hill comes this report:

'"Kingsley bin in?" You might well ask. This is his local though they don't bruit that about at the Queens. Kingsley – Sir Kingsley Amis that is – is quite often in the Queens and once wrote an article about it for the *New York Times*.

'It is a pleasantly situated house. On one side rises Primrose Hill with its trees, paths and walking people. On another its own brown Young's Brewery livery gives way to the yellows and pinks of the towny-pastoral Regents Park Road.

'The Queens stands on a corner at the very heart of Primrose Hill village, home over the years to writers, actors, musicians, artists, and, in more recent times, environmentally friendly shop people. Robert Stephens gets in. Denis Quilley has a drink here. So do Gayle

Hunnicutt, Simon Jenkins, Robert Plant of Led Zeppelin...

'Nine out of ten of the 170 or so Young's pubs in and around London play no music. So it is with the Queens. This does not dissuade young hearties from piling in after cricket, softball or whatever on the hill. It can get very busy.

'Manager Dave Williams looks on his domain as a place to which sensible older people resort. So Sir Kingsley is well suited.'

OPEN: Mon-Sun. **HOURS:** 11.00am-3.00pm and 5.00-11.00pm Mon-Fri; 11.00am-11.00pm Sat; 12.00-3.00pm and 7.00-10.30pm Sun. **CREDIT CARDS** Accepted: All major cards. **BAR FOOD AVAILABLE:** 11.30am-2.30pm. **SET PRICE SUN LUNCH:** £6.50. Wheelchair access (but not lavatory). Tables outside seat 18. Private room seats 45. **BEERS AVAILABLE:** Young's Bitter, Young's Special, Young's Oatmeal Stout, Young's Premium Lager, Young's London Lager, Tennent's Extra, Red Stripe, Castlemaine, Guinness. **NEAREST TUBE STATION:** Chalk Farm.

The Queen's Arms 217

94 Draycott Avenue, SW3 **071-589 4981**

'Slap bang in the centre'

A chap I know in these parts told me all about the Queen's Arms Tavern. 'It is a pool table with a pub round it,' he said.

The pool table is slap bang in the centre of the bar which also has gaming machines, a jukebox, a satellite TV, and a sort of dart-board snug. Scottish and Newcastle haven't had it for long. They mean to do it up a bit some time...

OPEN: Mon-Sun. **HOURS:** 12.00-11.00pm (12.00-3.00pm and 7.00-10.00pm Sun). **CLOSED:** Christmas Day. **CREDIT CARDS ACCEPTED:** All major cards except AmEx. **BAR FOOD AVAILABLE:** 12.00-10.00pm. Wheelchair access (but not lavatory). Tables outside seat 20. **BEERS AVAILABLE:** Courage Best, Courage Directors, John Smith's, Foster's, Budweiser, Holsten, Carlsberg, Guinness. **NEAREST TUBE STATION:** South Kensington. **MAP REF:** 2, D/3

The Railway Tavern 218

15 Liverpool Street, EC2 **071-283 3598**

'The grand Railway Tavern of the main-line terminus'

Is there a self-respecting town in all the land that does not have a Railway Tavern? London has eighteen. This and the one that follows can stand for them all.

First the grand Railway Tavern of the main-line terminus. This one is opposite Liverpool Street, a big, impressive high-ceilinged bar with a roomy games room upstairs – dartboards, pool table, fruit machines, jukebox and pizzas to eat here or take away. There is also a small wine bar, its two floors linked by a spiral staircase.

Service is swift and efficient. The staff know well that customers have either a job to go to or a train to catch.

This Railway Tavern has been so much a part of Liverpool Street station for so many years that it has become known as Platform 19. 'Meet you on Platform 19,' older commuters say. Liverpool Street, you will gather, has 18 platforms.

OPEN: Mon-Fri. **HOURS:** 11.00am-11.00pm. **CLOSED:** Christmas Day, Boxing Day. **CREDIT CARDS ACCEPTED:** All major cards. **BAR FOOD AVAILABLE:** 11.00am-3.30pm. **RESTAURANT FOOD AVAILABLE:** 11.00am-10.00pm. Private room seats 120. **BEERS AVAILABLE:** Boddingtons, Heineken, Stella Artois. **NEAREST TUBE STATION:** Liverpool Street.

The Railway Tavern

219

18 Clapham High Street, SW4 **071-622 1696**

'A Railway Tavern's Railway Tavern'

Here in Clapham High Street we have the classic local Railway Tavern, to be found wherever railways run. It has everything one asks from Railway Taverns. Firstly a railway station, in this case Clapham High Street. Secondly a railway bridge. Road traffic belts past in front and trains rollick by at the side and inside there's a jukebox, fruit machines, Sky TV . . .

The lunchtime ham and eggs get good marks in this one, as do the draught Bass and Charrington IPA. There is darts in the bar and pool upstairs. Long-lost station name signs are nailed securely to the wall: Lydd Town. Durham. Baker Street. Has Lydd Town station noticed?

Everyone smokes non-stop in Railway Taverns. In Clapham High Street a prewar fug starts building up in the morning and can be sliced and gift-wrapped by the middle of the evening. No one minds. Quite the contrary. It is, in short, a Railway Tavern's Railway Tavern.

OPEN: Mon-Sun. **HOURS:** 11.00am-11.00pm (12.00-3.00pm and 7.00-10.30pm Sun). **BAR FOOD AVAILABLE:** Lunchtimes Mon-Sat. **BEERS AVAILABLE:** Draft Bass, Charrington IPA, a guest beer. **NEAREST TUBE STATION:** Clapham Common.

The Raj

220

40 Holland Park Ave, W11 **071-727 6332**

'Traces of each passing civilization can be found'

For most of its life this big Victorian public house was the Mitre, a good-looking red-brick Victorian pub devoting itself, I have no doubt, to good works and the prosperous stucco villas around it. A decade or so ago it got a radical going over. It briefly closed and reopened as the Raj, one of the early theme pubs. Nostalgia for British India, that was the theme and the big lounge at the back became an Indian restaurant.

Alas, it was not the hit that had been expected so out went British India, the restaurant, the gazebo and the Indian waiters, in came pool tables, arcade games, a jukebox permanently on, Sky TV never off.

Traces of each passing civilization can be found. Portland stone mitres from its days as the Mitre decorate the roof. Framed 70-year-old gossip about Sir Hari Singh hangs in the bar.

The day belongs to pool, though. While the jukebox competes with Sky TV the five pool tables are in constant use and the two bars, a short flight of steps between them, get packed as the week wears on.

The Raj seems due for a new name again, the Cue Ball? The Inn Off the Black? In the meantime its customers may find reassurance in the large handwritten poster pinned behind the bar counter. It bears an existential message: I Drink Therefore I Am.

OPEN: Mon-Sun. **HOURS:** 12.00-11.00pm (12.00-3.00 and 7.00-10.30 Sun). **CLOSED:** Christmas Day. **CREDIT CARDS ACCEPTED:** None. Wheelchair access. Tables outside seat 36. **BEERS AVAILABLE:** Carlsberg, Holsten, Budweiser, Foster's, Becks, John Smith's, Courage Directors. **NEAREST TUBE STATIONS:** Holland Park. **MAP REF:** 3, B/1

The Ram

221

34 High Street,
Kingston

081-546 4518

'Dark and traditional'

A plain, comfortable Victorian beer house, dark and traditional, with a conservatory and a long paved garden leading down to the river. This is a pleasant spot to watch the Thames go by on summer afternoons.

OPEN: Mon-Sun. **HOURS:** 11.00am-11.00pm (12.00-2.30pm and 7.00-10.30pm Sun). **CLOSED:** Christmas Day. **CREDIT CARDS ACCEPTED:** All major cards. **BAR FOOD AVAILABLE:** 12.00-2.30pm. Beer garden seats 70. **BEERS AVAILABLE:** Theakston, Courage Best, Courage Directors, Holsten, Foster's, Kronenbourg, Guinness. **NEAREST BR STATION:** Kingston.

The Rat and Parrot

222

24 Tavistock Street, WC2

071-497 2796

'Loud music and bottled beer'

There are a number of Rat and Parrots. There's a rather rakish one in Kensington Church Street, a lively one in Putney High Street, a smart one in Earls Court Road. This one is the noisy, boozy one. It is, in the judgement of at least one observer, one of the noisiest, booziest pubs in London. The observer I have in mind is the manager.

To look at it now you'd think it had always been a pub but actually it found its true vocation late in life. For its first 100 or so years this Rat and Parrot was part of Covent Garden market. It was a warehouse, long and narrow, crammed with cut flowers, open at Tavistock Street at one end and Exeter Street at the other. Latterly Joe Allen's was underneath.

Chef and Brewer made it into a pub in the late Eighties and there's still quite a lot of the warehouse left. The stout wooden floor, the heavy double doors, the black metal windows and the obligatory warehouse ramp could hardly be improved upon Rat and Parrotwise . . .

The week starts quietly in Tavistock Street as a rule but it rapidly gains momentum and is soon rocketing towards Friday, THE day of the Rat and Parrot week. On Friday nights the place heaves with people, all the seating removed, impatient queues outside, strong men at the door and music at full blast.

The scrum has two things in mind, to reach the bar and to meet the immediate just-glimpsed object of their desire. Most manage these feats repeatedly. The drink is bottled lager from the bottle or the glass and landlord Gordon Inglis likes to see his customers enjoying themselves. 'We give them a bit of leeway here,' he says. 'If someone wants to dance and scream and shout we let them do it. Everyone else is here to do the same thing.'

There's food but just at lunchtime. People don't come here to eat though they might go for a bowl of chips at £1.50. Melted cheese or chilli on top is extra.

OPEN: Mon-Sun. **HOURS:** 11.00am-11.00pm (12.00-3.00pm and 7.00-10.30pm Sun). **CLOSED:** New Year's Day. **CREDIT CARDS ACCEPTED:** All major cards. **BAR FOOD AVAILABLE:** 12.00-3.00pm. Wheelchair access (but not lavatory). **BEERS AVAILABLE:** Theakston, Courage Best, Courage Directors, John Smith's, Heineken, Foster's, Kronenbourg, Guinness. **NEAREST TUBE STATION:** Covent Garden. **MAP REF:** 1, F/1

The Red Lion

223

Duke of York Street, SW1 **071-930 2030**

'Flower girls would offer their services for 2d a time'

This is the most glittering of Red Lions. On all sides brilliant-cut and bevelled glass flashes and sparkles. It is a real star, a small Victorian gin palace of a most superior kind, almost totally unspoiled. 'Uncommonly well preserved,' wrote Sir Nikolaus Pevsner. That was high praise from him.

Did I mention it was small? It is small. There is just 300 square feet of it, not a lot. In summer it spills onto the pavement but the rest of the year sees Londoners reverting to one of their most profoundly held beliefs: there's always room for one more inside.

Mr Michael Browne, who has run the pub for ten years, likes to see it really full. He will tell you that he sells more beer per square foot than any other Ind Coope pub, indeed, he says, he sells more real ale per square foot than any other pub in Piccadilly. That's good going.

In its bohemian past Jermyn Street flower girls would offer their services for 2d a time in the private bar. The Red Lion, robbed of its private bar, is the height of respectability these days and you see unexpected people pushing through the crush. Clint Eastwood. Andrew Lloyd Webber. Mr Lloyd Webber is said to like it because there is never any music of any sort.

You can eat here too. Well, you can get a sandwich. There's not room for much else.

OPEN: Mon-Sat. **HOURS:** 12.00-11.00pm. **CLOSED:** Bank holidays. **CREDIT CARDS ACCEPTED:** None. **BAR FOOD AVAILABLE:** 12.00-2.30pm. Wheelchair access. **BEERS AVAILABLE:** Tetley, Burton, Greene King, Nicholson's, Bass. **NEAREST TUBE STATION:** Piccadilly Circus.

MAP REF: 1, D/1

The Red Lion

224

318 High Street, Brentford **081-560 6181**

'The pub doesn't open at all during the day'

In 1967 the Red Lion, Brentford, was just two years old, not just a new pub, a new kind of pub. The *Evening Standard* at the time described it as a socko, roll-em-in-the-aisles, top-of-the-pops fun palace and most controversially announced that this was its first-ever Pub of the Year.

It divided the judges like nothing has since. We had seen some lovely old pubs and here was this young, noisy, uppity pub where you could hardly move and couldn't hear yourself speak. There were two live bands every night, Country and Western in one bar, rock 'n' roll in another and the cocktail bar upstairs was linked to the saloon bar by closed circuit television. That wasn't all. 'When groups aren't playing,' I wrote in surprised tones, 'gramophone records are.'

We also took note of the food counter, a model of speedy service. Customers moved along it with plates, being given bits of this and bits of that. 'It's like the army,' said the manager happily, 'only better.'

Then 26 years passed and I went back.

It looks, I have to say, a bit grim. Graffiti on the cement rendering. Heavy curtains drawn all day. Posters stuck in every pane of glass all advertising the bands that would be playing that week: the Boogie Brothers, Stiff Pilchards, Road Runner, Sally's Slightly Smaller Than Usual Hat. 'Every Saturday It's 8.30 'til Late Rock Party', declares a banner across the front.

The house style now is rockin' blues, pop and indie and the music is so all-consuming that the pub doesn't open at all during the day. It doesn't bother with food either. Only one bar remains, the original saloon bar, and this opens at 6.30. The music room opens at 9pm and the bands are on until midnight or 1am. You pay to get in, how much depends on the night and who is on.

So the Red Lion is still moving along. No one will believe it used to have a cocktail bar.

OPEN: Mon-Sun. **HOURS:** 6.30pm to late (12.00-2.00pm and 7.30-10.30pm Sun). **BEERS AVAILABLE:** London Pride, Chiswick, draught and bottled lagers. **NEAREST BR STATION:** Brentford.

The Red Lion

225

1 Waverton Street, W1 **071-499 1307**

'Totally gentrified'

There's a proud pride of Red Lions in London, at least 24 of them, but socially this is surely the one that has done best. It is the Mayfair Red Lion and it is very smart these days. To see it now with its quiet restaurant, its old prints, its panelled walls and its well-heeled regulars it is hard to imagine the rough boozer it was.

In those days – it is the 17th century we are talking about now – it stood on a muddy unmade road just by the boundary of Chesterfield House, lordly seat of the earls of Chesterfield. Its customers were toughs from the notorious May Fair, street traders from Shepherds Market, grooms from the big house. Then the workmen building Berkeley Square, Hill Street and Chorley Street made it their own. That was a step up all right and, as the exclusive Mayfair of the 19th century took shape, it became the favoured pub of the great army of domestic servants that kept the place going.

Now, of course, the basements they worked in and the attics they slept in are expensive Mayfair apartments and it is the occupants of these who fill today's totally gentrified Red Lion with a hum of quiet conversation.

It is a charming pub. 'Quite unspoiled,' people say. That's not it. Vastly improved is what it is. In winter the seats to get are the winged settles near the fire. In the summer people crowd the forecourt.

Chesterfield House was demolished in 1937. Its low-life neighbour it was that survived.

OPEN: Mon-Sun. **HOURS:** 11.00am-11.00pm (11.00am-3.00pm and 6.00-11.00pm Sat; 12.00-3.00pm and 7.00-10.30pm Sun). **CLOSED:** Christmas Day, Boxing Day. **CREDIT CARDS ACCEPTED:** All major cards. **BAR AND RESTAURANT FOOD AVAILABLE:** 12.00-3.00pm and 6.00-10.00pm. (restaurant closed Sat lunch). **SET PRICE LUNCH:** £15.95. Wheelchair access. **BEERS AVAILABLE:** Theakston, Greene King IPA, Flowers IPA, Abbot Ale, Courage Best, Courage Directors, Wadworth, Foster's, Holsten, Kronenbourg. **NEAREST TUBE STATION:** Green Park. **MAP REF:** 1, B/2

The Red Lion

226

23 Crown Passage, SW1 **071-930 4141**

'Every bit as old as it seems'

Crown Passage is a narrow alley just opposite St James's Palace. It is lined with useful little shops. Some go up it for the ironmonger, the cobbler or the tobacconist, others use it as a short cut from Pall Mall to King Street. Quite a few never get past the Red Lion.

This tiny black timber-fronted pub with its leaded glass windows, hanging baskets and antique lanterns looks too picturesque to be true but it is every bit as old as it seems. It has been there for more than 400 years, has the second oldest beer licence in London and is still very much in business.

The small, panelled bar, open all day, fills up quickly at lunchtime and again when people finish work, though there are always customers whatever the time of day.

There is a small pleasant room upstairs that seats 20 people and serves good plain pub food and on the last Saturday of every January the pub is packed with splendidly attired Cavaliers. They come together to mark the execution of their hero, King Charles I, on 30 January 1649. This is an event the Red Lion remembers well but it is with King Charles II that it is most closely associated. He lived in St James's Palace over the road and his lively mistress Nell Gwynne lived round the corner at 79 Pall Mall. Some discretion seemed appropriate so Nell would slip into the Red Lion, go down the cellar steps and through a tunnel – or so the story goes. At the other end the King would be waiting.

If it's not too busy the young landlord gives interested customers a tour of what is now called Nell Gwynne's cellar. It is worth having a look. That blocked-up arch. It could be the start of a tunnel. It IS the start of a tunnel says the landlord and everyone has the same thought.

Nowadays that tunnel would have had the King and pretty Nell on all the front pages.

OPEN: Mon-Sat. **HOURS:** 11.00am-11.00pm (11.00am-4.00pm Sat). **CLOSED:** Bank holidays. **CREDIT CARDS ACCEPTED:** Visa, Access. **BAR AND RESTAURANT FOOD AVAILABLE:** 12.00-2.30pm. Wheelchair access (but not lavatory). Tables outside seat 8. Private room seats 25. **BEERS AVAILABLE:** Old Speckled Hen, London Pride, Wadworth, Marston's Pedigree, Webster's, Kronenbourg, Carlsberg, Foster's. **NEAREST TUBE STATION:** Green Park. **MAP REF:** 1, C/1

The Red Lion

227

48 Parliament Street, SW1 **071-930 5826**

'Nervously visited by Charles Dickens when he was only eleven'

Of all the Red Lions this one lies nearest to the corridors of power. Around it are great ministries of state. Across the road is the Prime Minister. Round the corner are the Houses of Parliament themselves.

It is a very handsome pub indeed, eclectic Flemish baroque as you can see, a Grade II listed building, very classy pub and historical. The original Red Lion was built on this site in 1733, a similar pub actually, nervously visited by Charles Dickens when he was only eleven. The adventure appears in *David Copperfield*. 'What is your best – your VERY best – ale a glass?' 'Twopence-halfpenny,' says the landlord, 'is the price of the Genuine stunning ale.' 'Then,' says I, producing the money, 'just draw me a glass of the Genuine Stunning if you please . . .'

They pulled this Red Lion down in 1899 during the great pub boom and built a new one, this one, in its place, the very latest in pubs, no cost spared. It has changed hardly at all since then. Most of the original fittings are still in place and it's pretty well full all day, the bar walls covered in drawings, cartoons and photographs of famous politicians, mostly long departed.

There's a nice old-fashioned dining room upstairs with old-fashioned English food and a comfortable cellar bar where the Parachute Regiment has reunions. It was much liked by demonstrating miners and the pit banners they presented to the pub are now part of its history.

OPEN: Mon-Sun. **HOURS:** 11.00am-11.00pm (12.00-3.00pm and 7.00-10.30pm). **CLOSED:** Christmas Day. **CREDIT CARDS ACCEPTED:** All major cards, except AmEx and Diner's Club. **BAR FOOD AVAILABLE:** 11.00am-3.00pm. **RESTAURANT FOOD AVAILABLE:** 12.00-2.45pm. Wheelchair access (but not lavatory). Tables outside seat 70. Private room seats 35. **BEERS AVAILABLE:** Tapsters Choice, Tetley, Burton, Carlsberg, Lowenbrau, Castlemaine, Oranjeboom. **NEAREST TUBE STATION:** Westminster.

MAP REF: 8, D/1

The Ring

228

72 Blackfriars Road, SE1 **071-928 2589**

'Bombadier Billy Wells, Seaman Tommy Watson, the great Tommy Farr'

Photographs of boxers, chins in, fists up, cover the walls of this small, serious boxers' pub – Bombadier Billy Wells, Seaman Tommy Watson, the great Tommy Farr. Ben Foord waves from the train, Jack Doyle, boxer, singer, movie star, shakes hands with Len Harvey and in the bar old fighters gather and the talk is all of boxing then and now.

The Ring is run by Neville Axford, one-time army champion, 25 professional fights and still in the game. He's a coach now with young boxers in training. They work in the gym over the bar, no frills up there, a ring, some well-used punchbags and young hopefuls toiling and pummelling.

From the gym windows you can see the corner of the crossroads where the Blackfriars Ring once stood. London's Premier Arena said the posters, turbulent centre of boxing said the papers of the day. It was run for 25 years by Bella Burge, the world's only woman boxing promoter, but it was reduced to rubble in an air raid in 1940 and after the war an office block, Orbit House, replaced it.

It has been useful. The British Library keeps its Oriental and India Office collections there. But it's not the same, somehow.

OPEN: Mon-Sun. **HOURS:** 11.00am-11.00pm Mon-Fri; 11.00am-3.00pm and 7.00-11.00 Sat; 12.00-3.00pm and 7.00-10.30pm Sun. **CREDIT CARDS ACCEPTED:** None. **BAR FOOD AVAILABLE:** 12.00-3.00pm. Wheelchair access (but not lavatory). **BEERS AVAILABLE:** Tetley, Burtons, John Smith's, Castlemaine, Carlsberg, Kronenbourg, Guinness. **NEAREST BR STATION:** Waterloo.

MAP REF: 7, C/2

The Rising Sun

229

38 Cloth Fair, EC1 **071-726 6671**

'A rapscallionly youth'

This old Smithfield pub used to be picturesque to the point of almost falling over. Now it is very chipper, having been given a thorough going-over by Samuel Smith, the Yorkshire brewers.

The general feeling in the bar is now modishly Victorian, beefed up with non-stop music and flashing fruit machines. There is a quieter room above where you can have lunch. You feel you could almost touch St-Bartholomew-the-Great, the oldest church in the City outside the Tower, from the upstairs windows.

The Rising Sun had a rapscallionly youth with bodysnatchers slipping laudanum into drinks at the bar. This would not be allowed today. Nothing is allowed to spoil Sam Smith's good beer.

OPEN: Mon-Sun. **HOURS:** 11.30am-11.00pm (12.00-3.00pm and 7.00-10.30pm Sun). **CLOSED:** Christmas Day and Boxing Day. **CREDIT CARDS ACCEPTED:** Visa, Access. **BAR FOOD AVAILABLE:** 12.00-2.30pm Mon-Sun; 5.30-9.00pm Mon-Fri. **SET PRICE LUNCH:** £3.95. **SET PRICE DINNER:** £5.50. No smoking area. Wheelchair access (but not lavatory). Private room seats 50. **BEERS AVAILABLE:** All Sam Smith variants, Taddy Porter Stout, Oatmeal Stout, Natural Lager, Old Brewery Bitter, Museum Ale. **NEAREST TUBE STATION:** ST Paul's.
MAP REF: 6, B/2

The Rising Sun

230

46 Tottenham Court Road, W1 **071-636 6530**

'A bartizan is an overhanging turret. The Rising Sun has two of these'

Next time you are in Tottenham Court Road, you are bound to be there some time, have a look at the Rising Sun. It is just getting over a rather uncomfortable experience but it is, as you will see, a most remarkable pub.

It was designed by Treadwell and Martin, Victorian architects who are increasingly admired. The Rising Sun is said to be their masterpiece. The style is elaborate art nouveau Gothic and architectural critics speak with admiration of its delicate mouldings and cupids' heads, its rising suns, decorative gables and elegant bartizans. A bartizan is an overhanging turret. The Rising Sun has two.

In the early Eighties the owners of the day made what seems to be a bizarre decision. They changed its name to the Presley as in Elvis, lowered the ceiling by about two yards, anointed the walls with pictures of Elvis and turned it into a rock 'n' roll bozo.

It was an eccentric interlude which the next owners, Scottish and Newcastle, speedily put behind them. Earlier this year they closed the Presley for two months. When it reopened in May it was the Rising Sun again. Or almost. Treadwell and Martin would be pleased with the outside, carefully restored and painted cream, but very little was left of the once-luxuriant Victorian fittings inside and the designers started more or less from scratch. It is what is described as the Ale House Concept now which here, as elsewhere, means bare boards and a generous roster of real ales and speedy pies.

So that is the good news from this generally ill-favoured thoroughfare. Outside, a minor masterpiece rescued. Inside, well, at least the ceiling is back where it belongs.

OPEN: Mon-Sun. **HOURS:** 11.00am-11.00pm (12.00-3.00pm and 7.00-10.30pm Sun). **CLOSED:** Christmas Day, New Year's Day. **CREDIT CARDS ACCEPTED:** Mastercard, Visa. **BAR FOOD AVAILABLE:** 11.00am-10.00pm. **SET PRICE LUNCH AND DINNER:** £3.95. Wheelchair access (but not lavatory). Tables outside seat 16. **BEERS AVAILABLE:** Theakston, Holsten, Carlsberg. **NEAREST TUBE STATIONS:** Tottenham Court Road, Goodge Street.
MAP REF: 1, E/3

Robert Browning

231

15 Clifton Road, W9 **071-286 2732**

'"Would this wine had washed all over that body of yours ere I drank it"'

On one of his sorties from his Yorkshire stronghold seven years ago Sam Smith bagged a down-at-heel Victorian pub called the Eagle. He refurbished it from top to toe as he does and here it is now, a glossy Sam Smith pub called the Robert Browning. Locals still call it the Eagle.

As a young man Browning lived briefly nearby overlooking the canal and he would have been astonished to hear that pictures of him and his beloved would one day cover the upstairs bar of the boisterous new pub down the way, not to mention his passionate love letters and some of the poems he wrote for her. His marriage certificate too. 'Age: of full age. Rank or Profession: Gent.'

The young licensee of the reborn Robert Browning is every bit as ardent about his pub as Robert was about Elizabeth. The main bar downstairs is where the serious drinking is but the first-floor bar is the one that has his heart. 'I can honestly say,' he says as you go upstairs, 'that this will be the best room you've ever been in in your life.' It is a nice room, the long windows, the Sam Smith button-backed leather sofas, the mahogany tables, the lamps, mirrors, portraits. I see Robert Browning here with Elizabeth and a bottle of wine. He wrote:

There you stand
Warm too and white too;
Would this wine
Had washed all over that body of yours
Ere I drank it.

Is this what goes on at the Robert Browning?

OPEN: Mon-Sun. **HOURS:** 11.00am-11.00pm (12.00-3.00pm and 7.00-10.30pm Sun). **CLOSED:** Boxing Day, New Year's Day. **CREDIT CARDS ACCEPTED:** None. **BAR FOOD AVAILABLE:** 12.00-2.30pm and 5.00-9.00pm. **SET PRICE LUNCH:** £3.45. **SET PRICE DINNER:** £4.00. Wheelchair access (but not lavatory). Tables outside seat 60. Private room seats 90. **BEERS AVAILABLE:** Old Brewery Bitter, Museum Ale, Ayingerbrau. **NEAREST TUBE STATION:** Warwick Avenue. **MAP REF:** 4, A/2

The Rose and Crown

232

55 High Street, SW19 **081-947 4713**

'It keeps its powerful appeal for generation after generation'

The Rose and Crown in Wimbledon Village is one of south London's great pubs. The *Evening Standard* Pub of the Year judges thought so and gave it the crown in 1970.

It is an old pub. Charles I still had his throne and his head when it was built and it is as pretty a pub as you could hope to find. It keeps its powerful appeal for generation after generation. In its days as a coaching inn – the London coach began and finished here – it was as popular as it is now.

Inside are old maps of Wimbledon, prints of 18th-century London and a complete set of Hogarth's 'Idle Prentice'. They add to the pub's historical feel but nothing does this more than the benign, ghostly presence of its two most famous regulars. Leigh Hunt and Swinburne were both leading figures in Bohemian London. Swinburne not only a poet but a notoriously dissipated poet. Such was the life he led, it was said, that his health had broken down. That is why he lodged at 2 The Pines, Putney, and walked across heath and common to the Rose and Crown.

Sightseers started gathering at the Rose and Crown to see the dying poet. It was a predicament as familiar then as now and he found a satisfactory solution. He simply moved his chair upstairs. The chair is still upstairs, though his table continues to do service in the bar. He lived to 72.

The bar goes on drawing crowds. It is not the stage coaches for London or celebs walking from Putney. It is, I can only suppose,

the atmosphere, the congeniality and the beer.

There is a small no-smoking area in the Rose and Crown now, a new departure that would have puzzled Swinburne, a light, comfortingly plain lounge and a buttery serving hot and cold food. At the back a conservatory leads to a little garden, paved, ivy-walled and thoroughly charming. Families recuperate here after constitutionals on the common, young lovers hopefully seek a quiet table, people read papers and chat. Poets, their health ruined by dissipation, may also take their chances.

OPEN: Mon-Sun. **HOURS:** 11.00am-11.00pm (12.00-3.00pm and 7.00-10.30pm). **CREDIT CARDS ACCEPTED:** None. **BAR FOOD AVAILABLE:** 12.00-2.30pm and 5.30-10.00pm (12.00-10.00pm Sat; no food Sun). No smoking area. Wheelchair access. Beer garden seats 100. **BEERS AVAILABLE:** Young's, Castlemaine, Tennent's Extra. **NEAREST TUBE STATION:** Wimbledon.

The Rose and Crown

233

88 High Street, N6 **081-340 6712**

'None of the old customers have been seen since'

The charitable view on this little Highgate pub used to be that it was an honest boozer. Others said rowdy boozer. A boozer, at any rate, is what it was before the arrival of Billy Hunter, 25, and his exceptionally pretty wife Dana, 23.

Billy and Dana, surely two of London's youngest licensees, had a week or two of crowds of youths noisily knocking back the lager and then, in April, the pub closed. It reopened, three and a half weeks and £78,000 later, a very different place. 'Rose and Crown' still appeared, rather small, on the fascia. 'WINE ALE AND CIDER HOUSE' appeared very large. None of the old customers have been seen since.

The Rose and Crown has become a smart, upmarket, modern tavern – six real ales on offer, fourteen wines sold by the glass, two draught ciders and an up-to-the-minute cappuccino machine on the counter. All the gaming and pinball machines are gone, also the jukebox. Now there's background music produced by a compact disc machine controlled by a computer with strong views about what should be heard when.

The new Rose and Crown opens for breakfast at 8.30am, killer English or kinder continental, and from midday onwards crudités, dips, pâtés and the like appear on the menu. Steaks too and daily specials. A patio with picnic tables is at the back.

Will Highgate like its new Wine, Ale and Cider House? Will the computer take over? Will Dana get a film contract? Watch this space.

OPEN: Mon-Sun. **HOURS:** 8.30am-11.30pm (10.00am-10.30pm Sun). **CLOSED:** Christmas Day. **CREDIT CARDS ACCEPTED:** All major cards. **BAR FOOD AVAILABLE:** 12.00-9.00pm. Wheelchair access (disabled lavatory). Tables outside seat 75. **BEERS AVAILABLE:** Old Speckled Hen, London Pride, Boddingtons, Flowers Original, Heineken, Stella Artois, Murphy's. **NEAREST TUBE STATION:** Highgate.

The Rose of York

Petersham Road,
Richmond 234

081-948 5867

'A view so beautiful it has been painted by Turner and Reynolds and thousands of times by Sunday painters'

When Samuel Smith, the Yorkshire Brewers, set its cap on London its first pub was this one. It was an old cavalry barracks which had been made into a pub called Tudor Close and Sam Smith really went to town on it. The Tudor fakery was stripped away, new cellars were excavated and a team of craftsmen from Yorkshire worked on it for sixteen months. The Rose of York emerged as from a chrysalis and almost at once became the *Evening Standard* Pub of the Year.

Fourteen years later it is still a most appealing country pub with its big comfortable bar, its good traditional food, its lovely sheltered courtyard and a view of Petersham meadows and the bend in the Thames so beautiful it has been painted by Turner and Reynolds and thousands of times by Sunday painters.

There was quite a lot of space in the old barracks and the Rose of York has been letting a few rooms for bed and breakfast as old inns used to. It has been adding to them and in November it will have nine bedrooms with en suite bathrooms. En suite bathrooms? You would have done well to get a bowl and a jug of hot water in the old inns of England.

OPEN: Mon-Sun. **HOURS:** 11.00am-11.00pm (12.00-3.30pm and 7.00-10.30pm Sun). **CLOSED:** Christmas Day, Boxing Day. **CREDIT CARDS ACCEPTED:** All major cards except AmEx. **BAR FOOD AVAILABLE:** 12.00-3.00pm and 6.30-9.30pm (12.00-3.30pm Sun). **SET PRICE LUNCH:** £4.30 (Sun only). No smoking area. Wheelchair access. Beer garden seats 150. **BEERS AVAILABLE:** All Samuel Smith variants, including Old Brewery, Museum Ale, Ayingerbrau. **NEAREST TUBE STATION:** Richmond.

The Round House

235

1 Garrick Street, WC2

071-836 9838

'A thorough going-over'

The Round House, the substantial Victorian pub on the corner of Garrick Street, recently turned over a new leaf. It was, how shall I put this, rather rough but the new owners hope it now has a whole new personality.

Scottish and Newcastle, for it is they, closed it, gave it a thorough going-over and reopened it as the first of their new real ale houses. This meant an entirely new interior, a nice wooden floor, plain wooden furniture and pies with puff pastry tops floating up from the kitchen.

A wide sweep of pavement outside the front door is a compelling invitation to drink al fresco, which customers of all kinds love to do. The police say no drinking outside on pain of your licence. So the occasional Friday night doormen have two tasks – one to keep lager louts out, the other to keep real ale drinkers in.

A potted history on the front has a bold theory about the name. It wascalled the Round House, it says, because of its shape. But it isn't round. It is elbow-shaped. It should be called the Elbow.

Please note: THIS is the pub. The Garrick Club is further down.

OPEN: Mon-Sun. **HOURS:** 11.00am-11.00pm (12.00-3.00pm and 7.00-10.30pm Sun). **CREDIT CARDS ACCEPTED:** None. **BAR FOOD AVAILABLE:** 12.00-4.00pm. **AVERAGE COST:** £5.00. Wheelchair access (but not lavatory). **BEERS AVAILABLE:** Theakston Best, Theakston Old Peculier, Marstons Pedigree, Younger's IPA, Becks, McEwans, Guinness. **NEAREST TUBE STATIONS:** Leicester Square, Covent Garden. **MAP REF:** 1E/1

The Round Table

236

St Martin's Court, WC2 **071-836 6436**

'A doorman to discourage such horsy fighting men as may pass by'

St Martin's Court, the little pedestrians-only cut between St Martin's Lane and Charing Cross Road, has old book shops, the restaurant and oyster bar Sheekey's, the stage doors of the Albery and Wyndham's and this extremely pleasant Victorian pub.

There is a history of it on the outside wall, rather rumbustious apparently. These parts were the resort of 'horsy and fighting men' and prize fights were arranged in local taverns. The original Round Table put up the American champion John C Heenan to contest the belt with the valiant Tom Sayers. It doesn't say who won.

However those days ended with the Queensberry Rules and the Round Table, rebuilt in 1877, became more theatrical than sporting. So it is today. It is a civil, good-looking pub with downstairs and upstairs bars, both very busy at times and the landlord, Norman Gregory from Manchester, uses a doorman to discourage such horsy fighting men as may pass by.

It has become known for its cask ales. Big blackboards have lists of the guest beers coming soon and serious beer drinkers can have two-pint or four-pint jugs. It is a very good place to eat too. The pies come complete with layers of potato and vegetables under a flaky pastry crust. They are very good pies.

OPEN: Mon-Sun. **HOURS:** 11.00am-11.00pm (12.00-3.00pm and 7.00-10.30pm Sun). **CLOSED:** Christmas Day. **CREDIT CARDS ACCEPTED:** None. **BAR FOOD AVAILABLE:** 12.00-4.00pm and 6.00-8.30pm (12.00-2.30pm and 7.00-8.30pm Sun). Wheelchair access (but not lavatory). Beer garden seats 30. Private room seats 40. **BEERS AVAILABLE:** Theakston, Theakston Old Peculier, Young's, Flowers IPA, Marston's Pedigree, Bulmer's, Belgian Trappist beers, Becks, McEwans. **NEAREST TUBE STATION:** Leicester Square.

MAP REF: 1, E/1

The Running Footman

237

5 Charles Street, W1 **071-499 2988**

'The pub sign shows a running footman. He seems most unsuitably dressed'

This interesting Mayfair pub, properly called I Am the Only Running Footman, commemorates a job no longer on offer in the Job Centres of the nation. In the 18th century seriously grand persons employed footmen to run before their carriages, lighting the way, paying tolls, preventing collisions and generally showing what fine fellows their masters were. The running footmen and indeed footmen of all kinds met here. It was originally the Running Horse, renamed by the fourth Duke of Queensberry, the one they called Old Q. He was infamous for his shameless debaucheries and he was a great swell. A footman always ran ahead of *him*.

The new name has served the pub well for 200 years and it still brings people in. The pub itself is totally changed. It was almost entirely rebuilt in the 1930s, but it looks as old as you could wish with its dark panelling and bottle-glass windows. Tourists love it.

The pub sign shows a running footman, of course. He seems most unsuitably dressed. He wears a powdered wig, a feathered hat, knee breeches and buckled shoes. The running footman in the big painting inside is even more encumbered. He carries a tall cane topped with a silver ball containing a little something to keep him going and blows a horn as he lopes along. The painting used to be over the fireplace in the saloon bar but you could easily miss it now. In the last redecoration they stuck it on the ceiling.

OPEN: Mon-Sun. **HOURS:** 11.30am-11.00pm Mon-Fri; 6.00-11.00pm Sat; 12.00-3.00pm and 7.00-10.30pm Sun. **CLOSED:** All bank holidays. **CREDIT CARDS ACCEPTED:** All major cards. **RESTAURANT FOOD AVAILABLE:** 11.00am-3.00pm and 6.00-9.30pm Mon-Fri; 6.00-9.30pm Sat; 7.00-9.30pm Sun. **AVERAGE COST:** £10.50. Wheelchair access (but not lavatory). Tables outside seat 20. Private room seats 20. **BEERS AVAILABLE:** Courage Best, Courage Directors, John Smith's, Theakston Best, Foster's, Kronenbourg, Holsten, Budweiser, Guinness. **NEAREST TUBE STATION:** Green Park.

MAP REF: 1, B/2

The Rutland

238

Lower Mall, W6 **081-748 5586**

'Oriel College, Oxford, bagged the balcony...'

The Rutland, a big lively pub on Hammersmith's riverside, was an early recruit to the olde English ale house look. It has been bare boards and ancient timbers for years and more changes are on their way.

A new staircase – it will look a very old staircase – will bring the first floor function room into the pub. This has three big French windows opening onto a fine balcony running the full width of the building so this is quite a prize for a pub that gets as crowded as the Rutland does. It is particularly popular on sunny days when all the doors open wide and local office workers flock to the tables outside.

Like all five pubs along this short stretch of river it does brilliantly on boat race days. This is just halfway along the course and the crowds are prodigious. The police estimated 25,000 people packed the riverside at Hammerside this year to watch the boats flash by. Oriel College, Oxford, bagged the balcony with its incomparable view and the Rutland, allowed a marquee for the first time to ease the crush, sold more beer in one day than ever before. Plastic glasses only.

OPEN: Mon-Sun. **HOURS:** 11.00am-11.00pm (12.00-3.00pm and 7.00-10.30pm Sun). **CLOSED:** Christmas Day. **CREDIT CARDS ACCEPTED:** All major cards. **RESTAURANT FOOD AVAILABLE:** 12.00-8.00pm. Wheelchair access. Tables outside seat 200. Private room seats 100. **BEERS AVAILABLE:** Budweiser, Holsten, Foster's, Theakston, Wadworth, Courage Best, Guinness. **NEAREST TUBE STATION:** Hammersmith.

The Salisbury

239

90 St Martin's Lane, WC2 **071-836 5863**

'A path to the bar mysteriously opens before you when the need is greatest'

The Salisbury is sometimes said to be the most beautifully preserved Victorian public house in London. It certainly has lovely windows, brilliant-cut, acid-etched, delicately engraved, and Nikolaus Pevsner admired its lincrusta ceiling, the art nouveau bronze figures of alluring maidens, the flower stalks and flowers out of which electric bulbs grew.

You have to go early to get a proper look at this famous pub as it is packed to the doors a lot of the time. Every evening and often lunchtimes too doormen check who comes in and on occasion who goes out, an anti riff-raff move apparently.

The surprising thing is that anyone can get a drink at all in a pub so popular and so populated. In the thick of the crush, however, with theatre and theatregoers talking ten to the dozen all round you, a path to the bar mysteriously opens before you when the need is greatest.

Some very patient customers actually find seats. Curved banquettes form shallow niches with copper-topped tables, one of the bronze figures Pevsner liked between each, but most people accept that in the Salisbury you stand.

Should you by miraculous osmosis emerge at the far end of the big main salon you may find yourself in a rather dull room often partitioned off for private parties. There is also an excellent little theatre bar with a door onto St Martin's Court.

The Salisbury has had various owners since the third Marquess of Salisbury sold the lease in 1892. He was usually prime minister but not then actually. It is his face on the pub's inn sign.

The Salisbury is now owned by Scottish and Newcastle who got it and 1,653 other pubs when they did the famous deal with Chef and

Brewer last year. This means you can get Newcastle Brown Ale in the Salisbury, something no one thought they would live to see.

OPEN: Mon-Sun. **HOURS:** 11.00am-11.00pm (12.00-3.00pm and 7.00-10.30pm Sun). **CREDIT CARDS ACCEPTED:** All major cards. **BAR FOOD AVAILABLE:** 12.00-7.30pm. No smoking area. Wheelchair access (but not lavatory). Tables outside seat 32. Private room seats 26. **BEERS AVAILABLE:** Theakston, Tetley, Burton Ale, Carlsberg, Skol, Castlemaine, Lowenbrau. **NEAREST TUBE STATION:** Leicester Square. **MAP REF:** 1, E/1

The Salutation Inn

240

154 King Street, W6 **081-748 2365**

'The Queen Mother pulled a few pints'

Walk far enough along King Street in Hammersmith and you will come to this agreeable pub. Old coaching inn, rebuilt 1909, listed building. Go in. I think it will surprise you.

The bar is all right. It is a very nice bar and the home-cooked meals are good and I expect you'll like the conservatory but what is so unexpected is what lies beyond. It is a beautiful walled garden, colourful, tranquil, immaculate, the perfect place for a quiet bosky drink on a warm afternoon away from the workaday reality of Hammersmith.

It has earned the Salutation Inn umpteen accolades. It has been Fuller's Garden of the Year seven times and has won London in Bloom contests time and again. So much admired is this garden that the Queen Mother, patron of the Horticultural Society, came to see it in 1989, congratulated everyone in sight and pulled a few pints.

As I write, though, the garden is closed. The only way out was through the pub. A fire risk said the Fire Officer.

There was much gloom in the Salutation but they have a solution now. Fuller's have bought a strip of the property next door, just enough to give the garden an entrance of its own. The Salutation breathes again.

OPEN: Mon-Sun. **HOURS:** 11.00am-11.00pm (12.00-3.00pm and 7.00-10.30pm Sun). **CREDIT CARDS ACCEPTED:** None. **BAR FOOD AVAILABLE:** 12.00-2.00pm. Wheelchair access. Beer garden seats 40. **BEERS AVAILABLE:** All Fuller's variants. **NEAREST TUBE STATIONS:** Ravenscourt Park, Hammersmith.

Sawyers Ale House

241

8-9 London Street, W2 **071-723 0685**

'Nook upon nook and cranny upon cranny'

Sawyers, if you wondered, are persons who saw timber. Two such are engaged in doing this on the inn-sign of this remarkable pub which has clearly kept an army of sawyers fully engaged. Floors, walls, ceilings, partitions, steps, stairs, half-landings, whole landings, galleries, nooks upon nook and cranny upon cranny, chairs, stools, benches, tables, everything is sawn timber in the Sawyers Ale House.

You never saw a pub that provided so many different places to sit, all wood, every inch. Even the decorations are made of wood – barrels, crates piled high, an old hand plough hanging from the ceiling.

Paddington Station is just down the road. If you miss your train have a look at the Sawyers.

OPEN: Mon-Sun. **HOURS:** 11.00am-11.00pm (12.00-3.00pm and 7.00-10.30pm Sun). **CREDIT CARDS ACCEPTED:** All major cards except AmEx. **BAR FOOD AVAILABLE:** 11.00am-9.30pm (12.00-3.00pm and 7.00-9.30pm Sun). Wheelchair access. **BEERS AVAILABLE:** All variants of Scottish and Newcastle brewery. **NEAREST TUBE STATION:** Paddington.

MAP REF: 5, C/2

The Scarsdale

242

23a Edwardes Square, W8 **071-937 1811**

'If there is an award going it gets it'

The Scarsdale is one of London's most admired pubs – if there is an award going it gets it. It has been the *Evening Standard* Pub of the Year of course. It is a lovely pub.

You find it in Edwardes Square in Kensington, a French Arcadia said the poet Leigh Hunt, who lived at No. 32. The square was built in 1812 by Louis Changeur, a speculative French builder, and people whispered that it was for officers of Napoleon's army when they arrived. Happily they didn't.

People warm to the Scarsdale as soon as they see it. As I write its impeccable Georgian façade is covered in trailing ivy, erica and winter cyclamen, the greenery and flowers spilling from the hanging baskets and window boxes. In the spring these will be filled with daffodils and in the summer with fuchsias, lobelia and geraniums, watered all night by means of ingenious arrangement devised by a previous landlord. It is as attractive inside as out, with high ceilings, a rich gleam of mahogany and brass, wooden fans and the original etched glass.

It is all traditional beers at the Scarsdale and this being Edwardes Square there is a brisk gin and tonic trade. They do well with wine too – six reds, six whites, three champagnes – and lunchtimes are busy with steaks, chops and burgers from a grill at the far end.

There's no music of any sort but some years ago two fruit machines slipped in somehow. They are hidden away round a corner at the back.

OPEN: Mon-Sun. **HOURS:** 12.00-11.00pm (12.00-3.00pm and 7.00-10.30pm Sun). **CREDIT CARDS ACCEPTED:** Visa, Access. **BAR FOOD AVAILABLE:** 12.00-2.00pm and 6.00-10.00pm (12.00-2.00pm and 7.00-10.00pm Sun). Tables outside seat 30. **BEERS AVAILABLE:** Holsten, Foster's, Carlsberg, John Smith's, Courage Best, Courage Directors, Theakston. **NEAREST TUBE STATIONS:** High Street Kensington, Earl's Court. **MAP REF:** 3, D/1

The Sekforde Arms

243

34 Sekforde Street, EC1 **071-253 3251**

'A prosperous air'

This is a pleasant street-corner local in Clerkenwell, a bit of London that has had more than its share of ups and downs.

It is having a bit of an up at the moment and the Sekforde wears a prosperous air with window boxes and fresh paint and new tables on the pavement. It is a real village pub and it plays a central part in local life. The local Rotarians meet in the first-floor restaurant and the staff and students from the City University seek daily inspiration in its comfortable bar.

There is a Sekforde Arms in the little Suffolk town of Woodbridge too. Thomas Sekforde, a 16th-century worthy, was a lawyer there, then retired to Clerkenwell. Many years later the two pubs, so many miles apart, quite independently took his name.

OPEN: Mon-Sun. **HOURS:** 11.00am-11.00pm (12.00-4.00pm Sun). **CLOSED:** Bank holidays. **CREDIT CARDS ACCEPTED:** All major cards. **BAR FOOD AVAILABLE:** 12.00-9.00pm (12.00-4.00pm Sun). **RESTAURANT FOOD AVAILABLE:** 12.00-3.00pm. Wheelchair access (but not lavatory). Private room seats 38. **BEERS AVAILABLE:** Young's, Labatts, Becks, Guinness, Beamish, Steinlager, Rolling Rock, Castlemaine, Tennent's Extra, Stella Artois, Lowenbrau. **NEAREST TUBE STATIONS:** Farringdon, Angel. **MAP REF:** 5, A/1

The Seven Stars

244

53 Carey Street, WC2 **071-242 8521**

'Much used by lawyers'

You're not doing too well? You're heading for Carey Street. This little back street is where the bankruptcy courts are and many a man facing financial disaster has slipped into the Seven Stars to buck himself up. It is a charming little wooden-fronted old pub, one of the smallest in London, two small bars, a few tables and chairs, much used by lawyers. It has been there since 1663.

OPEN: Mon-Fri. **HOURS:** 11.00am-9.30pm. **CLOSED:** Bank holidays. **CREDIT CARDS ACCEPTED:** None. **BAR FOOD AVAILABLE:** 11.00am-7.00pm. Wheelchair access (but not lavatory). **BEERS AVAILABLE:** Courage Best, Courage Directors, Foster's, Kronenbourg, Budweiser, Holsten Pils, Molsen, Tiger, Grolsch. **NEAREST TUBE STATIONS:** Chancery Lane, Holborn.

MAP REF: 6, A/2

Shelley's

245

10 Stafford Street, W1 **071-493 0337**

'It is nice to have a pub named after a poet'

This most tasteful and elegant public house is named, you might well suppose, after Percy Bysshe Shelley, poet and good egg. His likenesses are all over, also pictures of his wife, his holiday home, his tomb. Several of his poems are on the walls too in a handsome italic script, his portrait in oils hangs above the fireplace in the panelled doubles bar and there he is, at his most romantic, on the inn sign outside.

And he might have known the house. He did stay at Cooke's Hotel round the corner in Albermarle Street, indeed a letter he wrote from there hangs near the bar counter. It is an interesting letter about money and his great expectations.

All the same I think Shelley's was named after Fred Shelley. You may laugh. You may think I'm making Fred Shelley up but I promise you there was a Fred Shelley and he bought this pub in Stafford Street in 1862, 40 years after poor Percy Bysshe had drowned. It was the King John's Head in those days. It was still the King John's Head when someone called J Shelley assigned it to E H Barnes in 1888. By 1895 it had been upgraded to Shelley's Hotel. Which Shelley though?

There has been many a change of owner since, the hotel bit has long since been dropped and Percy Bysshe has carried the day, the current owners, Nicholsons, are quite adamant about that. Fred Shelley? Do you mind?

Anyway it is nice to have a pub named after a poet, and such a poet, and this one is very pleasant with its basement wine bar, its busy Victorian bar and its handsome function room upstairs.

Nikolaus Pevsner included it in his great book on London. He called it 'a pub in a thoroughly debased style.' Sir Nikolaus! Language!

OPEN: Mon-Sat. **HOURS:** 11.00am-11.00pm. **CLOSED:** Bank holidays. **CREDIT CARDS ACCEPTED:** Access, AmEx, Visa, Switch. **BAR FOOD AVAILABLE:** 12.00-9.00pm. **SET PRICE LUNCH:** £4.50. Private room seats 60. **BEERS AVAILABLE:** Adnams Extra, Landlord Timothy Taylor, Tetley, Nicholson's Best, John Bull, Lowenbrau, Castlemaine, Carlsberg, Tennent's Pilsner, Becks, Molson, Budweiser. **NEAREST TUBE STATION:** Green Park.

MAP REF: 1, C/1

The Sherlock Holmes

246

10 Northumberland Street, WC2 **071-930 2644**

'"Moriarty's grilled mushrooms"'

Sherlock Holmes has us in thrall. The stories sell round the world. They are tirelessly staged, filmed and televised and members of far-flung Sherlock Holmes societies arrive all summer to pay tribute to the great man.

They all end up with notebooks and cameras at the Sherlock Holmes in Northumberland Street to find the bar filled with other travellers on other Sherlock Holmes tours mingling with locals on Sherlock Holmes walks and television crews filming everything. Robert Davie, the licensee, and his family have been wakened at 3am to find someone taking pictures of the pub outside. 'It must be the most photographed pub in London,' he says.

The Sherlock Holmes is a smartly turned out pub in the modern Victorian style with a comfortable restaurant upstairs and a unique tourist attraction: Holmes' study as it appeared one foggy night in *The Empty House*, every item supplied by the Conan Doyle family. There it is, the cosy cluttered room, Holmes by the window shot through the head by the vile Col Moran, Moriarty's right-hand man. See the hole the bullet made. But of course Holmes had foreseen it all. Moran had shot a mannequin. He was no match for Holmes.

This tableau was one of the big hits of the Festival of Britain in 1950 and subsequently toured America. Then, happily, Whitbread's bought it and installed it in their pub, where it has been much enjoyed by students of Holmes law ever since. The smallest change, the slightest error and they are on it like a shot.

In Sir Arthur Conan Doyle's day the pub was part of the Northumberland Hotel. It was a place he liked and he put it into *The Hound of the Baskervilles*. He also had Holmes and Watson use the Turkish bath next door. This is now a branch of Barclays Bank.

The Northumberland Hotel did not survive the Twenties. Part of it – this part – then became the Northumberland Arms and in 1957 it changed its name again. Calling it the Sherlock Holmes was a brilliant stroke. It ensured customers in droves.

Holmes, not a modest man, would surely have approved of all the hoopla, the brisk sale of specially made Holmes' memorabilia and dishes on the menu like 'Inspector Lestrade's spinach and mushroom lasagne' and 'Moriarty's grilled mushrooms'.

You will recognize the lean hawk-nosed figure on the pub sign, smoking a curved pipe. Peter Cushing as I live and breathe!

OPEN: Mon-Sun. **HOURS:** 11.00am-11.00pm (12.00-3.00pm and 7.00-10.30pm Sun). **CLOSED:** Christmas Day, Boxing Day. **CREDIT CARDS ACCEPTED:** Access, Visa, Diner's Club, AmEx. **BAR FOOD AVAILABLE:** 12.00-10.30pm. **RESTAURANT FOOD AVAILABLE:** 12.00-3.00pm and 5.30-10.45pm. No smoking area. Wheelchair access (but not lavatory). Tables outside seat 30. **BEERS AVAILABLE:** Sherlock Holmes Ale, Boddingtons, Flowers Original, Flowers IPA, Brakspear, Murphy's, Stella Artois, Heineken. **NEAREST TUBE STATION:** Embankment. **MAP REF:** 8, D/2

The Ship

247

10 Thames Bank, SW14 **081-876 1439**

'A lake of lager, an ocean of bitter beer'

From the saloon bar of the Ship at Mortlake you get a fine view of a yellow pole sticking out of the river. This is the finishing post for the Oxford and Cambridge Boat Race and for one moment on Boat Race Day it becomes the most important post sticking out of any river anywhere.

Boat Race Day is when it all happens at the Ship. By the time it opens its doors there's a wall of people on both sides of the river and right across Chiswick Bridge and the pub is under siege. Boat Race watchers get through a lake of lager and an ocean of bitter beer and keep a team of cooks working flat out at the barbecue long after the two crews have collapsed over their oars.

The Ship is a handsome pub on the Surrey side of the river with deep bay windows and balustrading right round the eaves. It is painted cream and has a substantial bar, a patio that can seat 300 and a garden with rabbits and a slide and a bouncy castle for children.

The Ship has plenty of big occasions through the year. The river overflows. Summer pig roasts draw the crowds. There's St Patrick's Day with Irish session musicians and Guinness and oysters and Burns Night with the haggis, the ode to the haggis and David Morgan the manager, a Limerick man, in a kilt. But it's the Boat Race that has made the Ship famous, the boat race that gets the adrenalin going. It is the day of days in Mortlake.

OPEN: Mon-Sun. **HOURS:** 11.00am-11.00pm (12.00-3.00pm and 7.00-10.30pm Sun). **CREDIT CARDS ACCEPTED:** Mastercard, Visa, AmEx. **BAR FOOD AVAILABLE:** 12.00-2.30pm and 6.00-9.30pm (12.00-3.00pm and 7.00-9:30pm Sun).. Wheelchair access. Beer garden seats 100. Private room seats 20. **BEERS AVAILABLE:** John Smith's, Courage Best, Theakston XB, Wadworth, Foster's, Carlsberg, Budweiser, Holsten, Guinness. **NEAREST BR STATION:** Mortlake.

The Ship Inn 248

41 Jew's Row, SW18 **081-870 9667**

'Parachute in'

The one problem presented by this remarkable pub is finding it. This is not easy. It is set back from the river, hemmed in by a cement works, a bus depot and a car park and no one lives in Jew's Row or has any idea where it is. The faint-hearted have been known to give up.

All the same on a sunny summer's afternoon there might be fully 600 customers in and around the Ship Inn at Wandsworth, so it can be reached. Try this. Drive across Wandsworth Bridge, go round the roundabout and just before you reach the bridge again take the little slip road on the left. That's the Ship on your right with the figurehead. On the other hand you could parachute in.

The figurehead juts over the door to the public bar, an endangered species but this one thrives with cheaper beer, bacon and eggs at lunchtime and a pan of sausages sizzling on the range in the evening. Beyond that is a big airy conservatory with sofas and lots of tables, a harmonium, an open fire in the winter and french windows opening on to the beer garden in the summer.

The Ship goes great guns on lunches all year round but Sunday lunch on a fine summer's day is when it all comes together, everyone outside in the sun, the river slipping by and the barbecue in full spate producing prodigious quantities of steaks, chops, sausages and burgers.

You get an extraordinary number of people there. Every year, for instance, the Ship celebrates the last night of the proms with a big 12-foot television screen rigged up in the garden. More than 1,000 have been known to crowd in, extroverts doing karaoke conducting, everyone swaying, waving arms and belting out 'Land of Hope and Glory' and there's a great fireworks display on Guy Fawkes' Night.

The beer is Young's which shares the credit with Charles and Linda Gotto who rescued the place from what seemed like certain oblivion. The Gottos are now tenants of four Young's pubs. (See also the Alma and the Coopers Arms.)

An *Evening Standard* Pub of the Year.

OPEN: Mon-Sun. **HOURS:** 11.00am-11.00pm (12.00-3.00pm and 7.00-10.30pm Sun). **CREDIT CARDS ACCEPTED:** All major cards except Diner's Club. **RESTAURANT FOOD AVAILABLE:** 12.00-3.00pm and 7.30-10.00pm. Wheelchair access. Tables outside seat 400. Private room seats 100. **BEERS AVAILABLE:** Young's Special, Young's Bitter, Tennent's Extra, London Lager, Castlemaine. **NEAREST BR STATION:** Wandsworth Town.

The Ship Tavern 249

27 Lime Street, EC3 **071-626 7569**

'The Ship now seems beached rather far inland'

Ship Tavern Passage, an alley in the City, leads to just one place, the Ship Tavern. It is an historic old pub said to have been originally built in 1447 though much has happened to it along the way, principally the loss of its ground floor. This is an unusual mishap for even the oldest pub.

The Ship Tavern now seems beached rather far inland but in the 18th and 19th centuries it had close connections with the sea and seamen. Generations of ship-owners and sea captains met there to discuss the urgent business of the moment. Those were its great days.

Today it is left with its cellar which provides a good-sized panelled bar, one side kept for diners-only every lunchtime. The bar counter is shaped like the side of a ship's boat, portraits of long-forgotten admirals in fine uniforms and powdered hair abound, a prominently hung etching is titled *A Moderate Gale* and there is a large model of an 18th-century fighting ship in a glass case.

OPEN: Mon-Fri. **HOURS:** 11.00am-9.30pm Mon-Wed; 11.00am-10.30pm Thur-Fri. **CLOSED:** Bank holidays. **CREDIT CARDS ACCEPTED:** All major cards. **RESTAURANT FOOD AVAILABLE:** 12.00-2.30pm. **BEERS AVAILABLE:** John Smith's, Courage Best, Courage Directors, Theakston Best, Theakston XB, Miller, Foster's, Budweiser, Hoffmeister, Guinness. **NEAREST TUBE STATION:** Monument.

The Silver Cross

250

33 Whitehall SW1 **071-930 8350**

'Is it really haunted by the Tudor maid whose portrait hangs above the carved fireplace?'

This lively old pub, a brothel in the reign of Charles I, a tavern since the reign of Charles II, is the repository of much myth and legend including, quite possibly, the brothel bit. Is it really haunted by the Tudor maid whose portrait hangs above the carved fireplace, murdered, they say, dumped in the Thames and not best pleased? 'Certainly it is,' says landlord cheerfully.

There are three pubs in a row in this bit of Whitehall and this is the oldest, also the smallest. Now that the bar has been moved to the far end though there's room enough. Alterations of this sort can be made but preservation orders are in place to protect the important bits, the ceiling for instance. The ceiling is the great prize of the Silver Cross. It is a beautiful barrel-vaulted ceiling. Barrel vaulting is special. The barrels over the bar are just barrels.

When these three pubs were built they were within what was called the Verge of the Court and all three licensees must present themselves at Buckingham Palace once every three years to face the Board of the Green Cloth. They arrive at 11am, just after the changing of the guard when the crowds of sightseers outside are thickest, going in by the front entrance and being escorted along corridors to the room where, behind a table covered by green cloth, the Master of the Household and his colleagues wait.

The licensees get closely questioned. Their licences depend on this examination so it is a bit of an ordeal. Still it's better than going to the licensing justices as everyone else has to. Nearer too.

OPEN: Mon-Sun. **HOURS:** 11.00am-11.00pm (12.00-3.00pm and 7.00-10.30pm Sun). **FOOD AVAILABLE:** Daily. **BEERS AVAILABLE:** Courage Best, Courage Directors, John Smith's, Foster's, Holsten, Carlsberg. **NEAREST TUBE STATION:** Charing Cross. **MAP REF:** 8, D/2

Sir George Robey

251

240 Seven Sisters Road, N4 **071-272 5356**

'They are too young to have heard of George Robey at the George Robey'

George Robey, Prime Minister of Mirth, observes the comings and goings at the Sir George Robey from the inn sign with his once-famous quizzical smile. He wears his once-famous bowler, collarless frock coat and black eyebrows but he needn't have bothered. They are too young to have heard of George Robey at the George Robey and just call it the Robey. I expect there are annoying people around who still call it the Clarence which is what it used to be.

A raver writes: 'The Robey is near Finsbury Park station. Everyone knows it. Johnny Rotten goes there. It has a bar and a music room and two beer gardens, one at the front, one at the back. The music room is dark with black walls, a fair-sized stage and there's room to dance. You can get 300 ravers in. It closes at 11pm during the week but on Friday and Saturday it turns into a club and stays open till 6am. Soft drinks only after 2am.

'On Friday nights it's the Freaky Club which is indie-dance and on Saturdays its either Night of the Living Dub, a sort of reggae, or the Far Side which is trippy, trancey, techno, deep house. You don't have to be a member. They aren't clubs like that.'

OPEN: Mon-Sun. **HOURS:** 11.00-12.30am Mon-Thur; 11.00-6.00am Fri-Sat; 12.00-3.00pm and 7.00-10.30pm Sun. **CLOSED:** Christmas Day. **CREDIT CARDS ACCEPTED:** None. **BAR FOOD AVAILABLE:** All opening hours. Wheelchair access. Beer gardens seat 150. **BEERS AVAILABLE:** Grolsch, Newcastle Brown Ale, Labatts, Stella Artois, Rolling Rock, Budweiser, Becks, Castlemaine, Lowenbrau, Tetley, Guinness. **NEAREST BR STATION:** Finsbury Park.

Sir Richard Steele

252

97 Haverstock Hill, NW3 **071-722 1003**

'The ordinary outside gives no hint of the surprises within'

It would be easy to miss this Victorian pub on its corner between Chalk Farm and Belsize Park tube stations. The ordinary outside gives no hint of the surprises within.

Every inch of wall, shelf and ceiling is taken up with bric-a-brac. There are toys, clocks, paintings, drawings, sketches, violins, sewing machines, mirrors, railways signs, old tin advertisements, bottles, tennis rackets, thousands of books, a whole armadillo and a moose's head and that is just the main bar. The back room with its hand-painted window and real fire has a whole collection of its own. There is not much lighting. All the tables have candles stuck in old wine bottles. It is very cosy.

They don't do food here. This is a drinker's pub. People come for a good time and a few pints which would have suited Sir Richard Steele, an 18th-century dramatist – author of *The Funeral or Grief à la Mode* – and rather a goer in spite of the high moral tone that kept creeping in.

That is him observing the passing scene from the inn sign and from the big stained-glass window in the main bar. His house was here. Dr Johnson described him as 'The most agreeable rake that ever trod the rounds of indulgence.' This could probably be said for most of the clientele today.

OPEN: Mon-Sun. **HOURS:** 11.00am-11.00pm (12.00-3.00pm and 7.00-10.30pm Sun). **CREDIT CARDS ACCEPTED:** None. **BAR FOOD AVAILABLE:** 12.00-2.30pm. Wheelchair access. Tables outside seat 12. **BEERS AVAILABLE:** Budvar, Courage Best, Courage Directors, John Smith's, Flowers IPA, Foster's, Kronenbourg, Guinness. **NEAREST TUBE STATIONS:** Belsize Park, Chalk Farm.

The Slug and Lettuce

253

16 Putney High Street, SW15 — **081-785 3081**

'A full-sized white lion still stands high on the façade looking neither like a slug nor a lettuce'

The Slug and Lettuce would seem the pub name least likely to succeed. It has, in fact, proved quite otherwise. There are twelve of them now, six in London, and more are in the offing.

They are all a bit like this one, big Victorian pubs restyled and renamed. This is a Slug and Lettuce class of '93. It was the White Lion until then and a full-sized white lion still stands high on the decorative Victorian façade looking neither like a slug nor a lettuce.

The style is old English ale house, bare floorboards, plain furniture, a good range of cask ales and food from 11am till late. There is a garden with picnic tables at the back and live bands, jazz, soul and blues, on Wednesdays and Fridays. It gets very lively at weekends.

The menus include the slug cheese platter for £2.95 and the giant slugburger for £3.75. The giant slugburger, on a bun with salad mayonnaise and relish, is a popular item at the Slug and Lettuce.

OPEN: Mon-Sun. **HOURS:** 11.00am-11.00pm (12.00-3.00pm and 7.00-10.30pm Sun. **CREDIT CARDS ACCEPTED:** Visa, Access. **RESTAURANT FOOD AVAILABLE:** 11.00am-10.00pm. Wheelchair access (but not lavatory). Beer garden seats 40. Private room seats 150. **BEERS AVAILABLE:** Courage Best, Courage Directors, Boddingtons, Gale's HSB, Kronenbourg, Foster's, Miller Lite, Guinness, Beamish. **NEAREST TUBE STATION:** Putney Bridge.

The Spaniard's Inn

254

Spaniard's Road, NW3 **081-455 3276**

'Dick Turpin stabled his horse in the toll gate that still causes daily traffic jams in both directions'

The Spanish Ambassador to the Court of James I is said to have lived here. In the middle of Hampstead Heath? Well, it's more a theory really but it would explain the name.

The Spaniard's is a 16th-century weatherboarded house with many additions and alterations, none of which has spoiled it in any way. It has been a tavern for 400 years, most of that time deep in the countryside and very remote. All the same life has not been without its drama or its glamour.

Highwaymen, who, like modern New Yorkers, could be great company when not actually shooting you, were often there. Dick Turpin stabled his horse in the toll gate that still causes daily traffic jams in both directions and a musket ball he fired while holding up the Royal Mail is on show in the bar. They used to have his pistols too but they were nicked, ironic really.

Then there were the rifles left behind by the Gordon rioters who were boozing in the bar when the soldiers arrived and marched them off to Newgate jail. They were on show in the bar for well over 100 years but they walked too.

Well, things are usually more peaceful than this in the Spaniard's. Shelley, Keats and Byron all went there and so, of course, did Dickens. In *The Pickwick Papers* this was where Mrs Bardell and her friends plotted Mr Pickwick's downfall.

You can imagine Mr Pickwick in the saloon bar with its low ceilings, old panelling and cosy alcoves. Bar stools surround the old wooden bar and there is a charming panelled room upstairs with original beams and shutters and a splendidly sloping floor. There are real fires in winter and in the summer one of the best pub gardens you will ever see with its raised lawn and its roses, its pergola and terrace of picnic tables. At the bottom of the garden a flock of budgies noisily lead busy lives in a big aviary. Children love them and are welcome here.

It is a pub worth making any sort of detour to visit. Mind the toll gate.

OPEN: Mon-Sun. **HOURS:** 11.00am-11.00pm (12.00-3.00pm and 7.00-10.30pm Sun). **CREDIT CARDS ACCEPTED:** Visa, Access, Mastercard. **BAR FOOD AVAILABLE:** 12.00-3.00pm and 6.00-9.30pm (12.00-9.30pm Sat; 12.00-3.00 and 7.00-9.30 Sun). Wheelchair access (but not lavatory). Beer garden seats 250. Private room seats 30. **BEERS AVAILABLE:** Bass, London Pride, Hancock's, Worthington, Carling Black Label, Tennent's Extra, Grolsch. **NEAREST TUBE STATIONS:** Hampstead, Golders Green.

The Sporting Page

255

Camera Place, SW10 **071-352 6465**

'Friendly, extrovert and sporty'

Life in the Sporting Page is, as the name suggests, friendly, extrovert and sporty. The crowd is clearly there to enjoy itself and so is the staff.

It is a light cheerful modern pub between the King's Road and Fulham Road, formerly one of the many Red Lions. Outside it is whitewashed walls and big windows with blue canopies, inside varnished pine floors, furniture and bar. There are light-hearted sporting prints, sporting paintings and sporting murals and rugby internationals on a big screen fill the bar to scrum-like capacity.

The tables and benches from the bar appear outside in the summer and the kitchen is busy all year round. Espresso coffee is on offer and free hot snacks circulate in the evening.

OPEN: Mon-Sun. **HOURS:** 11.00-3.00pm and 5.30-11.00pm (12.00-3.00pm and 7.00-10.30pm Sun). **CLOSED:** Christmas Day and Boxing Day. **CREDIT CARDS ACCEPTED:** None. **BAR FOOD AVAILABLE:** 12.00-2.30pm and 7.00-10.00pm. Wheelchair access (but not lavatory). Beer garden seats 40. **BEERS AVAILABLE:** Boddingtons, Wadworth, Webster's, Holsten, Foster's, Carlsberg, Guinness. **NEAREST TUBE STATION:** Sloane Square, South Kensington.

MAP REF: 2, B/2

The Stage Door

256

3 Allington Street, SW1 **071-834 7055**

'A white-gloved, top-hatted stage-door Johnny carrying a bunch of flowers'

Allington Street runs up one side of the Victoria Palace Theatre and opposite the stage door is the Stage Door. It is a handsome Victorian pub with a big saloon bar featuring a speedy food counter, video games, Sky TV, and two digital wall-mounted jukeboxes (3 plays £1). It is handy for the theatre, fairly handy for Victoria Station.

The pub looks best from across the narrow street. Its inn-sign shows a white-gloved, top-hatted stage-door Johnny carrying a bunch of flowers, a native species now extinct, and in gilt letters across the confident fascia are Dr Johnson's famous words: 'There is nothing which has yet been contrived by man by which so much happiness is produced as by a good tavern or inn.'

OPEN: Mon-Sun. **HOURS:** 11.00am-11.00pm (12.00-3.00pm and 7.00-10.30pm Sun). **CLOSED:** Christmas Day. **CREDIT CARDS ACCEPTED:** None. **BAR FOOD AVAILABLE:** All opening hours.. Wheelchair access (but not lavatory). **BEERS AVAILABLE:** Wadworth, John Smith's, Theakston Old Peculier, Courage Best, Courage Directors, Holsten, Carlsberg, Guinness. **NEAREST BR STATION:** Victoria. **MAP REF:** 8, A/2

The Star and Garter

257

4 Lower Richmond Road, SW15 **081-788 0345**

'Beside themselves with excitement'

On the last Saturday of March getting on for 1,000 people press into the Star and Garter on the river at Putney. It is a huge Victorian pile, a landmark, five storeys high with a tower making six and the great windows in the big saloon bar have a brilliant view of the start of the Oxford and Cambridge boat race.

The Star and Garter is well prepared. It takes all the furniture out, puts away the real glasses and produces big boxes of plastic ones. A platoon of barmen lines the 40-foot counter, one of the longest in London, and then the doors are open and the pub is instantly overflowing.

The big ground-floor windows are wide open and that's where everyone wants to be. They are front stalls for the drama ahead and, as the big moment approaches, they are filled with faces, as, indeed, are the smaller windows of the cellar bar. Both bars are a mass of people, beside themselves with excitement as the race begins. The boats are around the bend and away in no time but they can be seen all the way to the finish on the big television screens over the bar counters.

The rest of the year, you might think, must be an anti-climax. Still it is a busy pub with a big young following and ordinary weekends can be hopping at the Star and Garter. The bar is quite a sight at any time. So thickly covered in every kind of object is the high ceiling that it is years since anyone has seen it.

Its original architects had great social plans for the Star and Garter. The entire first floor was a ballroom, high, wide and elegant with classical mouldings and long windows overlooking the river. This is now the home of the Riverside Gymnasium: gold card membership £250 a year.

OPEN: Mon-Sun. **HOURS:** 11.00am-3.00pm and 5.00-11.00pm (11.00am-11.00pm Sat; 12.00-3.00pm and 7.00-10.30pm Sun). **CREDIT CARDS ACCEPTED:** None. **BAR FOOD AVAILABLE:** 12.00-2.30pm and 5.00-7.30pm. Wheelchair access (but not lavatory). Private room seats 100. **BEERS AVAILABLE:** Tetley, Courage Directors, Kronenbourg, Foster's, Budweiser, Miller, Guinness, Beamish. **NEAREST TUBE STATION:** Putney Bridge.

The Stargazey

258

236 Fulham Road, SW10 **071-376 5827**

'It seemed clear that banks were made for pubs'

Fuller Smith and Turner, the Chiswick brewers, will be watching the Stargazey closely. Will this be the pub of the 1990s? If so, we'll be seeing a lot more like it.

It opened last summer, the first of Fuller's new brainwave chain, the Ale and Pie Houses, a new generation of pubs, much discussed, carefully designed and marketed. 'Concept' is the buzz word as in 'has Fuller's got the concept right?' Bang on, I would have thought.

First there's the building. It was a National Westminster bank until Fuller's took it, 2000 square feet, twice the size of your average pub, and on a big main road corner site with vaults perfect for cellars, kitchens and storerooms. It was murder drilling through the thick reinforced walls but apart from that it seemed clear that banks were made for pubs. Were there any more going?

There were. What about that Barclays in Earls Court Road? (See the Blackbird).

So now, after a 10-week transformation scene, we have the Stargazey, a wide-open, attractive, youthful pub. The outside walls are a continuous run of sliding doors which fill it with light and slide open in a most satisfactory way on sunny days, and on every side the designers have given a modern gloss to traditional pub features. How nice to see granite counter tops, leather benches, Welsh chapel chairs, and modern partitions forming big bays for eating and drinking.

The ale is Fuller's, of course, and the pies, central to the success of the exercise, are pretty good too. A stargazey is apparently a sort of Cornish pie in which little fish poke their heads through the pastry. Thankfully they don't do this dreadful-sounding pie at the Stargazey but the fish pie they do do – white fish, smoked fish and prawns – is very popular. Like all the pies it comes on an ash trencher, a wooden plate with grooves, but pies are by no means the only things on offer and you can eat here very reasonably until 9pm. After that the pub side really takes over.

OPEN: Mon-Sun. **HOURS:** 11.30am-11.00pm (12.00-11.00pm Sat-Sun). **CREDIT CARDS ACCEPTED:** Access, Visa, Mastercard. **BAR FOOD AVAILABLE:** 12.00-9.00pm (12.00-8.00pm Fri-Sat; 12.00-2.30pm Sun). No smoking area. Wheelchair access (disabled lavatory). **BEERS AVAILABLE:** London Pride, ESB, Chiswick Bitter, Hock, Summer Ale, Mr Harry, Grolsch, Tennent's Extra, Heineken, Carling Black Label, Scrumpy Jack, Guinness, Murphy's. **NEAREST TUBE STATIONS:** Earl's Court. **MAP REF:** 2, A/3

The Star Tavern

259

6 Belgrave Mews West, SW1 **071-235 3019**

'Actors, gangsters, the Gaekwar of Baroda'

The Star Tavern was built for the household servants of the nobility. There were plenty of both in 19th-century Belgravia. Four dukes lived round the corner in the newly built Belgrave Square and the local servant population was enormous. The Star Tavern had to be big. It was every bit as hierarchical as the great town houses around it. Saloon bar, private bar, public bar or snug, the butlers, valets, footmen and coachmen understood exactly which was for them and which was not.

A couple of wars and the partitions came down and after that you didn't know whose shoulder your shoulder might be rubbing. Actors, gangsters, the Gaekwar of Baroda, it was a rich mix in the saloon bar of the Star Tavern and you were never sure if Paddy Kennedy would even let you in. Kennedy ruled the Star Tavern in the 1950s and '60s and would not serve you if he did not like the cut of your jib. He was particularly particular about who used the upstairs bar where, they say, the Great Train Robbers planned their deed.

Kennedy made a few bob in his day, lived well, spent freely but the horses were his undoing. He died broke in the licensed trade's home.

Bruce and Kathy Taylor run the pub now and it is comfortable, familiar, agreeably old-fashioned. On winter evenings you still look for a table near one of the open fires and on a summer evening customers like to take their drinks into the mews where there are tubs of geraniums, hanging baskets of lobelia and little traffic. Other London pubs have had to stop their customers drinking outside, often after the complaint of a single neighbour, but hopefully, in spite of rumbles, this pleasant custom will continue in Belgrave Mews West.

The Star Tavern's food is a draw and it is a Fuller's house so the beer is a big plus.

It was the *Evening Standard* Pub of the Year in 1992.

OPEN: Mon-Sun. **HOURS:** 11.30am-3.00pm and 5.00-11.00pm Mon-Thur; 11.30am-11.00pm Fri; 11.00am-11.00pm Sat; 12.00-3.00pm and 7.00-10.30pm Sun. **CLOSED:** Christmas Day and Boxing Day. **CREDIT CARDS ACCEPTED:** None. **BAR FOOD AVAILABLE:** 12.00-2.30pm and 6.30-8.45pm. Wheelchair access (but not lavatory). Private room seats 30. **BEERS AVAILABLE:** ESB, London Pride, Chiswick Bitter. **NEAREST TUBE STATION:** Knightsbridge. **MAP REF:** 2, F/3

The Sun

260

63 Lamb's Conduit Street, WC1 **071-405 8278**

'A labyrinth of vaults and catacombs'

The Sun in Lamb's Conduit Street doesn't care what it looks like and truthfully it can look pretty rough. Beer is what matters at the Sun and few pubs anywhere take that more seriously.

Observe the old U-shaped counter, a bit battered, nothing to write home about, but the hand pumps now, what a sight for sore eyes they are, black and gleaming, seven on one side, nine on the other, sixteen cask ales on offer at any one time and it can and does do more. It likes to claim that no other pub sells a greater range of real ales.

What makes this possible are its cellars, a labyrinth of vaults and catacombs under the streets of Bloomsbury, a priceless asset. The Sun can store up to 70 different real ales there in perfect conditions and can make up to twenty available at any one time.

These are remarkable cellars and Gary Brown, the manager, might well take you down there if you ask. He often has a group going round in the early evening. If he can't take you for some reason, well, you will have seen a good old London pub and possibly had a beer you never tried before. They will fit you in another time.

Alarming rumours of a refurbishment are, I am assured, just rumours. A coat of paint to the outside is all that is intended.

OPEN: Mon-Sun. **HOURS:** 11.00am-11.00pm (12.00-3.00pm and 7.00-10.30pm Sun). **CLOSED:** Christmas Day, Boxing Day. **CREDIT CARDS ACCEPTED:** None. **BAR FOOD AVAILABLE:** 12.00-2.30pm and 6.00-10.00pm. Wheelchair access (but not lavatory). Tables outside seat 20. **BEERS AVAILABLE:** Tanglefoot, Adnams Broadside, Ruddells County, Brakspear, Foster's, Holsten, Carlsberg, Budweiser. **NEAREST TUBE STATIONS:** Russell Square, Holborn.

The Sun in Splendour

261

7 Portobello Road, W11 **071-727 6345**

'There aren't many open-air pool tables in London. When it rains there's a rush to put the cover on.'

A Victorian local on the corner of Portobello Road, particularly lively every Saturday with much coming and going of stall-holders, collectors, bargain-hunters and tourists. The locals have it the rest of the week.

The bar has gaming machines, a spectacular compact disc Wurlitzer and the sporting event of the moment on television. A high-walled triangular yard at the back is an unexpectedly pleasant place for a quiet lunch on weekdays and a noisy one on Saturdays. A pergola covered in ivy and honeysuckle gives dappled shade on hot summer days. Taking up its share of room is a pool table. There aren't many open-air pool tables in London. When it rains there's a rush to put the cover on.

Two yellow notices in the bar suggest the sort of problems pubs can encounter. 'Cash on these premises is protected by an anti-hold up device,' they read. 'Staff cannot override or affect its operation . . .'

OPEN: Mon-Sun. **HOURS:** 11.00am-11.00pm (12.00-3.00pm and 7.00-10.30pm Sun). **CREDIT CARDS ACCEPTED:** None. **RESTAURANT FOOD AVAILABLE:** 12.00-3.00pm and 6.00-8.00pm. **SET PRICE LUNCH AND DINNER:** £3.95. Wheelchair access (but not lavatory). Beer garden seats 40. **BEERS AVAILABLE:** Bass, London Pride, Tennent's Pilsner, Tennent's Extra, Carling Black Label, Guinness, Caffreys. **NEAREST TUBE STATION:** Notting Hill Gate.

The Sun Inn

262

7 Church Road, SW13 **081-876 5893**

'A warren of little rooms, a jumble of nooks and snugs'

First find Barnes Green. Note the willow which grows aslant the brook, the avenue of horse chestnuts, the house, on the left, where Henry Fielding lived. Take a turn round the pond and there's the Sun, a pretty Georgian building with a mansard roof, a pergola, window boxes and hanging gardens.

Before you go in, though, go round the back and have a look at Barnes Bowling Club, still owned by the brewers. It has a very rare, old-fashioned green, a sort of inverse crown with the centre lower than the sides. Here, so the story goes, Elizabeth I was taught to play.

Inside the Sun little seems to have changed since its days as an 18th-century coaching inn. There is a warren of little rooms, a jumble of nooks and snugs divided by rails, pillars, stained-glass panels and sliding leaded windows. There are wooden floors on different levels, beams, low ceilings, stuffed owls, a piano, a huge stuffed pike, old prints, old bottles, old rugs, bric-a-brac of all sorts and a ghost.

This fussy spirit is thought to be a former landlord. He moves plates behind the bar and alters clocks but no one minds and during opening hours the Sun couldn't be livelier. Barnes is peopled by celebrated persons of a musical and theatrical sort and this is where they drink.

The Sun is really a country pub, the perfect object of a walk. The dog will be welcomed, many are counted among the regulars. They are happy to see children too, at lunchtime anyway.

There is no dartboard at the Sun, no pool table, no jukebox or television or other distractions of that kind. A no smoking area is planned. It gets very crowded, of course, but that is what you would expect. Sunday lunch, traditional roast, is particularly popular.

OPEN: Mon-Sun. **HOURS:** 11.00am-11.00pm (12.00-3.00pm and 7.00-10.30pm Sun). **CREDIT CARDS ACCEPTED:** None. **RESTAURANT FOOD AVAILABLE:** 12.00-2.30pm. Wheelchair access. Tables outside seat 72. **BEERS AVAILABLE:** Tetley, Burton Ale, Young's Ale, Carlsberg, Lowenbrau, Castlemaine, Labatts, Guinness. **NEAREST BR STATION:** Barnes Bridge.

The Surprise

263

6 Christchurch Terrace, SW3 **071-352 4699**

'The surprise about the Surprise...'

The Surprise was the name of the frigate that took Charles II to safety in France, a voyage commemorated on the pub sign. There is the frigate heaving to, there the king being rowed out to board her. He stands heroically in the prow, his wig understandably askew. This happened in Falmouth 200 years before this handsome Victorian pub was built but the Surprise remains properly grateful to its namesake and there are lots of pictures of the graceful fighting ship or of others like her in the bar, lots of pictures of old Chelsea too and the surprise about the Surprise is to find so little changed by the years.

The black oak bar with its painted frieze still serves the public bar with its bare floorboards, its dartboard and shove-ha'penny board on one side and the saloon bar with its carpet and most of the windows on the other. Change would be met with outrage. There were even some grumbles when they brought the gents in from the yard.

OPEN: Mon-Sun. **HOURS:** 11.00am-11.00pm (12.00-3.00pm and 7.00-10.30pm Sun). **CREDIT CARDS ACCEPTED:** None. **BAR FOOD AVAILABLE:** 12.00-2.30pm. Wheelchair access. Tables outside seat 10. **BEERS AVAILABLE:** Worthington, Bass, Hancock HB, London Pride, Grolsch, Tennent's Extra, Tennent's Pilsner, Carling Black Label. **NEAREST TUBE STATION:** Sloane Square. **MAP REF:** 2, D/2

The Sussex 264

20 Upper St Martin's Lane, WC2 **071-836 1834**

'A grim reminder . . .'

This busy West End pub was the scene of a violent and tragic event that put it on every front page. On 12 October 1992 the IRA planted a bomb in the men's lavatory. Five customers were injured, one died days later. It was a grim reminder that public houses are from time to time in the front line.

The Sussex replaced its windows, mended its shattered bar and got on with it. It remains the decent, friendly, useful pub it has always been.

OPEN: Mon-Sun. **HOURS:** 11.00am-11.00pm (12.00-3.00pm and 7.00-10.30pm Sun). **BAR FOOD AVAILABLE:** 12.00-2.00pm and 7.00-9.00pm. **BEERS AVAILABLE:** Courage Best, Courage Directors, John Smith's, Foster's, Holsten, Beamish, Guinness. **NEAREST TUBE STATION:** Leicester Square. **MAP REF:** 1, E/1

Sussex Arms 265

London Street, W2 **071-402 9602**

'A crowded, jolly, boozy boozer'

Gaming machines, pinball machine, jukebox, darts, sport on Sky, pool in pool lounge upstairs monitored by closed circuit TV on the bar. A crowded, jolly, boozy boozer.

The glum chap in the beret and dressing gown on the inn-sign outside isn't getting into the spirit of things at all.

OPEN: Mon-Sun. **HOURS:** 11.00am-11.00pm (12.00-3.00pm and 7.00-10.30pm Sun). **CLOSED:** Christmas Day. **CREDIT CARDS ACCEPTED:** None. **BAR FOOD AVAILABLE:** All opening hours. Wheelchair access. Tables outside seat 16. Private room seats 40. **BEERS AVAILABLE:** Tetley, Burton Ale, Castlemaine, Lowenbrau, Carlsberg, Guinness. **NEAREST TUBE STATION:** Paddington. **MAP REF:** 4, C/2

The Swan 266

66 Bayswater Road, W2 **071-262 5204**

'No wonder the terrace gets packed'

Tourists love the Swan. They come in time and again during their holiday here and years later come back and tell the barmen about it. They were staying in a hotel just round the corner, they will say, and on their very first day they found the Swan. It was the first English pub they had ever seen . . .

The Swan is genuinely pretty and genuinely old. It was there in the 18th century, or anyway some of it was, and it looks its age. Pubs try to do that. It was built as a coaching inn, then became the Floral Tea Gardens, then happily it went back to being a tavern and today, though bigger, it is still a nice domestic size, just two storeys, with a handsome swan painted on the stucco and lanterns and hanging baskets and wooden picnic tables on a deep terrace.

This terrace is a tremendous asset. It stretches to the pavement, much of it sheltered by a glass canopy so let it rain, and the traffic roars by but let it roar. This is London after all. Kensington Gardens are just across the road and after dark they light the gas lamps and you could almost be back a hundred years. No wonder the terrace gets packed all day long in summer.

The bar is comfortably English, so is the food. There's roast beef and Yorkshire pudding every lunchtime and in the room at the back there is a copy of a big old painting of a typically English scene. Look closely, there is the Swan and there is Bayswater Road, just a country lane in those days you will notice, and the small tree in the picture is probably the large tree just outside and that group of redcoats is allowing felons one last drink before taking them to Tyburn to get hanged.

The locals used to enjoy that and entertainment is still provided at the Swan. Every evening from Monday to Saturday there is a typical English sing-song in the back room. Everyone, whether they are from Tokyo, Texas or Tottenham Court Road, ends up joining in.

OPEN: Mon-Sun. **HOURS:** 11.00am-11.00pm (11.00am-3.00pm and 7.00-10.30pm Sun). **CLOSED:** Christmas Day and Boxing Day. **CREDIT CARDS ACCEPTED:** All major cards. **BAR FOOD AVAILABLE:** 11.00am-10.00pm. Wheelchair access (but not lavatory). Beer garden seats 66. **BEERS AVAILABLE:** Courage, John Smith's, Theakston, Carlsberg, Foster's, Holsten, Budweiser, Guinness, Becks, Holsten, Molsen, Sol, Newcastle Brown Ale. **NEAREST TUBE STATION:** Lancaster Gate. **MAP REF:** 4, D/1

The Swan

267

46 Hammersmith Broadway, W6 **081-748 1043**

'Unflinching confrontations and draconian bannings'

Look at this noble pub on its commanding peninsular, dominating if anything could the big unlovely road junction at the heart of Hammersmith. It is a prime example of Victorian gin palace baroque. No money was spared by the builders who went to town with marble and etched glass and a magnificence of mahogany and there is no identity crisis here. There are painted swans on the inn sign, a flamboyant swan on the gable, a stuffed swan in a case over the bar . . .

It has a beady eye, the swan in the bar, but this has not always been enough to keep the peace. The dignified Swan got decidedly rough not long ago, takings fell and Victorian worthies turned in graves. But a no-nonsense new manager cured this in a surprisingly short time with unflinching confrontations and draconian bannings and today you can again take your aunt. Choose one that enjoys the new generation of gaming machines. There are three of these.

The Swan is an early starter. It opens for breakfast at 7am. A Big

Breakfast there is two eggs, two sausages, two rashers of bacon, black pudding, baked beans, fried tomato, fried bread, toast, tea or coffee and costs £3.25. Secretaries on their way to the office usually settle for coffee and toast. But not always. Lunches take over at 11.30am and there are evening snacks till 9pm. The big kitchen is kept at it.

There is a handsome function room upstairs. People have wedding receptions, annual general meetings, parties and goodness knows what else in it. Hammersmith finds it very useful.

OPEN: Mon-Sun. **HOURS:** 11.00am-11.00pm (12.00-3.00pm and 7.00-10.30pm Sun). **CREDIT CARDS ACCEPTED:** Visa, Mastercard, Eurocard. **BAR FOOD AVAILABLE:** 7.30am-7.00pm. No smoking area. Wheelchair access. Private room seats 60. **BEERS AVAILABLE:** Charrington variants, Grolsch, Caffreys. **NEAREST TUBE STATION:** Hammersmith.

The Swan

268

77-80 Gracechurch Street, EC3 **071-283 7712**

'Probably the smallest'

For twenty-three years Franco and Maria Ferrer ran the Rossetti in St John's Wood. It was big, sunny and Mediterranean, more a trattoria than a pub really. It is still there but Franco and Maria are not. Two years ago they came to a crossroads. The Rossetti was being sold, Franco was getting no younger and was homesick for Spain. So he and Maria took early retirement and went back home to Barcelona.

They had a nice house there. The beach was nearby. The sun shone and a year passed. They were bored. They missed their three daughters, grown up now and living in Mill Hill. They missed their busy lives. They were homesick for London.

So it is that Franco and Maria are back in London and running a pub again. It is the Swan, cosy, Dickensian and probably the smallest pub in the City of London.

If a chap of moderate girth stands at the downstairs bar another chap of moderate girth can hardly squeeze by. One has a strange urge to shout 'Move right down the bus please.' Nevertheless, every lunchtime from Monday to Friday substantial gents from City institutions line this bar drinking pints of Fuller's Chiswick, eating Mrs Ferrer's big filled baps and breathing in whenever a newcomer arrives. I don't believe it myself but Franco says he gets 38 people in the downstairs bar every lunchtime and at least another 40 upstairs.

Ah yes, upstairs. There is a bar there too exactly twice the size. It crosses the alley to form an archway, a very nice bar indeed, rich mahogany, thick carpet and a bit of space. Downstairs it is beer only. Upstairs you can get the usual as long as the usual isn't too unusual.

The cellar is tiny and crammed high with barrels delivered once a week at 6am and the Ferrers, living above the pub as they have for most of their lives together, say how lovely it is to get so much time off. City pubs close at 9pm and don't open at all at weekends.

They are, in short, busy as bees and in their element again.

OPEN: Mon-Fri. **HOURS:** 11.00am-9.00pm. **CREDIT CARDS ACCEPTED:** Visa, Access. **BAR FOOD AVAILABLE:** 11.00am-8.30pm. Wheelchair access (but not lavatory). **BEERS AVAILABLE:** London Pride, ESB, Chiswick Bitter, Grolsch, Tennent's Extra, Heineken, Guinness, Becks, Steinlager, Molson, Budweiser, Rolling Rock. **NEAREST TUBE STATION:** Bank.

The Swan

269

215 Clapham Road, SW9 **071-978 9778**

'Every night is Friday night'

The young and free who flock to this massive Irish pub in Stockwell drink fast and hope to score.

A hopeful scorer writes:

'A couple of lagers and the search is on for the opposite sex. You don't have far to look. There's the huge bar downstairs and the Swan's Nest upstairs is just as big, lots of room, lots of possibilities, plenty of time. The Swan doesn't close till midnight early in the week and not until 2am from Thursday to Saturday.

Big-name Irish acts like the Commitments play here so check your programme, otherwise every night is Friday night at the Swan. Watch the doormen, though. They failed O-level charm.'

OPEN: Mon-sun. **HOURS:** 11.00am-12.00am (11.00am-2.00am Thur-Sat; 12.00-3.00pm and 7.00-10.30pm Sun). **CLOSED:** Christmas Day, Good Friday. **CREDIT CARDS ACCEPTED:** Barclaycard. **BAR FOOD AVAILABLE:** All opening hours. **SET PRICE LUNCH:** £3.50. **SET PRICE DINNER:** £4. Wheelchair access. Private room seats 200. **BEERS AVAILABLE:** Ruddells Best, John Smith's, Foster's, Carling Black Label, Holsten, Guinness, Beamish. **NEAREST TUBE STATION:** Stockwell.

(Ye Olde) Swiss Cottage

270

98 Finchley Road, NW3 **071-722 3487**

'It is to this distant craze that we owe this agreeably dotty pub'

For about ten minutes when Queen Victoria was very young there was a fashion for pseudo-Swiss chalets. People thought they were just darling and Prince Albert brought one over from Switzerland in sections. It was reassembled in the grounds of Osborne and the children had tea parties there.

It is to this distant craze that we owe this agreeably dotty pub, a household name in London. In 1840 Finchley Road was being built and they put a pub in the shape of an outsize chalet on the key junction. They called it the Swiss Cottage and it was the last word in chic. It gave its name to the new bus terminus, then to the Metropolitan Line station when it opened and soon to the entire district.

People always liked it and it was rebuilt on an even bigger scale after the war. It is huge now, 6000 square feet of public space, four bars, a private pool club, a terrace with picnic tables, a deep wooden balcony around three of its sides.

Samuel Smith bought it in 1986 and there has been lots of refurbishing, of course. The Victoria Bar (with music) and the Albert Bar (without) are now big, comfortable rooms with sofas and armchairs grouped around widely spaced coffee tables.

The Tap Room is plain and pleasant and well used by the locals, and you could give a ball in the vast upstairs bar. A flight of wooden Swiss-type steps leads up to the wide Swiss-type balcony on the first floor where people take their drinks on sunny days and the pool club, known as the Swiss, has been a notable success. The big Swiss-type hall it occupies was a venue for live bands and a disco at one time but now pool players pay £25 a year membership and 50p a game and the six tables are permanently occupied every evening.

I see they have taken to calling it Ye Olde Swiss Cottage now. Dottier and dottier. But good old Swiss Cottage, all the same. They don't build pubs like this any more.

OPEN: Mon-Sun. **HOURS:** 11.00am-11.00pm (12.00-3.00pm and 7.00-10.30pm Sun). **CREDIT CARDS ACCEPTED:** None. **BAR FOOD AVAILABLE:** 12.00-3.00pm. Wheelchair access. Beer garden seats 100. Private room seats 100.. **BEERS AVAILABLE:** Old Brewery Bitter, Museum Ale, Ayingerbrau. **NEAREST TUBE STATION:** Swiss Cottage.

Tattersalls Tavern

271

Knightsbridge Green, SW1 **071-584 7122**

'Horsey prints and fruit machines'

There is no green at Knightsbridge Green. The pavement gets a bit wider, that's all. There are, however, luxuriant window boxes all round Tattersalls Tavern, also two fertile tubs on either side of its front door.

Tattersalls is a comparatively modern pub. It is on the Knightsbridge Green end of the big Texaco building that caused such a stir when it opened in 1958. Alas for Tattersalls, Texaco moved to Canary Wharf in February 1993, taking its staff of 1,000 with it. Things seemed strangely quiet in Tattersalls for a while.

Tattersalls has found new customers now. There are other offices in Knightsbridge, lots of shops, a great many shoppers. Tattersalls, named after the rather better known Tattersall's whose famous auction rooms used to be here, greets them with horsy prints, fruit machines, a pinball ball and piped music. There is a restaurant downstairs.

OPEN: Mon-Sat. **HOURS:** 11.00am-11.00pm. **CLOSED:** Sun and 5 days at Christmas. **CREDIT CARDS ACCEPTED:** All major cards. **BAR FOOD AVAILABLE:** 11.00am-6.00pm Mon-Fri (11.00am-3.00pm Sat). **RESTAURANT FOOD AVAILABLE:** 12.00-2.45pm and 6.00-8.45pm. No smoking area. Wheelchair access. Private room seats 50. **BEERS AVAILABLE:** Courage Directors, Wadworth, Courage Best, John Smith's, Foster's, Holsten, Carlsberg. **NEAREST TUBE STATION:** Knightsbridge. **MAP REF:** 2, F/4

The Tattershall Castle

272

King's Reach,
Victoria Embankment, SW1 **071-839 6548**

'A million pounds was spent on unbarnacling her bottom'

For 40 years the Tattershall Castle, a popular and successful London pub, ferried passengers across the Humber. This is unusual for a pub.

There are in fact two floating pubs in central London, old salts both. The Queen Mary worked on the Clyde, and this one, the Tattershall Castle, made eight trips a day between Hull and New Holland across what can be quite boisterous waters. She was a coal-fired paddle steamer and could, indeed frequently did, carry 1,050 people plus cars and livestock. First-class passengers travelled in what is now the wardroom bar, second-class passengers in what is now the buffet restaurant, third-class passengers in what is now the kitchen and the horses in the nightclub.

By 1973 the old paddle steamer needed urgent repairs to her boiler. Too costly, said British Rail Sea Link. So she was replaced and what happened next must have surprised her. Instead of being scrapped she was given a radical refit and a prime mooring in London.

She has certainly taken to life in the big city. A million pounds was spent on her only three years ago, a lot of it on unbarnacling her bottom, and she seems extremely perky now with a new taste for nightlife. During the week she keeps pub hours but at weekends the nightclub in the stern gets going and stays open until 3am. It gets queues.

The pub is the thing, though, and once you are in the saloon bar a pub it unmistakably is. The Tattershall Castle can't keep traditional ales but two lagers and a bitter are piped into ten big tanks in the barge moored alongside. These have to be refilled twice a week in the summer when the decks are crowded and the demand for lager seems insatiable.

There is a buffet downstairs, bar food in the bar, a barbecue on deck on fine days and on Sunday afternoons they do teas. There is something romantic and rather rakish about a paddle boat, even if what you are having is just Sunday tea. That's how it is on the Tattershall Castle.

OPEN: Mon-Sun. **HOURS:** 11.00am-11.00pm (12.00-10.30pm Sun). **CLOSED:** Christmas Day, Boxing Day, New Year's Day. **CREDIT CARDS ACCEPTED:** All major cards, except Diner's Card. **BAR FOOD AVAILABLE:** 12.00-10.00pm. **SET PRICE LUNCH:** £4.95. Wheelchair access. Tables outside seat 150. **BEERS AVAILABLE:** John Smith's, Beamish, Newcastle Brown Ale, Foster's, Holsten, Budweiser, Becks, Molsen Dry. **NEAREST TUBE STATION:** Embankment. **MAP REF:** 8, D/2

Thomas à Becket

273

320/322 Old Kent Road, SE1 **071-252 7605**

'Time and again the Thomas àBecket has been on the ropes'

There was a time when the Thomas à Becket was one of the best known pubs in London. It was a renowned boxing pub and for a time every world champion worked out in the gym on the first floor. Muhammad Ali hit those punch bags. Henry Cooper threw punches in that ring as did Mike Tyson, Frank Bruno, John Conti, Dave Charnley, Terry Downes, Alan Minter, Joe Bugner . . .

Goodness knows what happened to the old pub along the way but time and again the Thomas à Becket has been on the ropes. Each time a rescuer has appeared in the nick of time and we have read stories about vast sums about to be invested, about a refurbished gym and a boxing museum and the return of the good old days.

At the time of writing the Thomas à Becket is bracing itself for yet another comeback. The famous gym with its boxing ring, its tall bright windows on two sides, its showers and its sauna is locked and unused. There are no customers to speak of in the big downstairs bar and hardly any beer in the cellar. But, as always, a rescuer is at hand.

A local businessman is hoping to establish the old pub as a leading music venue and there are hopeful signs of the area picking up a bit. The huge new Tesco on the other side of the road will surely bring new customers and a retail park on the next corner is well on its way.

As for the famous gym, there seem, for the moment, to be no plans for that.

OPEN: Mon-Sun. **HOURS:** 11.00am-3.00pm Mon-Sat; 7.00-11.00pm Mon-Wed; 8.00pm-2.00am Thur-Sat; 12.00-3.00pm and 7.00-10.30pm Sun. **CLOSED:** Christmas Day. **CREDIT CARDS ACCEPTED:** None. **BAR FOOD AVAILABLE:** All opening hours. **SET PRICE DINNER:** £6.95. Wheelchair access. **BEERS AVAILABLE:** Theakston, Courage Best, Kronenbourg, Foster's, Newcastle Brown Ale, Grolsch, Diamond White, Holsten, Budweiser, Becks, Sol, Rolling Rock. **NEAREST TUBE STATION:** Elephant and Castle.

The Three Greyhounds

274

25 Greek Street, W1 **071-734 8799**

'Transformed'

Some pubs mirror the personality of the licensee. This one was transformed by the arrival of the charismatic Roxy Beaujolais.

The Three Greyhounds is the Tudory one on the corner of Greek Street and Old Compton Street, a genuinely old pub faked up with half-timbering in the 1920s. It was distinctly rough before Roxy took over in 1992. She brought glamour and oysters, cocktails, interesting snacks, cosmopolitan customers. She won't have music, gaming machines or crowds of lads. She made the white curtains herself and when someone pinched her stuffed piranha fish there was a tremendous rumpus.

She doesn't open till noon but she keeps the food going till 10.30pm. There's a variety of ales, wine starts at £7.10 a bottle, they serve coffee. *Time Out* thinks it is more a continental café than a pub but it's a pub all right. If you are going to the theatre you could start off here.

OPEN: Mon-Sun. **HOURS:** 12.00-11.00pm (12.00-3.00pm and 7.00-10.30pm Sun). **CLOSED:** Christmas Day. **CREDIT CARDS ACCEPTED:** Visa. **BAR FOOD AVAILABLE:** 12.00-7.30pm. Wheelchair access (but not lavatory). Private room seats 16. **BEERS AVAILABLE:** Adnams, Young's, Nicholson's, Carlsberg. **NEAREST TUBE STATION:** Leicester Square. **MAP REF:** 1, E/2

The Three Stags

275

67-69 Kennington Road, SE1 **071-928 5974**

'Lovable cockneys having a knees-up'

Charabancs deliver loads of tourists to the Three Stags on Friday and Saturday evenings in the summer. The tourists go there to see lovable cockneys having a typical knees-up and they are not disappointed. The manager, Gary Finnis, lays on exactly what they have in mind and before the night is out everyone is singing lovable cockney songs and doing the Lambeth Walk, oy. If this appeals to you give Mr Finnis a ring to make sure it's on before setting out, oy.

The Three Stags is a nice old Victorian pub opposite the Imperial War Museum and next door to the house Captain Bligh lived in. It hasn't changed much over the years.

Charlie Chaplin has a rather sad story about it in *My Early Years.* He says he was passing the pub one evening and an urge prompted him to peek inside. He opened the saloon door just a few inches and saw his father sitting in the corner looking very ill.

'I was about to leave, but his face lit up and he beckoned me to him,' wrote Chaplin. 'I was surprised at such a welcome for he was never demonstrative. He was most solicitous, enquiring after Mother and Sydney, and before I left took me in his arms and, for the first time, kissed me. That was the last time I saw him alive.'

Charles Chaplin Snr was a music hall artist who had topped the bill in happier days. He died of drink in St Thomas's Hospital three weeks after this encounter in the Three Stags. He was only 37.

OPEN: Mon-Sun. **HOURS:** 12.00-3.00pm and 6.00-11.00pm (7.00-10.30pm Sun). **CREDIT CARDS ACCEPTED:** None. **BAR FOOD AVAILABLE:** 12.00-2.30pm. **BEERS AVAILABLE:** Greene King variants. **NEAREST TUBE STATION:** Lambeth North. **MAP REF:** 7, B/2

The Tottenham

276

6 Oxford Street, W1 **071-636 7201**

'What publicans call a refurb'

London's pub population has been going down for years. Oxford Street used to have twenty. Now it has only one. This one.

The Tottenham is, as you might suppose, at the Tottenham Court Road end, just opposite Tottenham Court Road underground. Its Victorian architect wanted the best for it and quite a lot of its birthright has survived – some good decorated mirrors, three tapestry panels representing the seasons, lots of carved mahogany, a striking skylight. The Tottenham has just had what publicans call a refurb. This mainly involved reorganizing the cellar to double the number of real ales on tap and giving the ground floor bar and the plainer cellar bar a much-needed paint job. All the original features just mentioned survived. That is something to write home about. Refurbs quite often wipe out every original feature in sight.

Traditional pub food is served all day. Has anyone seen the missing tapestry?

OPEN: Mon-Sun. **HOURS:** 11.00am-11.00pm (12.00-3.00pm and 7.00-10.30pm Sun). **CLOSED:** Christmas Day. **CREDIT CARDS ACCEPTED:** All major cards. **BAR FOOD AVAILABLE:** 11.00am-3.00pm. **SET PRICE LUNCH:** £4.50. Wheelchair access. Private room seats 30. **BEERS AVAILABLE:** Tetley, Burton, Castlemaine, Lowenbrau, Carlsberg, Carlsberg Export. **NEAREST TUBE STATION:** Tottenham Court Road. **MAP REF:** 1, E/2

The Town of Ramsgate

277

62 Wapping High Street, E1 **071-488 2685**

'Just tied to the post and left to drown'

This dark little pub, the scene of many grisly events, still stands its corner in this narrow cobbled street, pinioned between the mass of

Oliver's Wharf and the dank alley known as Wapping Old Stairs. At the end of the alley old stone steps go bleakly down into the river. Judge Jeffreys, the notorious hanging judge, was captured here in disguise in 1688. He was trying to sneak off to Hamburg in a collier when he was recognized, almost lynched and dragged off to the Tower.

A succession of unfortunates stumbled down Wapping Stairs to be hanged on execution dock. This was the fate of the handsome, dashing privateer Captain Kidd. Others fared, if it is possible, even worse. They were just tied to a post in the river and left to drown as the tide rose and spectators jeered.

Then there was Captain Bligh. He and Fletcher Christian drank here before the Bounty sailed and press gangs kept their unwilling crews manacled in the cellars until their boats could take them. They just keep the beer down there these days, they say.

The Town of Ramsgate is a listed building now. It is a narrow old pub with a wooden ceiling and a small deck over the river at the back. There is a sinister black post sticking out of the yellow water. Was this the post on which the pirates died? The Town of Ramsgate isn't saying.

Some serious drinking goes on in the Town of Ramsgate. 'Don't be a mug, buy it by the jug' says a notice over the bar and regulars often do. A four pint jug of Bass is £5.44, a saving of 20p a pint.

OPEN: Mon-Sun. **HOURS:** 11.30am-11.00pm (12.00-3.00pm and 7.00-10.30pm Sun). **CREDIT CARDS ACCEPTED:** Access, Barclaycard. **BAR FOOD AVAILABLE:** 12.00-2.30pm and 6.00-9.00pm. Wheelchair access. Tables outside seat 30. **BEERS AVAILABLE:** Carling Black Label, Tennent's Pilsner, Tennent's Extra. **NEAREST TUBE STATION:** Wapping.

The Trafalgar 278

200 Kings Road, SW3 **071-352 1076**

'For teenagers of all ages'

Vast, lively, deafening, for teenagers of all ages. Bands, DJs, records, big-screen telly, pool, darts, pin-ball, arcade games, beefburgers, jumbo sausages, baked potatoes, steakwiches, extra chips £1. Fridays and Sundays resident DJ doing his 60s and 70s thing, everyone up dancing. Up dancing again Saturdays, Dinosaurs of Rock night, head banging favourites Quo, Deep Purple, Dire Straits, live bands Spin Doctors, Black Crowes, Joe Satriani.

Army of uniformed staff – uniform bright red polo shirts. Regular doormen to keep out riff-raff.

Built in ancient times, 1930s, as boring pub called the Lord Nelson, atmosphere, said *Evening Standard* of day, provincial hotel. Hard to imagine.

OPEN: Mon-Sun. **HOURS:** 11.00am-11.00pm (12.00-3.00pm and 7.00-10.30pm Sun). **CREDIT CARDS ACCEPTED:** All major cards. **BAR FOOD AVAILABLE:** 12.00-3.30pm Mon-Sat. No smoking area. Wheelchair access (but not lavatory). **BEERS AVAILABLE:** Grolsch, Tennent's Extra, Carling Black Label, Bass, London Pride, Toby's, Caffreys. **NEAREST TUBE STATION:** Sloane Square. **MAP REF:** 2, C/2

The Trafalgar Tavern

279

Park Row, SE10 **081-858 2437**

'A whole new lease of life. Even the whitebait dinners are back'

Pub is hardly the word for the Trafalgar Tavern, or tavern either. Seat, perhaps, or Place or even Hall would be better, so large it is and imposing with its parade of noble bars and its great ballroom on the floor above.

They call this the Nelson Room and it is a vast room of quite astonishing splendour with classical mouldings, elegant windows and curved wrought-iron balconies overlooking the river. It has elaborate swagged curtains and no fewer than eight chandeliers.

The Trafalgar was built in 1837 in this dashing Regency style to attract free-spending grandees from London which indeed it did. It was one of a number of whitebait taverns, noted for their whitebait dinners. Whitebait – the fry of herring, did you know that? – was the local speciality. It is said that at Greenwich they were heaved out of the river, seasoned, floured and dumped straight into cauldrons. Whitebait dinners were hugely popular and very expensive and none did them better or charged so much as the Trafalgar Tavern.

The gallants and the bloods careered down to Greenwich in their four-in-hands, the great and the good came more sedately. Thackeray, Wilkie Collins, Macaulay and Dickens were all regulars and Ministerial Whitebait Dinners became part of political life. Guests, including the prime minister of the day, arrived by Ordnance Barge. The Trafalgar and its competitors flourished.

The whitebait taverns had a good run but with the turn of the century they went out of business one by one. The Trafalgar lasted longer than most but in 1915 it succumbed too. For the next 50 years it was used as a home for old seamen and as a working men's club. Then in 1965 it was restored, relicensed and alleluia reopened and there it is on the river, full of swank and swagger again, enjoying a whole new lease of life. Even the whitebait dinners are back. The Saints and Sinners Club gives one in the Nelson Room every October – 250 members and guests, members of the cabinet usually present, the whitebait served with a flourish as the second of five courses and some of the most amusing after-dinner speakers in England doing their stuff.

The Nelson Room is much in demand for wedding receptions, but most of the action is in the lofty main bars downstairs. There all is space, comfort, lamb cutlets and most excellent bitter beer.

OPEN: Mon-Sun. **HOURS:** 11.00am-11.00pm (12.00-3.00pm and 7.00-10.30pm Sun). **CREDIT CARDS ACCEPTED:** Visa, Mastercard, Access. **BAR AND RESTAURANT FOOD AVAILABLE:** 12.00-3.00pm and 6.00-10.00pm. No smoking area. Wheelchair access. Private room seats 250. **BEERS AVAILABLE:** Ruddles County, Courage Best, Courage Directors, John Smith's, Foster's, Carlsberg, Budweiser, Kronenbourg, Beamish, Guinness. **NEAREST BR STATIONS:** Greenwich, Maze Hill.

Tut 'n' Shive

280

235 Upper Street, N1 **071-359 7719**

'A pub that sets out to turn the generation gap into the Grand Canyon'

A funny thing happened to the Angel and Crown this year. This unremarkable high street pub in Islington closed for a couple of weeks. When it reopened it had turned into the Tut 'n' Shive.

Were the old regulars surprised? 'Surprised?' says the new young landlord. 'They were shell-shocked . . .'

The Tut 'n' Shive is a pub that sets out to turn the generation gap into the Grand Canyon. Clearly a wild party has just finished and desperate repairs have been done before the next one starts. Old doors hold the counter up, graffiti is scrawled on peeling paint, corrugated iron sheets are pinned to the ceilings and piped music gets steadily louder until, about 9pm, it flattens you against the wall.

This, surprisingly, is a Whitbread pub, the first of a chain in its early days. It is run by Mark Clayton and Vanessa Bridger, an apparently tireless young couple who seem to be permanently planning another party. This is their first pub and it certainly has been in at the deep end. Upstairs it's comedy nights, titter at the Tut, and psychic nights, read your nut at the Tut, while shipwreck nights, spaghetti western nights and such gallivant in the bar. Music's the thing, non-stop music, music as loud as you like. 'That's what people want,' says Clayton. 'That's why they come. No music no pub.'

The Tut has music all right and lots of jokes. A life-size Frankenstein monster greets you as you arrive, stirring on his high shelf in the bar, coming to disconcerting life in a shroud of dry ice. An open coffin on its end is a peculiarly unappealing seat, the lavatories are labelled Willy's Room and Fanny's Place . . .

The Tut gets serious only about its cask ales. There are ten on offer, three changing behind the bar and seven regulars on the pumps and

herein lies the big drawback about managing the Tut 'n' Shive. You are forever having to explain the name. Let me try. The tut is the breathing hole in the cask. The shive is the plastic ring around it. I think that's right but it hardly matters. The pub is already just known as the Tut.

OPEN: Mon-Sun. **HOURS:** 11.00am-11.00pm (12.00-3.00pm and 7.00-10.30pm Sun). **CREDIT CARDS ACCEPTED:** None. **BAR FOOD AVAILABLE:** 12.00-3.00pm. Wheelchair access. Tables outside seat 15. Private room seats 40. **BEERS AVAILABLE:** Flowers Old Peculier, Flowers IPA, Boddingtons, London Pride, Summer Lightning, Heineken, Stella Artois, Guinness, Murphy's. **NEAREST TUBE STATION:** Highbury & Islington.

The Two Chairmen

281

39 Dartmouth Street, SW1 — **071-222 8694**

'The taxis of their day'

Sedan chairs were the taxis of their day. They were slow and swayed a lot and the men who carried them were often drunk but the streets were foul and dangerous and people threw unspeakable things from the upper windows. Lud, Madam! I think I'll take a chair!

The chairmen picked up fares at fixed points in London and this pub was one of them. Most of one wall in the bar is covered by a large painting showing a customer being given a bad time by two red-faced chairmen in the green greatcoats they wore. On second thoughts I think I'll walk.

Those chairmen wouldn't be allowed in the Two Chairmen nowadays, not in that state. It is a well-mannered up-market pub in the heart of St James's frequented mostly by civil servants. Quiet conversation is the thing. You get the impression that little has happened there lately, not since 1756 when it was last rebuilt.

There it is then, a quiet, dignified pub, at ease among its government offices. The small restaurant upstairs is popular at lunchtimes and it is a big spirit house. Few pubs sell more pink gins.

OPEN: Mon-Sun. **HOURS:** 11.00am-11.00pm (11.00am-6.00pm Sat; 12.00-3.00pm Sun). **CLOSED:** Bank Holidays. **CREDIT CARDS ACCEPTED:** All major cards. **BAR FOOD AVAILABLE:** 11.00am-10.30pm. **RESTAURANT FOOD AVAILABLE:** 12.00-10.00pm. Wheelchair access. **BEERS AVAILABLE:** Theakston Best, Courage Directors, John Smith's, Webster's, Holsten, Foster's, Miller Lite. **NEAREST TUBE STATION:** St James's Park. **MAP REF:** 8, C/1

The Viaduct Tavern

282

126 Newgate Street, EC1 — **071-606 8476**

'Interesting but grisly. You may need a drink'

On your way to the City or possibly to the Old Bailey you will find this singular pub, a small gin palace built in 1869, the year Queen Victoria opened Holborn Viaduct. It was the height of fashion, decorated mirrors, neo-Classical paintings, a beaten copper ceiling supported by a cast-iron Corinthian column, an ornate manager's stall behind the bar. The landlord's wife would sit enthroned in it, issuing tokens for drinks. The staff was not trusted with money.

Wan soulful ladies gaze down from the wall representing banking, agriculture and the arts. The arts has been holed. A drunken soldier from the London Regiment did it in the First World War. Some say he shot it, others say he charged it with a bayonet and look at the ceiling. This was the first public building in London to have an electric light and that was the old connecting point.

Yes, well you may prefer the cellars. There is something very nasty down there, to whit the debtors' cells. They were once part of Newgate Prison but they are part of the Viaduct Tavern now. The cells are tiny and they used to cram sixteen people into each of them. Ventilation holes in the ceilings opened onto the pavement in Newgate Street and prisoners would push their hands through, clutching at passers-by.

One prisoner appears to have been left behind. The landlord takes groups down there from time to time. It is interesting but grisly. You may need a drink afterwards.

OPEN: Mon-Sun. **HOURS:** 11.00am-11.00pm (12.00-3.00pm and 7.00-11.00pm Sat; 12.00-3.00pm and 7.00-10.30pm Sun). **CLOSED:** Christmas Day. **CREDIT CARDS ACCEPTED:** All major cards. **BAR FOOD AVAILABLE:** 12.00-8.00pm. Wheelchair access (but not lavatory). **BEERS AVAILABLE:** Carlsberg, Castlemaine, Tennent's Extra, 5 real ales. **NEAREST TUBE STATION:** St Paul's.
MAP REF: 6, B/2

The Warrington

283

93 Warrington Crescent W9 **071-286 2929**

'How was the church to know about its raunchy double life?'

The Church of England is down to just a handful of pubs now, a shame really. It used to have so many. Still, it could be a troublesome portfolio.

The Warrington in Maida Vale is a good example. How was the church to know about its raunchy double life? It was so stately, so grand, how to explain that those lively young ladies besporting themselves on every floor were not, well, ladies?

The Warrington had long since put its past behind it by the time the church sold it to David and Charles Williams in 1983. Their family had run the Warrington for years. Everyone thought it was their pub. Now it is.

It is a tremendous star turn, constantly appearing in movies and television ads. It plays what you might call walking-in parts. Cameras love it, delighting in its photogenic entrance with its faience pillars, its rich art nouveau tiling, its mosaic steps flanked by huge wrought-iron standard lamps made by Biggs and Co of Southwark and as for the saloon bar, it is a sight to behold. The great high room with its cherubs and marble pillars, the marble-topped counter with its ornate canopy, the frieze, the art nouveau glass, the handsome fireplace, lofty ceiling, sweeping mahogany staircase, film cameras find it irresistible.

I like the tap room myself but you would not have found Marie Lloyd in here. The main salon was created for great music hall stars like her and on a shelf over the fireplace you will see an empty champagne bottle, the last she consumed there. She was in her element in the Warrington.

Upstairs, in what was the naughtiest bit in the old days is now in the hands of Mr Songklod Boonyachalayont, known as Ben, whose large smiling staff provides delicious Thai food from 7pm onwards. It is very popular. You have to book.

The Warrington is much admired, not least by English Heritage who recently made a grant towards its repair. Listed Grade II buildings like this take a lot of looking after. It does not take itself too seriously though. It remains a lively and popular pub and seems to be under siege on sunny days with crowds outside and the big grassy road island covered by its younger customers. I have no hesitation in saying that as often as not this is the most densely populated road island in London.

OPEN: Mon-Sun. **HOURS:** 11.00am-11.00pm (12.00-3.00pm and 7.00-10.30pm Sun). **CREDIT CARDS ACCEPTED:** None. **BAR FOOD AVAILABLE:** 12.00-2.30pm and 6.00-11.00pm. **RESTAURANT FOOD AVAILABLE:** 6.00-10.30pm (7.00-10.00pm Sun). Tables outside seat 200. **BEERS AVAILABLE:** Fullers ESB, Young's Special, Brakspear Special, Ruddells County, Grolsch, Tennent's Extra, Foster's, Guinness. **NEAREST TUBE STATIONS:** Maida Vale, Warwick Avenue. **MAP REF:** 4, A/1

The Water Rat

284

1 Milman's Street, SW10 **071-351 4732**

'For fans of Absolut Mars Bar'

You can't miss the Water Rat in high summer. Such masses of flowers spill from window boxes, baskets and tubs that the Royal Borough of Kensington and Chelsea gives it prizes.

Even without the flowers this is a good-looking pub, three-storeyed, whitewashed, well-proportioned. This comes from being built in the 1830s when they took pains with these things.

Inside there is a big bar with a wallful of small-paned windows, taped music and Sky TV for big sports events. It is a freehouse so real ales rule. Absolut Vodkas are big there too with home-made variations that include Absolut Mars Bar, Absolut Hot Chilli Pepper and Absolut Raspberry. They are all sold in shot glasses at £1.30 a slam.

Dennis and Denise Timms, tenants of the Water Rat, have the River Rat on Albion Quay in Battersea too. It scores well with its river views and nautical air and also caters for fans of Absolut Mars Bar.

Should Milmans Street and Albion Quay seem a little far-flung and the need be great you can make it yourself. You chop up a Mars Bar, add the vodka and let it stand until the Mars dissolves. This takes about twenty-four hours. Chill it well.

OPEN: Mon-Sun. **HOURS:** 11.00am-11.00pm (12.00-3.00pm and 7.00-10.30pm Sun). **CREDIT CARDS ACCEPTED:** None. **BAR FOOD AVAILABLE:** 12.00-2.30pm (12.00-3.30pm Sat). Wheelchair access. Tables outside seat 48. **BEERS AVAILABLE:** Old Speckled Hen, Yorkshire Bitter, Guinness, Carlsberg, Holsten, Kronenbourg. **NEAREST TUBE STATION:** Sloane Square.

MAP REF: 2, B/2

The Water Rats 285

328 Grays Inn Road, WC1 **071-837 7269**

'Dress to sweat'

With heroic disregard for their hearing music journalists nightly seek out the next big thing on our behalf. The Water Rats at the King's Cross end of Gray's Inn Road is one of their most fruitful staging posts.

A band tracker writes: 'A youthful and lively buzz goes round the front bar. Bands at the top of the indie charts play in the back room. It is frequently packed to the rafters so dress to sweat. Stays open late as the Splash Club at weekends. It is currently the best music pub in town.'

OPEN: Mon-Sun. **HOURS:** 11.00-12.00am Mon-Fri; 7.00pm-12.00am Sat; 7.00-10.30pm Sun. **CLOSED:** All bank holidays. **CREDIT CARDS ACCEPTED:** None. **BAR FOOD AVAILABLE:** 12.00-2.30pm. Wheelcbair access (but not lavatory). Beer garden seats 8. Private room seats 60. **BEERS AVAILABLE:** Young's Ordinary, Young's Special, Courage Directors, John Smith's, Foster's, Kronenbourg, Hoffmeister, Guinness, Beamish. **NEAREST BR STATION:** King's Cross.

The Waterside Inn 286

82 York Way, N1 **071-837 7118**

'A wide stretch of glassy water'

A railway needs warehouses and there are some new ones behind King's Cross, a group of modern red-brick buildings of a strictly necessary kind with high railings to keep you out. The end one is rather different though. It has a large board inviting you in. 'The Waterside' it says. A pub sign yet.

So go in. This is not what you have been led to expect. There is a large 19th-century barn inside that red brick shell, oak frame roof beams, timber and brick walls, old black plank floor. Left-over timber has been made into plain tables and benches. Uses have been found for old brass fittings and the cider press that used to sit in the middle of the barn does so still. You can't believe the building is only twelve years old

Go through the big doors at the end and you find that the Waterside is indeed on the waterside. Beyond the deep brick terrace covered in picnic tables is a wide spread of glossy water. This is Battlebridge Basin, a working siding for canal boats. The terrace narrows and follows the basin to its junction with the Grand Union Canal. There is a place behind the railings here where men and boys sit fishing for hour after hour. Do they catch anything? No one knows.

The pub has its own canal boat, Waterside Lady, gaily painted and moored off the terrace. This is a restaurant and opens in the evenings. There's a barbecue on the terrace too and a food servery in the bar which opens at lunchtime. Cheesy nut burgers. Stuffed baguettes.

It is an excellent and unexpected pub. It greatly cheers a glum bit of London.

OPEN: Mon-Sun. **HOURS:** 11.00am-11.00pm (12.00-3.00pm and 7.00-10.30pm Sun). **CREDIT CARDS ACCEPTED:** Visa, Access, Mastercard. **BAR FOOD AVAILABLE:** 12.00-3.00pm and 6.00-9.00pm. Wheelchair access (but not lavatory). Beer garden seats 120. **BEERS AVAILABLE:** Boddingtons, Flowers IPA, Greene King, Abbot Ale, Marston's Pedigree. **NEAREST TUBE STATION:** King's Cross.

The Wellington

287

351 Strand, WC2 **071-836 0513**

'The pub stays loyal if the rest of us do not'

The good news about the Lyceum Theatre is good news for the Wellington. The once-great theatre has been rotting away for years. Now it is to be restored on a grand scale and could soon be filling the little pub next door again.

It is a small pub but it has an excellent position at the end of the Strand and a strong character of its own. Its public and saloon bars each have their own street entrance and there is no mistaking which is which. The public bar has the wooden floor and the saloon bar has the carpet.

The old duke is the star of course. There are lots of pictures of him and a notice says that miniatures of the inn sign, a brightly coloured ducal portrait, are for sale but no one ever asks. 'That was in the days when I was just a gleam in a Ford Cortina,' says the barman.

Hot meals are served in the upstairs bar, a pleasant room with a front window that looks directly across Waterloo Bridge.

OPEN: Mon-Sun. **HOURS:** 11.00am-11.00pm (12.00-3.00pm and 7.00-10.30pm Sun). **CREDIT CARDS ACCEPTED:** All major cards. **BAR FOOD AVAILABLE:** 12.00-3.00pm. Wheelchair access (but not lavatory). Tables outside seat 15. **BEERS AVAILABLE:** Boddingtons, Courage Best, Courage Directors, Fosters, Kronenbourg, Budweiser, Guinness. **NEAREST TUBE STATION:** Charing Cross. **MAP REF:** 1, F/1

The Westminster Arms

288

9 Storey's Gate, SW1 **071-222 8520**

'MPs can find safety in numbers'

There are nine bars in the House of Commons, one for every 72.2 MPs, and they have to share eight of them with visitors and the like, rather a squash but luckily there is a pub or two a short walk away as well. This is one of them.

Until the new Queen Elizabeth Conference Centre was built the Westminster Arms had a clear view of Big Ben and of Westminster Abbey. Now what it sees is the side of the conference centre, not a good swap. On the other hand it gets wave after wave of custom from the new building and is extraordinarily busy most of the time. MPs can find safety in numbers and reassurance from the division bell in the bar.

The bar, crowded most of the day, looks much as it did when the pub was rebuilt in 1913 but the cellar bar, thoroughly done over in the modern manner this year, is back with a flagstone floor, drinking booths round the walls, old panelling, benches and wooden tables. There is a pleasant restaurant on the first floor and tables and chairs stand on the pavement outside all summer.

It is a free house, has seven real ales on the hand pumps and makes a big effort to keep prices down. A pint of Westminster Best, the one the pub has specially brewed, is £1.60 a pint and on the last Tuesday in the month landlord Roger Burston has a good deal going – he does five pints for £5. Regulars put it in their diaries and on the last Tuesday in the month they are there.

OPEN: Mon-Sun. **HOURS:** 11.00am-11.00pm (12.00-3.00pm and 7.00-10.30pm Sun). **CREDIT CARDS ACCEPTED:** All major cards. **BAR FOOD AVAILABLE:** 12.00-10.00pm Mon-Fri; 12.00-6.00pm Sat; 12.00-3.00pm Sun. **RESTAURANT FOOD AVAILABLE:** 12.00-3.00pm Mon-Fri. Wheelchair access (but not lavatory). Tables outside seat 15. Private room seats 40. **BEERS AVAILABLE:** Adnams, Brakspear, Wadworth, Theakston, Westminster Best, Bass, Tennent's Pilsner, Tennent's Extra, Foster's, Guinness. **NEAREST TUBE STATIONS:** Westminster, St James's Park. **MAP REF:** 8, C/2

Wetherspoons 289

Victoria Station, SW1 **071-931 0445**

'Not a hint of Queen Victoria'

This is a rarity, a pub built in the 1990s in the style of the 1990s. It is light, leafy and minimalist with not a hint of Queen Victoria anywhere to be seen.

It is in the middle of Victoria station on the first floor of the new building it shares with W H Smith. It has its own short escalators to take you up and bring you down again and there is a terrace on either side. From one you look down on the South Central Concourse and get a full view of the departure board and from the other you can look down on platforms 6, 5, 4 and 3 and watch your train leaving without you.

It is an unexpectedly quiet and civilized spot in this hectic place.

OPEN: Mon-Sun. **HOURS:** 11.00am-11.00pm (12.00-3.00pm and 7.00-10.30pm Sun). **CREDIT CARDS ACCEPTED:** Access, Visa, Delta, Switch. **BAR FOOD AVAILABLE:** 11.00am-11.00pm (12.00-3.00pm and 7.00-9.30pm Sun). **SET PRICE LUNCH AND DINNER:** £3.95. No smoking area. Wheelchair access. Tables outside seat 30. **BEERS AVAILABLE:** Theakston Best, Theakston XB, Younger Scotch Bitter, Courage Directors, Wadworth 6X, Becks, McEwans, Foster's. **NEAREST TUBE STATION:** Victoria.

The White Horse

290

1-3 Parson's Green, SW6 **071-736 2115**

'Now it is itself the destination'

Old coaching inns, their original occupations gone, often adapt brilliantly to our times. Look at the White Horse on Parsons Green. Three hundred years ago it was the last stop for a meal and a change of horses before the long hard journey from London to Exeter and Bristol. Now it is itself the destination.

It is an extrovert, cheerful place. The big, comfortable, U-shaped bar has huge draped windows, leather sofas and eating booths, there is a billiard room upstairs and a regularly changing team of young Australian and New Zealand athletes behind the bar. They arrive for six months or so, live in, work hard and move on having made friends for life in London.

The charismatic manager, Sally Cruickshank, has transformed the place in her years there and she has a unique asset in Mark Dorber, by day successful City analyst, by night White Horse cellarman. He is a serious bespectacled man totally enthused by the beer in his charge – the soft, fruity draught bass, the dry and aromatic Adnams, the velvety Highgate mild, the delightfully hoppy Harveys Sussex bitter and the guest beers that change every month. When Adnams Extra became Britain's champion beer this year the White Horse was the only London pub to have it, quite a coup. Lots of others have now.

A lot goes on at the White Horse. Big beer festivals have spread its reputation far beyond London but it is locally famous for the excellence of the beer and the robustness of its home-made cooking. Its breakfasts on Saturdays and Sundays are amazing – 11 items on the plate. They do a good Sunday lunch too. There are some notable trenchermen in Parsons Green.

An *Evening Standard* Pub of the Year.

OPEN: Mon-Sun. **HOURS:** 11.30am-3.00pm and 5.00-11.00pm (11.00am-4.00pm and 7.00-11.00pm Sat; 11.00am-3.00pm and 7.00-10.30pm Sun). **CREDIT CARDS ACCEPTED:** All major cards. **BAR FOOD AVAILABLE:** 12.00-2.45pm and 5.00-10.30pm (11.00am-2.45pm and 7.00-10.30pm Sat; 11.00am-2.45pm and 7.00-10.00pm Sun). **RESTAURANT FOOD AVAILABLE:** 12.00-2.00pm Sun, Oct-Apr. **SET PRICE LUNCH:** £10. Wheelchair access (but not lavatory). Beer garden seats 80. Private room seats 60. **BEERS AVAILABLE:** 15 Belgian and Dutch beers, Harveys Sussex, Highgate Mild, Bass, Adnams Extra. **NEAREST TUBE STATION:** Parsons's Green.

The White Swan

291

The Riverside,
Twickenham **081-892 2166**

'Shirts of the great and ties of the famous'

After the match the discerning rugby supporter will go for a walk. He will make his way through the Georgian streets of Old Twickenham, past the church with its medieval stone tower, past Thomas Twining's Dial House of 1726, along a brick-walled sunken lane and down to the river. On his right will be the wooded, tapering end of Eel Pie Island and on his left the old pub he has been making for.

The White Swan has been there since 1690. It is all terraces and balconies and railings and crooked windows and accretions and hanging baskets and troughs of flowers. Inside all is old wood and real ale. Bizarre collections cover the walls. 'Everything has a story behind it,' says Steve Roy, the landlord, 'but don't print this one . . .'

There are two bars, the main bar and the rugby bar. This being the pub it is the rugby bar comes first. In there it is prints of scrums and photographs of great tries, it is shirts of the great and ties of the famous, autographed oval balls and Paul Ackford's shorts which in themselves make this a shrine for toilers in the engine room.

The best table is the triclinium. A triclinium, explains Roy, is a room with three walls, the fourth being open, or a table with seats on three sides. This is both a snug spot for serious drinking and real conversation with a fine view of the river and the terraces.

Food is important at the White Swan. At lunchtimes a buffet is laid out on a huge table with a great ham, cooked on the premises, taking pride of place. On summer evenings and Sunday lunchtimes Steve Roy mans the barbecue and in the winter he cooks a corking Sunday lunch.

Some people, after a drink at the White Swan, keep going along the river to Richmond, taking in Marble Hill. Others stay right where they are.

OPEN: Mon-Sun. **SUMMER HOURS:** 11.00am-11.00pm (12.00-3.00pm and 7.00-10.30pm Sun). **WINTER HOURS:** 11.00-3.00pm and 5.30-11.00pm Mon-Thur; 11.00am-11.00pm Fri-Sat; 12.00-3.00pm and 7.00-10.30pm Sun. **BAR FOOD AVAILABLE:** 12.00-3.00pm and 5.30-9.00pm. **SET PRICE LUNCH:** £4.25. Wheelchair access. Tables outside seat 20. **BEERS AVAILABLE:** Wadworth 6X, London Pride, Pedigree, Webster's, Old Speckled Hen, Holsten, Budweiser, Foster's, Carlsberg. **NEAREST BR STATION:** Twickenham.

The White Swan

292

25-26 Old Palace Lane,
Richmond **081-940 0959**

'Many monarchs lived in the old palace, three died there'

A country lane leads gently down to the river with cottages, perhaps 400 years old, all painted white, little front gardens overflowing with flowers. You see the river ahead, usually flowing by but sometimes coming up the lane you meet you. Large notices warn of flooding.

The White Swan, painted white like the cottages, is halfway along and it draws you inside on a cold day with its fires, dark panelling, low ceilings and old settles. It could hardly be more picturesque.

It started life as an ale house and until quite recently it could only sell beer. You can get a Scotch there now though and there have been other changes; a small conservatory has been added and there is a flagged garden with picnic tables. It is peaceful there on a summer afternoon and quite a surprise when planes roar overhead and trains thunder past apparently in the bushes.

Its original customers were the below-stairs staff of the royal palace that gave the lane its name. It stretched along the riverbank and the new little ale house faced its garden wall.

Many monarchs lived in the old palace, three died there – Edward III, Henry VII and Elizabeth I, who went there on the advice of her astrologer and died of a distemper.

OPEN: Mon-Sun. **HOURS:** 11.00am-3.30pm and 5.30-11.00pm (12.00-3.00pm and 7.00-10.30pm Sun). **CREDIT CARDS ACCEPTED:** None. **BAR FOOD AVAILABLE:** All opening hours. **SET PRICE LUNCH AND DINNER:** £3.50. Wheelchair access (but not lavatroy). Beer garden seats 60. Private room seats 35. **BEERS AVAILABLE:** Courage Best, Courage Directors, Kronenbourg, Foster's, Beamish, Guinness. **NEAREST TUBE STATION:** Richmond.

The White Swan

293

14 Vauxhall Bridge Road, SW1 **071-821 8568**

'The modish style known as Old English Ale House'

The White Swan is the big Victorian pub you pass as you drive in heavy traffic towards Vauxhall Bridge. The temptation to stop is sometimes great.

Drastic things have been happening there. It is now one huge bar in the modish style known as Old English Ale House, massive weather-worn timbers, bare floorboards, bare brick walls, chopping-board tables, pine benches, ceilings lowered a good yard with introduced bare rafters. The original Victorian ceiling can be glimpsed high above.

Real ales, robust traditional food and lots of room make for busy lunchtimes, the latest gaming machines, a jukebox and television get a lively young crowd in the evenings and a large white swan in a glass case keeps a beady eye on all around it.

OPEN: Mon-Sun. **HOURS:** 11.00am-11.00pm (12.00-3.00pm and 7.00-10.30pm Sun). **CREDIT CARDS ACCEPTED:** All major cards. **BAR FOOD AVAILABLE:** 12.00-5.30pm. **SET PRICE LUNCH:** £4.95. Wheelchair access. Tables outside seat 70. Private room seats 50. **BEERS AVAILABLE:** Courage Best, Courage Directors, John Smith's, Wadworth, Kronenbourg, Foster's, Carlsberg. **NEAREST TUBE STATION:** Pimlico. **MAP REF:** 8, A/1

The William IV

294

75 Hampstead High Street, NW3 **071-435 5747**

'William IV might have been surprised by the William IV of our day. He seems to have been staunchly heterosexual himself. On the other hand . . .'

Near the top of Hampstead's steep leafy High Street is one of North London's principal gay pubs, prosperous, respectable and middle class, mirroring, as pubs do, the community it serves.

The William IV stands four square on its corner, yellow London brick with black shutters, window boxes and hanging baskets bright with flowers. The interior is very smart, ceiling lincrusta'd, walls sponged, stippled, papered and panelled. A large notice headed 'Our Fabulous Wines' lists eight, one of them a champagne: Duc de Roucher £23.50.

There is a substantial island counter and a team of cheerful barmen dealing with four drinking areas, three used predominately by men and one sometimes by women. There is also its new Bar Verandah, billed as 'London's first and only non-smoking lesbian and gay bar'.

The food, which is good, is lunchtime only. An alternative is not far to seek. La Crêperie de Hampstead is on the pavement outside, tucked against the pub's garden wall though no crêpes are allowed in either the pub or the garden. You can have one at the tables on the pavement. The garden, large, pleasant and filled with tables, can count on a busy and sociable summer.

William lV, bluff and red-faced, looks down from the inn sign. He might have been surprised by the William IV of our day. He seems to have been staunchly heterosexual himself, lived for twenty-one years with the actress Mrs Jordan who bore him ten children. On the other hand he was known as the sailor king.

OPEN: Mon-Sun. **HOURS:** 11.00am-11.00pm (12.00-10.30pm Sun). **CREDIT CARDS ACCEPTED:** None. **BAR FOOD AVAILABLE:** 12.00-2.30pm Mon-Sat. No smoking area. Wheelchair access. Beer garden seats 50. Tables outside seat 16. **BEERS AVAILABLE:** 'Pink Willy' bitter, Courage Best, Courage Directors, Ruddells, Foster's, Carlsberg, Kronenbourg, Heineken, Guinness. **NEAREST TUBE STATION:** Hampstead.

Williamson's Tavern 295

1 Groveland Court, EC4 **071-248 6280**

'No place for ravers'

You can lose yourself and never be seen again searching for Williamson's Tavern, so let me tell you precisely where it is. It is the exact centre of City of London's square mile. A stone in what was the parlour marks the spot.

Williamson's has a remarkable history. It started off as a grand private house, so grand that it was the official residence of successive lord mayors. One of them entertained the King and Queen there, William and Mary who presented him with a truly royal knick-knack, a pair of wrought-iron gates. These are still in daily use.

The house became Williamson's in 1739 when Robert Williamson bought it and converted it into an hotel. They had just laid the foundation stone of the Mansion House so the lord mayors had to stay on for another 13 years until the new building was finished.

It seems to have made a good hotel. Anyway, it was always full. Matches, we are told, were banned because the ceilings were whitewashed cotton nailed to bare oak so guests had to light their pipes with tapers. Happily it did not burn down in spite of this and in the 1930s a new owner made it a pub.

It is a distinctly superior pub with a library, two fine panelled bars and the general air of a gentleman's club. It is very popular with City gents who know exactly how to get there, also with City women who like its unpubby atmosphere. Between them they fill all three big bars at lunchtime. There is a charcoal grill in one of them and some say its steak sandwiches are the best in London.

It is very peaceful in Williamson's in the afternoon with everyone back at work. Then it wakes up again as people look in for a snifter on their way home and it closes about 9pm as most City pubs do. The City of London is no place for ravers.

OPEN: Mon-Fri. **HOURS:** 11.30am-9.00pm. **CLOSED:** Bank holidays. **CREDIT CARDS ACCEPTED:** AmEx, Access, Diner's Club. **BAR FOOD AVAILABLE:** 11.30am-2.45pm. **SET PRICE LUNCH:** £3.95. Private room seats 50. **BEERS AVAILABLE:** Tetley, Nicholson's, Adnams, Wadworth, Brakspear, Castlemaine, Carlsberg. **NEAREST TUBE STATION:** Mansion House.

The Wilton Arms

296

71 Kinnerton Street, SW1 **071-235 4854**

'Some jolly good books in the bookcases'

Wilton Crescent, Wilton Place, Wilton Row, as good addresses go these are hard to beat and the Wilton Arms, named like the rest after the first Earl of Wilton, stands, most respectfully, a little apart.

It is just round the corner from Wilton Place in Kinnerton Street, that most desirable of mewses. I see it as the comptroller of the household, grand in its own right but knowing its place.

It was built with the rest of the street in 1826 and has shared its fortunes. In its early days Kinnerton Street was rough and malodorous with an open sewer and more horses than people, but those days are long gone and for many years the Wilton Arms has been a most superior public house. It got further improved in the Whitbread manner six years ago and high settles and bookcases now give the big bar a number of pleasantly separate drinking areas. There are some jolly good books in the bookcases. New Zealand Statutes. Public Acts of Tasmania.

There is a kitchen with a presiding chef on the first floor and hot food is served all day. You see friendly bar staff slipping down the street with covered plates, delivering lunch to elderly residents.

The Wilton Arms used to have a garden. This has been replaced by a conservatory to win more tables. One space has been left open to the sky with room for just one table and four chairs. When the sun shines this is the most sought-after place in the pub.

OPEN: Mon-Sun. **HOURS:** 11.00am-11.00pm (12.00-3.00pm and 7.00-10.30 Sun). **CREDIT CARDS ACCEPTED:** None. **BAR FOOD AVAILABLE:** 11.00am-11.00pm (11.30am-4.00pm Sat; 12.00-3.00pm Sun). Private room seats 20. **BEERS AVAILABLE:** Boddingtons, Flowers IPA, Abbot Ale, Heineken, Stella Artois. **NEAREST TUBE STATION:** Knightsbridge. **MAP REF:** 2, F/4

The Windmill on the Common

297

Clapham Common South Side,
SW4 **081-673 4578**

'A very genteel and good accustomed house'

You might not like to be called ye olde and some pubs don't either. This famous pub was called Ye Olde Windmill for a while but it is the Windmill on the Common now if you don't mind.

It is decidedly on the olde side all the same. It has been here, apparently, since at least 1665. Charles II. Full-bottom wigs. Richard Attenborough opening in *The Mousetrap*. Ye Olde.

The mid-17th century, then. There was this windmill standing in open countryside. The miller began to double as an ale house keeper and this side of the business gradually took over. Another 100 years and the windmill had gone and the Windmill Inn had replaced it – 'a very genteel and good accustomed house', a Mr Edwards wrote at the time.

It became a staging post and got bigger and grander. Youngs became involved in 1848 and bought the freehold fifty years later and here we are, another 100 years on and the Windmill is in terrific form with its big wandering bar, a spacious conservatory for non smokers, an excellent restaurant and an adjoining hotel that gets three stars from the AA and is highly commended by the English Tourist Board.

Things are always going on at the Windmill – quizzes, fiesta nights, jazz, opera in the conservatory. In the summer drinkers spill out onto the common and in the winter there's an open fire in the bar.

There are cask ales, draught lagers and a plentiful wine list, five reds, five whites, two rosés and two champagnes. The head chef of the attached restaurant does the bar food and makes his own bread.

The Windmill on the Common gets packed in the evenings and at weekends and no wonder.

OPEN: Mon-Sun. **HOURS:** 11.00am-11.00pm (12.00-3.00pm and 7.00-10.30pm Sun). **CREDIT CARDS ACCEPTED:** None. **BAR FOOD AVAILABLE:** 12.00-2.30pm and 7.00-10.00pm. **RESTAURANT FOOD AVAILABLE:** 7.00-10.00pm. No smoking area. Wheelchair access (disabled lavatory). Beer garden seats 50. **BEERS AVAILABLE:** All Young's variants.

The Windsor Castle

298

114 Campden Hill Road, W8 **071-727 8491**

'On a clear day you could see Windsor Castle'

You know at once that the Windsor Castle was meant to be a country pub and so it was in its young days. High on rural Camden Hill it was gravel pits, farms and a quiet life for the new tavern. On a clear day you could see Windsor Castle from an upstairs window though not perhaps the monarch. George IV would have been inside loosening his corsets. Now, surrounded by some of the most expensive real estate in London and with no view to speak of, the Windsor Castle is a prize, a pub of outstanding charm and character more admired today, perhaps, than any time in its long life.

It seems not to have changed at all. There used to be three bars, each clearly defined, the sherry bar for the local toffs, the private bar for the hoi polloi and the Campden bar for, well, the rest. This remains more or less the situation today. The three bars survive, each with its own entrance and its own customers, the Campden and the private bars with their heavy oak tables between high-backed settles, the sherry bar with more gentlemanly tables and chairs, all low-ceilinged and dark-panelled. The Campden Bar gets so packed in the evenings that movement is impossible though the staff in their black waistcoats and long white aprons somehow manage.

In the summer the garden opens and the capacity of the pub trebles. It is a splendid garden shaded by a old plane tree, two other trees coming along nicely for future generations. Visitors are shoulder-to-shoulder in the garden on hot days. The bankers, judges, lawyers and actors in the sherry bar are happy to stay just where they are. Should you brave the sherry bar the approved drink is the Huntsman – dry sherry with tomato juice, a milder Bloody Mary.

There is a roster of cooks and the food is outstanding – hot prawns, salmon fish cakes, chargrilled steak, lamb with couscous, steak and kidney pudding. You can get half a dozen oysters for a fiver and a bottle of champagne for £16. Sunday lunch in the Campden Bar – always roast rib of beef and Yorkshire Pudding – is so popular that lunchtime goes on until 4pm. Matthew O'Keefe, who runs it, proudly claims that on other days his kitchens never close. 'If we are open for drink we are open for food,' he says.

The gents is still outside. With luck it won't be raining.

OPEN: Mon-Sun. **HOURS:** 11.00am-11.00pm (12.00-3.00pm and 7.00-10.30pm Sun). **CLOSED:** Christmas Day and Boxing Day. **CREDIT CARDS ACCEPTED:** Visa, Access, AmEx. **BAR FOOD AVAILABLE:** All hours. No smoking Sunday lunchtimes. Wheelchair access (but not lavatory). Beer garden seats 60. **BEERS AVAILABLE:** Bass, Young's. **NEAREST TUBE STATION:** Notting Hill Gate. **MAP REF:** 3, C/2

The Wrestlers

299

North Hill, N6 **081-340 4297**

'One claim to up-to-dateness'

A plaque on the wall says there was a pub here in 1547 but this, clearly, was not it. This one was built in 1921, a solid, suburban public house. It recently took on modern times head on with a spell as a Slug and Lettuce but this didn't work at all and the Wrestlers was soon the Wrestlers again. Nowadays it contents itself with one claim to up-to-dateness each summer. 'Only Pub in Highgate with Air Conditioning' says a board outside.

Wrestlers wrestle on the inn sign. Elizabethan troopers stationed nearby says the landlord. They don't wrestle at the Wrestlers nowadays.

OPEN: Mon-Sun. **HOURS:** 12.00-11.00pm (12.00-3.00pm and 7.00-10.30pm Sun). **CREDIT CARDS ACCEPTED:** All major cards. **BAR FOOD AVAILABLE:** 12.00-2.30pm and 6.30-9.00pm. **SET PRICE LUNCH:** £3.95 (Sun only). **BEERS AVAILABLE:** Draught Bass, London Pride, Worthington Best, Grolsch, Tennent's Extra, Tennent's Pilsner, Carling Black Label, Guinness, Strongbow Cider. **NEAREST TUBE STATION:** Highgate.

The Yacht

300

Crane Street, SE10 **081-858 0175**

'Charles II liked it'

The original Yacht was a famous old pub. Charles II liked it. He would slip in there when the court was at Greenwich. It had a pleasant riverside garden and was growing old with much grace when, alas, Hitler got it.

The rebuilt version still has the fine site on the riverbank, the entrance romantically halfway along a narrow alley, but it is a pub for day trippers now.

A modern extension completely covers the old garden. Off the new room a narrow balcony over the water has room for a few standing drinkers in single file. You get a good view of the Canary Wharf tower from there. The Greenwich Meridian line runs through the building.

OPEN: Mon-Sun. **HOURS:** 12.00-11.00pm (12.00-3.00pm and 7.00-10.30pm Sun). **CLOSED:** Christmas Day. **CREDIT CARDS ACCEPTED:** All major cards. **BAR FOOD AVAILABLE:** 12.00-8.00pm. Wheelchair access. Tables outside seat 50. **BEERS AVAILABLE:** Ruddells Best, John Smith's, Courage Directors, Carlsberg, Holsten, Foster's, Budweiser. **NEAREST BR STATION:** Maze Hill.

Captain Kidd,
108 Wapping High Street, E1
071-480 5759

Dickens Inn,
St Katherine's Way, E1
071-488 1226

The Dove Inn,
19 Upper Mall, W6
081-748 5405

Flask,
77 Highgate West Hill, N6
081-340 7260

George Inn,
77 Borough High St,SE1
071-407 2056

Hamilton Hall,
Liverpool Street Station, EC2
071-247 3579

O'Hanlons,
18 Tysoe Street, EC1
071-837 4112

Waterside Inn,
82 York Way, N1
071-837 7118

Wetherspoons,
Victoria Station, SW1
071-931 0445

White Horse,
1-3 Parson's Green, SW6
071-736 2115

Windmill on the Common,
Clpham Common South Side, SW4
081-673 4578

Windsor Castle,
114 Campden Hill Road, W8
071-727 8491

Pubs with Theatres

King's Head

Man in the Moon

Old Red Lion, EC1
Orange Tree

Other pubs with theatres include:

Bush,
Shepherds Bush Green, W12. 071-740 0501.
Duke of Cambridge,
64 Lawford Road, NW5. 071-485 4303.
Finborough Arms,
118 Finborough Road, SW10. 071-373 3842.
Hen and Chickens,
109 St Paul's Road, N1. 071-359 1030.
Prince Albert,
(The Gate) 11 Pembridge Road, W11. 071-229 0706.
Latchmere,
503 Battersea Park Road, SW11. 071-228 2620.
Landor,
Landor Road, SW9. 071-924 5031.
Oxford Arms,
265 Camden High Street, NW1. 071-482 4857.
Rose and Crown,
61 High Street, Hampton Wick, Kingston. 081-224 2301.
Three Horseshoes,
28 Heath Street, NW3. 071-435 3648.
Union Tavern,
146 Camberwell New Road, SW9. 071-757 9053.
White Bear,
138 Kennington Park Road, SE11. 071-793 9193

Gay Pubs

Black Cap

Champion, W11
Coleherne

William IV

Other gay pubs include:

Angel,
65 Graham St, N1.
Brief Encounter,
41 St Martin's Lane, WC2.
Bromptons,
294 Old Brompton Road, SW5.
Comptons,
53 Old Compton Street, W1.
Duke of Wellington,
119 Balls Pond Road, N1.
Edward VI,
25 Bromfield Street, N1.
Father Redcap,
319 Gamborwell Green, SE5.
King's Arms,
23 Poland Street, W1.
London Apprentice,
333 Old Street, EC1.
Queen's Head,
27 Tryon Street, SW3.
Market Tavern,
1 Nine Elms Lane, SW8.
Royal Vauxhall Tavern,
372 Kennington Lane, SE11.
Salmon and Compasses,
58 Penton Street, N1.
Two Brewers,
114 Clapham High Street, SW4.
White Swan,
556 Commercial Road, E1

Pubs with Late-Night Opening

Please check pub entries for details

Albion, N16

Beaufoy Arms
Black Cap

De Hems
Dublin Castle

Friar and Firkin
Fusilier and Firkin

George Canning
Golden Lion, W1

King's Head, SW6
King's Head, N1

Monarch

O-Bar

Rose and Crown, N6

Sir George Robey
Swan, SW9

Thomas à Becket

Water Rats

Pubs with No Smoking Areas

Admiral Codrington
Albany
Albion, N1
Alexandra
Argyll Arms

Barley Mow, E14
Beehive
Bell & Crown
Blackbird
Britannia

Cat and Canary
Crooked Billett

Doggetts Coat and Badge
Drayton Arms

Freemasons Arms
Friar And Firkin

Gallery
Gatehouse
Guinea

Hamilton Hall *
Hand in Hand
Hare and Hounds
Hoop and Grapes
Hop Poles
Horniman's
J J Moon's

Lamb
Lamb Tavern

Man in the Moon
Melton Mowbray

Mitre
Moon and Sixpence
Moon under the Water

Old Bull and Bush
Old King Lud
Old Shades
Orange Tree

Paxton's Head
Phoenix and Firkin
Prospect of Whitby
Punch and Judy

Rising Sun, EC1
Rose and Crown, SW19
Rose of York

Salisbury
Sherlock Holmes
Stargazey
Swan, W6

Tattersalls Tavern
Trafalgar
Trafalgar Tavern

Waterside Inn *
Wetherspoons *
William IV
Windmill on the Common
Windsor Castle *

No smoking areas are now allotted thirty per cent of the space in all J D Wetherspoon pubs.

Riverside Pubs

Anchor
Angel

Bell and Crown
Black Lion
Blue Anchor
Bull's Head

City Barge
Cutty Sark

Dickens Inn *
Doggett's Coat and Badge
Dove Inn *
Duke's Head

Founders Arms

Gazebo
Grapes, E14

Mayflower

Old Ship

Prospect of Whitby

Rose of York
Rutland

Ship
Star and Garter

Town of Ramsgate
Trafalgar Tavern

White Swan, Twickenham

Yacht

Other riverside pubs include:

Barmy Arms,
Riverside Twickenham.
Bishop out of Residence,
Bishop's Hall, Thames Street, Kingston.
Gun,
27 Coldharbour Lane, E14.
London Apprentice,
62 Church St, Old Isleworth.
Pope's Grotto,
Cross Deep, Twickenham.
Samuel Pepys,
Brooks Wharf, 48 Upper Thames St, EC4.
Three Pigeons,
87 Petersham Road, Richmond.
Waterman's Arms,
1 Glenaffric Avenue, E14

Pubs with Car Parks

Albany
Albion, N16
Alma Tavern
Anchor Bankside
Angel

Barley Mow, E14
Black Lion
Bull
Bull's Head

Cat and Canary
City Barge
Cocoanut

Dove Inn *

Flower and Firkin

Gazebo
George Canning

Hare and Hounds
Henry Holland

Jack Straw's Castle

Old Bull and Bush
Outpost

Paddington Stop
Park Tavern

Rose and Crown, SW19
Rose of York

Ship Inn
Sir Richard Steele
Spaniards Inn
Sun Inn

Windmill on the Common *

Pubs with Live Music

Admiral Codrington
Albany
Albion, N16
Alexandra

Barley Mow, E14
Beaufoy Arms
Betsey Trotwood
Black Cap
Blue Anchor
Bull
Bull and Gate

Chelsea Potter
City Barge
Clutterbuck's
Coleherne
Cutty Sark

Drayton Arms
Dublin Castle

Eagle Tavern
Elephant and Castle

Ferret and Firkin
Finch's
Flask, N6 *
Flask, NW3
Flower and Firkin
Freemasons Arms
Friar and Firkin
Fulmar and Firkin
Fusilier and Firkin

George Canning
George Inn *
Goose and Firkin
Ground Floor Bar

Hare and Hounds
Henry Addington
Holly Bush
Hop Poles
Horse and Groom

Jack Straw's Castle

King's Head, N1
King's Head, SW6

Lamb and Flag
Leinster Arms

Magdela Tavern
Magpie and Stump, SW10
Marquess Tavern
Mitre
Monarch

Narrow Boat

O'Hanlons *
Old Bull and Bush
Old King Lud
Old Ship
Olde Surgeon
Orange Tree
Outpost

Paddington Stop
Park Tavern
Phoenix and Firkin
Prospect of Whitby

Queen's Arms

Railway Tavern, EC2
Ring
Robert Browning
Rose and Crown, N6
Rutland

Ship
Ship Inn
Sir George Robey
Sir Richard Steele
Slug and Lettuce
Stargazey
Swan, W2
Swan, W6
Swan, SW9
(Ye Olde) Swiss Cottage

Thomas à Becket
Three Greyhounds
Trafalgar
Trafalgar Tavern
Tut 'n' Shive

Water Rats
White Horse *
Windmill on the Common *

Yacht

Pubs with Beer Gardens

Admiral Codrington
Albany
Albion, N1
Anchor

Bell and Crown
Black Lion
Blind Beggar
Bull

Camden Head
Captain Kidd *
Cartoonist
Charlie Chaplin
Clarence
Cocoanut
Cutty Sark

Dickens Inn *
Dog and Fox
Doggets Coat and Badge

Enterprise

Flask, N6 *
Flask, NW3
Founders Arms
Fox and Pheasant
Freemasons Arms

Gatehouse
Gazebo
Gipsy Moth
Green Man

Hand in Hand
Hare and Hounds
Henry Addington
Henry J Bean's
Hereford Arms
Hillgate Arms

Jack Straw's Castle

King's Head, SW6

Lamb

Monarch
Monkey Puzzle

Nightingale

Old Ship
Orange Brewery

Outpost

Phene Arms
Phoenix and Firkin
Pineapple
Plumbers Arms
Prospect of Whitby

Queen Mary

Ram
Robert Browning
Rose and Crown, SW19
Rose of York
Round Table
Rutland

Salutation Inn
Scarsdale Arms
Ship
Sir George Robey
Slug and Lettuce
Spaniards Inn
Sporting Page
Sun in Splendour
Swan, W2
(Ye Olde) Swiss Cottage

Water Rats
Waterside Inn *
White Horse
White Swan, Twickenham
White Swan, Richmond
William IV
Windmill on the Common *
Windsor Castle